D1552938

The Economics of the Third Way

The Economics of the Third Way

Experiences from Around the World

Edited by

Philip Arestis

Professor of Economics, South Bank University, London, UK

and

Malcolm Sawyer

Professor of Economics, University of Leeds, UK

Edward Elgar

Cheltenham, UK • Northampton MA, USA

Published by
Edward Elgar Publishing Limited
Glensanda House
Montpellier Parade
Cheltenham
Glos GL50 1UA
UK

Edward Elgar Publishing, Inc.
136 West Street
Suite 202
Northampton
Massachusetts 01060
USA

A catalogue record for this book
is available from the British Library

Library of Congress Cataloguing in Publication Data

The economics of the third way : experiences from around the world / edited by
Philip Arestis, Malcolm Sawyer.
       p. cm.
    Includes bibliographical references and index.
    1. Economic policy—Case studies. 2. Mixed economy—Case studies. I. Arestis,
Philip, 1941- II. Sawyer, Malcolm C.

    HD87.E269 2001
    338.9—dc21

                                                                    2001023592

ISBN 1 84064 459 1

Printed and bound in Great Britain by Biddles Ltd, *www.biddles.co.uk*

Contents

Figures

Tables

Contributors

Philip Arestis, South Bank University, London, UK
Jesus Ferreiro, Universidad del Pais Vasco, Bilbao, Spain
Augusto Graziani, University of Rome I, Rome, Italy
Tim Harcourt, Australian APEC Study Centre, Melbourne, Australia
Jonathan Michie, Birkbeck College, University of London, UK
Vishnu Padayachee, University of Natal, Durban, South Africa
Pascal Petit, CEPREMAP, Paris, France
Robert Pollin, University of Massachusetts-Amherst, Amherst, United States
of America
Michael Rustin, University of East London, Dagenham, UK
Malcolm Sawyer, University of Leeds, Leeds, UK
Felipe Serrano, Universidad del Pais Vasco, Bilbao, Spain
Thanos Skouras, Athens University of Economics and Business, Athens,
Greece
Jim Stanford, Canadian Auto Workers, Toronto, Canada
Euclid Tsakalotos, Athens University of Economics and Business, Athens,
Greece
Ewald Walterskirchen, WIFO, Vienna

The views of the authors do not necessarily reflect the views of the institution
with which they are affiliated.

1. Economics of the 'Third Way': introduction

Philip Arestis and Malcolm Sawyer

'Third Way' is a term loosely used to describe the emergence of new social democracy governments throughout the world. Whilst it is easy to explain the term in this way, it is by no means a simple matter to analyse coherently. In view of this difficulty, and yet topicality, we decided to hold an international conference (26 May, 2000, University of East London) to which economists were invited from a number of countries where policies of the Third Way type had been implemented. In doing so we had thought we might be able to define Third Way and, more concretely, 'Economics of the "Third Way"'.

In the UK, for example, the emergence and then election of 'New Labour' has been closely associated with the development of the notion of the Third Way. 'New Labour is neither old left nor new right ... Instead we offer a new way ahead, that leads from the centre but is profoundly radical in the change it promises' (Blair, 1997, p. 1). In a similar vein, Giddens appears to locate the Third Way by reference to two other ways of 'classical social democracy' and neo-liberalism.

> Classical social democracy thought of wealth creation as almost incidental to its basic concerns with economic security and redistribution. The neoliberals placed competitiveness and the generating of wealth much more to the forefront. Third way politics also gives very strong emphasis to these qualities, which have an urgent importance given the nature of the global marketplace. They will not be developed, however, if individuals are abandoned to sink or swim in an economic whirlpool. Government has an essential role to play in investing in the human resources and infrastructure needed to develop an entrepreneurial culture. (Giddens, 1998, p. 99)

Hombach (2000, p. 1) talks of 'a policy that will steer a third course, a path between competing ideologies, a system that represents a realistic response to the changes that have taken place in the world', which supersedes 'the extremes of free market economics on the one hand and a centralized welfare state economy on the other'.

The idea of a third way (or 'middle way') between two major routes has surfaced a number of times. In relatively recent times it was often used to signify a way of a social democratic variety between free market capitalism and centrally planned socialism, though Franco and Tito, amongst others, used the term third way as a label for their own approaches. The current notion of a third way is between neo-liberalism and social democracy, and it is in this sense that we use the term (without implying that it is a viable way).

This chapter seeks to outline the type of economic analysis which we perceive to be involved in the ideas on the Third Way. We attempt to sketch out what we see as the analysis of a market economy that underpins the ideas of the Third Way. This is followed by some remarks on the role of the State which is also involved.

THEORETICAL FOUNDATIONS OF THIRD WAY

The exploration of the theoretical foundations of the Third Way, as with such an exploration for any other way, draws on analyses of the market economy and on analyses of the State and the role of State activity. Although there have been some notable contributions on the Third Way (for example Giddens, 1998, 2000), there has been rather little specifically on the economic analysis underpinning it, though speeches and other pieces by Blair and Brown provide some material. In this chapter we have to some extent to work back from the policies and policy pronouncements of governments (particularly in our case of the New Labour government) to seek to infer an economic analysis behind the Third Way. It is unlikely that there is a clear theoretical analysis of the economy in the minds of government ministers or their advisers. It is equally unlikely that economic policy pursued by any government is fully consistent either internally or with some theoretical paradigm. We would suggest, however, that in view of the approach adopted by those governments that purport to follow the Third Way, it can be variously described as 'new monetarism' (Arestis and Sawyer, 1998) or as interventionist neo-classical economics of a new Keynesian variety.[1] By this we mean firstly that the 'market failure' approach within neo-classical economics can be interpreted to support significant government intervention when market failures are viewed as widespread, though clearly there are neo-classical economists who would play down the significance of such market failures or who would counterpoise 'government failure' with market failure. Market failure is viewed as arising from the existence of externalities, the 'public good' nature of some goods and monopoly, and the emphasis on training and education by the new Labour government (and others) can be seen in this light of the government provision or encouragement of activities which would be underprovided by the market. We argue that the approach can be viewed as new Keynesian through its emphasis on the NAIRU (non-accelerating inflation rate of unemployment), its neglect of aggregate demand and of fiscal policy, the elevation of monetary policy and the concern over the 'credibility' of economic policies.

We postulate that the economics of the Third Way can be understood as based on the seven elements listed below which we would argue justify the description of interventionist neo-classical economics of a new Keynesian variety.[2] Giddens (2000) recognises this when he writes that

> the ideas of the new Keynesians allow us to make more sense of how the modern economy works, particularly at its cutting edge, the global financial economy. Suboptimal consequences can happen in any market sector as a result of the interaction of imperfectly competitive markets with the less than rational actions of individuals. In some situations, such as those found in the finance markets, the consequence can be extreme. The tendency of financial markets towards crisis is structural and needs to be coped with by collaborative intervention. (p. 37)

(i) The market economy is viewed as essentially stable, and that macroeconomic policy (particularly discretionary fiscal policy) may well destabilise the market economy.[3] Markets, and particularly the financial markets, operate with something like 'rational expectations'.[4] Specifically, financial markets make well informed judgements on the sustainability ('credibility') of economic policies.

(ii) Monetary policy can be used to meet the objective of a low rate of inflation. However, monetary policy should not be operated by politicians but by experts (whether banks, economists or others) in the form of an 'independent' Central Bank.[5] Politicians would be tempted to use monetary policy for short-term gain (lower unemployment) at the expense of long-term loss (higher inflation). An 'independent' Central Bank would also have greater credibility in the financial markets and be seen to have a stronger commitment to low inflation than politicians do.[6] It is argued that a policy which lacks credibility because of time inconsistency is neither optimal nor feasible (Kydland and Prescott, 1977). In situations of repeated games the authorities' are forced to take a longer-term view, since the future consequences of current policy decisions will influence the *reputation* of the authorities. In these situations, the authorities' incentive to renege is reduced because they face an intertemporal trade-off between the current gains from reneging and the future costs which inevitably arise from riding the Phillips curve. The overall conclusion is that the only credible policy is the one that leaves the authority no freedom to react to developments in the future, and that even if aggregate demand policies matter in the short run in this model, a policy of non-intervention is preferable. In view of the time-inconsistency and credibility problem monetary policy should be assigned to a 'credible' and independent Central Bank which should be given as its sole objective that of price stability.

(iii) The level of economic activity fluctuates around the NAIRU, and unemployment below (above) the NAIRU would lead to higher (lower) rates of inflation. The NAIRU is a supply-side phenomenon closely related to the workings of the labour market. The source of domestic inflation (relative to the expected rate of inflation) is seen to arise from unemployment falling below the NAIRU, and inflation is postulated to accelerate if unemployment is held below the NAIRU. However, in the long run there is no trade-off between inflation and unemployment, and the economy has to operate (on average) at the NAIRU if accelerating inflation is to be avoided. In this long run, inflation is viewed as a monetary phenomenon in that the pace of inflation is aligned with the rate of increase of the money supply.

(iv) The essence of Say's Law holds, namely that the level of effective demand does not play an independent role in the determination of the level of economic activity, and adjusts to underpin the supply-side determined level of economic activity (which itself corresponds to the NAIRU). Shocks to the level of demand can be met by variations in the rate of interest to ensure that inflation does not develop (if unemployment falls below the NAIRU). Fiscal policy has a passive role to play in that the budget deficit position varies over the business cycle in the well-known manner but fiscal policy is not required to either 'fine tune' or 'coarse tune' the economy. The budget (at least on current account) can be balanced over the course of the business cycle.

(v) The market system involves 'market failure' in the neo-classical sense of that term; that is markets do not reach an optimum outcome because of the presence of externalities, public and quasi-public goods (that is goods which are non-rivalrous in use and non-excludable), and monopoly situations. The policy conclusion is straightforward, namely that government seeks to correct externalities through appropriate taxation, subsidy and regulation, makes provision for 'public goods' either itself or through paying the private sector to provide the goods and competition policy can be used to reduce or restrain monopoly positions. The extent of government intervention may be extensive depending on views on the extensiveness of externalities and public goods and evaluation of the costs of 'government failure' (for example costs of government collecting relevant information and implementing appropriate policies, inefficiencies in government). This idea is, of course, not unique to the Third Way, and has been a central element in the neoclassical economics welfare economics. It is also the case that it is not the only idea motivating government intervention in a market economy.

(vi) Inequality has many dimensions and can be conceptualised and measured in many ways. It is, though, particularly significant to distinguish here what may be termed pre-market inequality and post-market inequality. The latter, which may also be seen in terms of inequality of outcomes (for example income), results from the former through inequality of 'initial endowments', through (partial or complete) exclusion from participation in the market (for example unemployment, discrimination) and through the ways in which the market rewards particular endowments. 'Recent discussion among social democrats has quite rightly shifted the emphasis towards the "redistribution of possibilities". The cultivation of human potential should as far as possible replace "after the event" redistribution' (Giddens, 1998, p. 101).

As the quote from Giddens illustrates, there has been a shift from concern over inequality of outcome to inequality of 'possibilities'. The former concern could be seen to be addressed through a progressive tax system and a redistributive social security system. The latter concern can be addressed through education and training (initial endowments), through 'employability' policies (for inclusion in the labour market and employment), and through seeking to change the rewards offered by the market. With the exception of the national minimum wage, it could be said that there has been little attempt to modify the rewards thrown up by the market. As Giddens (1998, p. 101) notes, a 'winner takes all' element in parts of the labour market means large inequalities. But also Giddens (2000, p. 86) perceives that 'that incentives are necessary to encourage those of talent to progress and that equality of opportunity typically creates higher rather than lower inequalities of outcome'.[7]

(vii) The final aspect refers to globalisation, and it has to be recognised that globalisation does not feature in new Keynesian economics but has been central to the analysis of the Third Way. The global nature of financial markets places constraints on the use of fiscal and monetary policy, at least in comparison with the constraints present in the 1950s and 1960s when exchange controls were in place. However, as discussed below, those constraints may be rather benign and take the form of providing well-informed market judgement on the validity or otherwise of the policies being pursued.

The rising ratio of international trade relative to GDP (at least again by way of comparison with the ratios of the 'golden age' of capitalism in the 1950s and 1960s) and the increased role of foreign direct investment by transnational corporations is an accepted (and indeed welcomed) 'fact of life'.

> Globalization, in sum, is a complex range of processes, driven by a mixture of political and economic influences. It is changing everyday life, particularly in the developed countries, at the same time as it is creating new transnational systems and forces. It is more than just the backdrop to contemporary policies: taken as a whole, globalization is transforming the institutions ofthe societies in which we live. (Giddens, 1998, p. 33)

Globalisation is viewed as limiting or ruling out a range of policies, such as domestic based fiscal policies. The nation state still has a role to play, though there are trends for moving government away from the nation state, sometimes in a downward decentralised direction (for example to regions within a country) and sometimes in an upward direction (for example to European

Union). But the role of government is seen to shift towards creating a favourable environment for transnational investment whether in the form of low taxation on profits, subsidies to inward investment or to creating a highly skilled work force. Giddens (2000, p. 73) speaks of the effects of globalisation on policy perspectives in terms of a shift from industrial policy and Keynesian demand measures favoured by 'old' social democracy but also from deregulation and market liberalisation emphasised by neo-liberals.

> Third way economic policy needs to concern itself with different priorities – with education. incentives, entrepreneurial culture flexibility, devolution and cultivation of social capital. Third way thinking emphasizes that a strong economy presumes a strong society, but does not see this connection as coming from old-style interventionism. The aim of macroeconomic policy is to keep inflation low, limit government borrowing, and use active supply-side measures to foster growth and high levels of employment.

'In a world of ever more rapid globalization and scientific changes we need to create the conditions in which existing businesses can prosper and adapt, and new businesses can be set up and grow' (Blair and Schröder, 1999, p. 163). 'It is not only the forces of globalization that demands the modernization of our institutions and political programmes, but, to no less an extent, changes in patterns of employment, in values and in demographic and social structures' (Hombach, 2000, p. 31).

It could be argued that the Third Way perceives globalisation as having virtually eliminated the possibilities of industrial policy (other than competition policy) and of macroeconomic policy. The mobility of industrial and financial capital is seen to preclude independent national economics policies in these regards. Labour, however, is much less mobile, and policies such as education and training are to be directed towards ensuring that the national economy is attractive for inward investment through the skills of the workforce.

THE ROLE OF THE STATE

There are many suggestions from the literature that the Third Way would not advocate the scale and range of the State being significantly larger than it is at present. In terms of the level of public expenditure, the general posture seems to be to hold the ratio of public expenditure to GDP at around its present level, but with some restructuring of the composition of public expenditure.

> The restructuring of government should follow from the ecological principle of 'getting more from less', understood not as downsizing but as improving delivered value. Most governments still have a great deal to learn from business best

practice - for instance, target controls, effective auditing, flexible decision structures and increased employee participation. (Giddens, 1998, pp. 74–5)

The state should not row, but steer: not so much control, as challenge. Solutions to problems must be joined up. Within the public sector bureaucracy at all levels must be reduced, performance targets and objectives formulated, the quality of public services rigorously monitored, and bad performance rooted out. (Blair and Schröder, 2000, p. 164)

Third way politics, it could be suggested, advocates a *new mixed economy*. Two different versions of the old mixed economy existed. One involved a separation between state and private sectors, but with a good deal of industry in public hands. The other was and is the social market. In each of these, markets are kept largely subordinate to government. The new mixed economy looks instead for a synergy between public and private sectors, utilizing the dynamism of markets but with the public interest in mind. It involves a balance between regulation and deregulation, on a transnational as well as national and local levels; and a balance between the economic and the non-economic in the life of the society. (Giddens, 1998, p. 100)

There is also considerable emphasis on the *investment* role of the State. 'Government has an essential role to play in investing in the human resources and infrastructure needed to develop an entrepreneurial culture' (Giddens, 1998, p. 99). Further, the guideline is investment in *human capital* wherever possible, rather than the direct provision of economic maintenance. In place of the welfare state we should put the *social investment state*, operating in the context of a positive welfare state' (Giddens, 1998, p. 117). Viewing public expenditure as investment provides a positive gloss. It suggests public expenditure has a positive effect and avoids the connotation of waste, and also links with the notion that borrowing can be used to finance public investment rather than current expenditure. It is also significant that investments in education and training (human resources) and in infrastructure are generally viewed as cases where the benefits of the investments cannot be fully appropriated by those who undertake the investments. Hence these investments suffer from a form of market failure and would be undertaken to a suboptimal extent by the private sector.

Further, the State can borrow for investment purposes but not for consumption ones as illustrated below in the discussion of fiscal policy. The rhetoric of the British Third Way has placed considerable emphasis on the so-called 'golden rule' - that over the course of the business cycle governments should only borrow to meet investment needs.[8]

There appears to be little positive role for public ownership, or indeed for social ownership alternatives to individual private ownership, on the Third Way. It is notable that in his first year as leader of the Labour Party, Blair successfully proposed the change of clause 4 of the Labour Party constitution which had stated the objectives of the Party to include 'to secure for the workers by hand or by brain the full fruits of their industry and the most equitable distribution thereof that may be possible upon the basis of common ownership of the means of production, distribution and exchange, and the best obtainable system of popular administration and control of each industry or service'. This was replaced by a clause which included the idea that 'where those undertakings essential to the common good are either owned by the public or accountable to them', and the last phrase has been interpreted in terms of regulation. Thus in keeping with the 'market failure' approach indicated above the presence of monopolies (as in the case of many utilities) is met by regulation. The Third Way of New Labour has meant not only accepting the privatisations of the previous Conservative government but also engaging in some of their own, albeit on a relatively small scale (which is more an indicator of few assets remaining in public ownership).

The Private Finance Initiative (PFI), which had been introduced by the previous Conservative government, has not only been continued but enlarged. The Labour Party (1997) manifesto spoke of the 'need to simplify the rules of PFI and engage with much greater creativity and energy in driving this project forward' (p. 13). The PFI can be viewed as privatisation not in the sense that previous publicly owned assets are sold to the private sector, but rather in the sense that the type of assets which had historically been owned and managed by the public sector (for example school buildings) may now be constructed, owned and managed by the private sector. The public sector then leases the assets from the private sector for a specified number of years.

Governments have always drawn on private finance: the cumulative effects of which is the national debt. But the PFI differs from bond-financed public expenditure in that the company constructing the asset borrows itself on the finance markets (usually at a higher interest rate than the government), creates the asset, and then leases the asset.

From these brief remarks, it could be said that the Third Way generally sees a somewhat reduced role for the State, and specifically a reduced role in the ownership and management of assets.

CONCLUDING REMARKS

We believe that the theoretical ingredients of the Third Way as just put forward constitute the theoretical foundations of the contributions that follow in this book. We had not sought to ask contributors to adhere to this way of thinking about the economy. On the contrary, the thrust of this introductory chapter was written after the conference. It was based on the contributions therein rather than used as the benchmark of the chapters in the book.

We would very much like to take this opportunity to thank all the contributors and participants to the conference. Their contributions and comments helped to shape up the contents of this book. The University of East London was generous in its hosting of the conference, as was June Daniels of the Department of Economics who generously provided that invaluable secretarial and related support. Our publishers, Edward Elgar and his staff, were as always absolutely excellent throughout the genesis of this book. We are both grateful to them all.

NOTES

1. It may appear strange that we use both the terms 'new monetarism' and 'new Keynesian' to describe the same approach. However, recall that new Keynesian economics does not involve any significant role for aggregate or effective demand, and shares the common feature of a labour market, supply-side determined equilibrium level of unemployment (the 'natural rate' or the non-accelerating inflation rate of unemployment).
2. The key elements of the new Keynesian research programme 'include the following five propositions:
    (i)   The frictions that prevent rapid and instantaneous price adjustment to nominal shocks are the key cause of business cycle fluctuations in employment and output.
    (ii)   Under normal conditions, monetary policy is a more potent and useful tool for stabilization than is fiscal policy.
    (iii) Business cycle fluctuations in production are best analyzed from a starting point that sees them as fluctuations around the sustainable long-run trend (rather than as declines below some level of potential output).
    (iv)   The right way to analyze macroeconomic policy is to consider the implications for the economy of a policy *rule*, not to analyze each one- or two-year episode in isolation as requiring a unique and idiosyncratic policy response.
    (v)   Any sound approach to stabilization policy must recognize the limits of stabilization policy, including the long lags and low multipliers associated with fiscal policy and the long and variable lags and uncertain magnitude of the effects of monetary policy' (De Long, 2000, pp. 83-4).
3. One of us (Sawyer, 1992) has argued elsewhere that the definition of 'the market' and hence of the market economy is problematic. We use the term 'market economy' here as shorthand for the interaction of privately owned enterprises.
4. It should be noted that most of the literature on 'rational expectations' and on credibility does not distinguish between different markets and hence all are assumed to hold rational expectations. However, it is the financial markets which are seen as crucial in determining whether a policy is deemed to be credible.
5. Further, from Rogoff (1985), there is the idea that those operating monetary policy should be more 'conservative' (that is place greater weight on low inflation and less weight on level of unemployment) than the politicians.
6. See Forder (2000) for an extensive discussion and critique of the notion of credibility.
7. It could though be argued that inequality of opportunity acts as a barrier for many to fulfil their potential. Those disadvantaged do not forego education because of a lack of incentives in terms of higher pay for the more educated but because of a range of barriers to their doing so. Greater opportunity would be expected to increase the supply of the well trained and so on, and reduce the pay of the well trained relative to the pay of the untrained.
8. It should though be noted that 'investment' in the context of the 'golden rule' is expenditure on fixed capital formation, whereas there is often reference to 'investment in education' or 'investment in health' which may be regarded as investment in human capital but expenditure on education and health which takes the form of salaries, purchase of materials and so on does not count as investment in the capital formation sense.

REFERENCES

Arestis, P. and Sawyer, M. (1998), 'New Labour, new monetarism', *Soundings*, 9 (Summer), 24–41.

Blair, T. (1997), Introduction to Labour Party (1997).

Blair, T. and Schröder, G. (1999), 'Europe: The Third Way/Die Neue Mitte' (reproduced in Hombach (2000), pp. 159–177; to which page numbers in text refer).

De Long, J. Bradford (2000), 'The triumph of monetarism?', *Journal of Economic Perspectives*, **14**(1), 83–94.

Forder, J. (2000), 'The theory of credibility: confusions, limitations, and dangers', *International Papers in Political Economy*, **7**(2).

Giddens, A. (1998), *The Third Way: The Renewal of Social Democracy*, Oxford: Polity Press.

Giddens, A. (2000), *The Third Way and its Critics*, Oxford: Polity Press.

Hombach, B. (2000), *The Politics of the New Centre*, Oxford: Polity Press.

Kydland, F. and Prescott, E.C. (1977), 'Rules rather than discretion: the inconsistency of optimal plans', *Journal of Political Economy*, **85**(3), 473–92.

Labour Party (1997), *New Labour Because Britain Deserves Better*, London: Labour Party.

Rogoff, K. (1985), 'The optimal degree of commitment to an intermediate monetary target', *Journal of International Economics*, **35**, 151–67.

Sawyer, M. (1992), 'The nature and role of markets', *Social Concept*, **6**(2) (reprinted with revisions in C. Pitelis (ed.), *Transactions Costs, Markets and Hierarchies*, Oxford: Blackwell, 1993).

2. The third sociological way

Michael Rustin

Does the Third Way belong, as a topic for social scientific study, to economics, political science, or sociology, or to all three of these? At moments of major transition, of which the politics of the Third Way seems to be at least a reflection, disciplinary boundaries often become blurred, as the different paradigms of social scientific explanation try to capture new or unexpected phenomena within their nets, and find themselves meeting in the course of their investigations.

Twenty years ago, problems of worldwide inflation provoked an intellectual turbulence similar to that which the era of 'globalisation' and the 'information age' have induced. Monetarism and neo-classical critiques of Keynesianism then emerged to explain inflation as a consequence of the follies and errors of governments, whose return to financial orthodoxy would, it was alleged, solve the inflation problem. Political scientists and sociologists developed a theory of governmental 'overload', arguing that the political system was unable to cope with the excessive demands being placed on it (Offe, 1984; Habermas, 1988). In a memorable intervention, the sociologist John H. Goldthorpe (1978) argued that the true explanation of inflation lay in changes in the underlying balance of social power in society. The loss of previous restraints on the working class derived from a hierarchical status order, norms of citizenship entitlements at that time extending into the sphere of employment, and the emergence of 'a mature working class' able to act in defence of its perceived interests, had brought a greater equality in the conditions of class conflict. Inflation represented both a reflection of and a partial solution to these conflicts, since a wages free-for-all encouraged sectionalism rather than class solidarity. No solution to the inflation problem would be found that did not take account of all these dimensions, Goldthorpe argued.

One strategy pursued during those years was to seek a normative, regulated basis for the resolution of industrial conflicts. Some recognition of the legitimacy of working class claims was offered by governments in exchange for 'solemn and binding' agreements by the trade unions to limit wage demands in the national economic interest. But this solution to the problem of inflation by means of 'corporatist' agreements or 'social contracts', as they were then called, pursued by successive governments during the 1960s and

1970s, collapsed in Britain in the 'winter of discontent' of 1978–79, mainly because the Callaghan government had tried to impose wage settlements in defiance of trade union claims to social justice.

A different solution was then effected, in Britain and the United States, by the governments of Thatcher and Reagan. These governments launched attacks on the idea of collectivist entitlements of citizenship, and set about undermining the capacity of working class organisations to defend their interests, through legislative changes, by means of some fierce industrial battles (with air traffic controllers in the USA, with miners in Britain), and by bringing an end to full employment, so crucial to working class bargaining power. Instead of seeking to reimpose restraints of status, however, these 'new right' governments sought to raise aspirations, but on an individual and competitive, not a collectivist, basis. This programme was largely successful, and its success has defined the political realities to which the strategies of New Labour and the New Democrats in the USA have been a deliberately conceived adaptation. There can be little doubt that social scientific debate on this earlier crisis was enriched by the cross-disciplinary trespassing by Goldthorpe and many others which took place. To explain the transitions which were going on during this period (from Fordism to post-Fordism, from 'consensus politics' to 'Thatcherism' and 'authoritarian populism', Hall and Jacques, 1983) and lately to a world of 'globalisation' and 'informational capitalism', the combined efforts of sociologists, political scientists, economists, and many others besides, have been more fruitful than any single academic discipline could have been by itself (Hirst and Thompson, 1996; Held et al., 1999). The changes opaquely reflected in the political programme of 'The Third Way' now equally require critical interdisciplinary attention.

THE THIRD WAY AND ITS PRECEDENTS

The Third Way has been invented more than once by socialists and social democrats, whose aim in this has been to resolve contradictions between political alternatives then deemed equally impossible. Social democracy was once itself such 'a third way' between communism and capitalism. Its aim was to combine the avowed commitment to equality and social justice of the first, with the goal of individual liberty within the framework of democracy of the second. The 'New Left' of the 1950s and 1960s also identified itself as a third way in its time. It defined a politics which was neither Stalinist nor merely Parliamentarist, instead focusing its energies on hitherto undeveloped sites of political action in civil society and cultural practice.

By the time New Labour came along with its Third Way of the 1990s, the spectrum of what was deemed to be politically possible had moved far to the right. Socialism itself, in any of its existing varieties, was now deemed to be one of two extremes to be avoided, the other being free market capitalism, or neo-liberalism, the antagonist of all the competing lefts. The state socialism of the Communist east, and the 'old social democracy' of Western Europe, were equally branded (or debranded) by advocates of the Third Way as the politics of a past era, as if there was little to choose between them. The near-century of antagonism between Leninism and Parliamentary Socialism was thus negated in a rhetorical stroke. Just when one might have anticipated that social democracy would, after the collapse of Communism in 1989, have the 'left field' to itself, it was summarily equated with the doomed mentalities of the East, and we were instructed to look elsewhere for political salvation.

Strategies defining themselves as a third or middle way characteristically proceed by castigating the received options to both left and right. The hope is that disillusion with existing and sometimes weary antagonisms, can be channelled into belief in a new untarnished alternative. In this and other respects the brief heyday of the SDP (Social Democratic Party) of Jenkins, Owen, Williams and Rodgers was a trial run for New Labour, which more effectively accomplished inside the Labour Party what the 'Gang of Four' had tried unsuccessfully to do in competition with it. These configurations of 'the new' are also rhetorical containers for a strategy of generational succession in the political class, since it may be possible to represent a third way as the path of the young, beaten out against the opposition of an arrogant or complacent generation of power-holders. This has certainly been central to the approach of Tony Blair, casting as his enemies, as he does, the 'old conservatisms' of both left and right.

The New Labour Third Way was an invention of political strategists and tacticians before it found its theoretical bearings. Tony Blair and his circle, with important debts to President Clinton and the New Democrats, decided on the necessity for a makeover of 'Old Labour' as the pre-condition of electoral success. They relied on the application of marketing disciplines to politics as their principal innovation. It is possible to see comparative political advantage as dependent on innovation in one activity or another, no less than competition in other spheres such as commercial markets or war. They thought it necessary to take account of the success of the 'new right' governments of Thatcher and Reagan in mobilising mass support, and to accept that the shift of public opinion which they had achieved, towards individualism and away from the collectivism of the postwar years, was now an irreversible fact. Only if the Labour Party could differentiate itself from its old identity as a party of class, public spending, high taxation, and welfare, did they believe it had a chance of re-election. Writings by members of the Blair circle, such as Peter Mandelson (Mandelson and Liddle, 1996) and Philip Gould (1998), indicate how these highly pragmatic and instrumental approaches to political warfare, although lightweight in their social analysis and vision, became powerful features of political thinking.

SOCIOLOGY AND THE THIRD WAY

Although the Third Way was conceived and marketed as a political 'brand' before it could be clearly specified what it stood for, there has since been a serious attempt to develop a theoretical basis for this new politics. The principal architect of this intellectual programme has been Anthony Giddens, whose two recent books, *The Third Way* and *The Third Way and its Critics*, are the most articulate theoretical statement of the case for New Labour politics. The first of these books was published virtually simultaneously with a Fabian Pamphlet by Tony Blair with the same title, and with very similar arguments, indicating the degree of cooperation, at that time at least, between the respective political and intellectual leaders of this programme. Anthony Giddens of course is a sociologist, not an economist. Since its invention as a social science discipline in the last decades of the nineteenth century, sociology has sought a 'third way' stance of its own, critical of Marxism on the one hand, especially in its institutionalised political forms, and of classical and neo-classical economics on the other.[1]

Sociology was and remains above all the discipline of the social and the normative, seeking causal explanation in structures of social relations and values, rather than in the competitive play of individual interests, or in their collectivisation as revolutionary class struggles. All social science disciplines struggle to impose their own dominant definitions or paradigms of reality, and to subordinate competitors. Where neo-classical economists see rational interests as the prime mover, sociologists see such interests as derived constructions of a normative order, dependent, as they hold markets themselves to be, on various 'social' boundary conditions. The history of the disciplinary traditions of sociology, economics and political science is relevant to understanding the goals and assumptions of the present Third Way.

What the New Labour opponents of the New Right needed, and found, in contemporary sociology, was a willingness to pay attention to what neo-classical economics left out of its models. That is, to dimensions of social solidarity, moral norms, and social cohesion. What they wished to keep at a distance was a theory which insisted on capitalist society's inherently divided and conflictual nature – the theory, that is, which has been chiefly embodied in the traditions of Marxism. The defeat of state socialism in 1989, and the flight from Marxism as an intellectual tradition which had preceded this collapse, made another renewal of this tradition seem an unlikely option in the 1990s.

The project of a Third Way required a focus on the dimensions of social life which were systematically neglected by neoclassical economics. New Labour drew attention to those aspects of competitive economic success which appeared to lie outside merely 'economic' explanation or the self-adjustments of the market. The inculcation of a work ethic and a sense of responsibility as well as rights among recipients of social benefit, presented as contributions to improving the efficacy of the labour market, is one example. The advocacy of 'education, education, education' and the priority intended to be given to investment in human capital is another. In fact, no such priority was visible for the first three years of the government's term of office. New Labour would also promote its greater sensitivity, compared with right-wing governments, to the social damage caused by unrestrained competition. In other words, the project of New Labour would be to create a dynamic capitalism in whose benefits *all* citizens would be able to share.

The sociological tradition had three other intellectual resources to bring to this Third Way programme, besides its generic interest in social norms and solidarity. The first was its theoretical pluralism, its insistence on the coexistence of at least three basic forms of social coordination. One of these was the organised means of violence, embodied in the power of the state. A second was the form of competition and coordination created by markets. A third was normative – the power of moral persuasion to maintain social cohesion and order, and even at times promote change. Anthony Giddens (1981, 1984, 1985, 1990) has been the most omnivorous and formidable practitioner of theoretical synthesis of his generation of sociologists. He is himself a Weberian pluralist by intellectual formation, who from early on in his writing career insisted that the essence of democratic capitalism lay in its systematic separation between the economic and political spheres, in contrast to their regressive fusion under state socialism.[2]

The potential resource which the repertoire of sociology provides for New Labour is thus considerable, though the politicians' anti-intellectualism has so far prevented its being deployed to full advantage. This sociological frame of thinking makes it possible to picture a society in which a strong democratic state, a vigorous and autonomous market economy, and a pervasive sense of moral community, must all coexist and have their necessary place. Government would in this frame of reference be justified in giving attention to all three of these fields of power. There would be real sense in a politics which was obsessed neither by the market, nor by the state, but recognised the importance of both, and also of civil society and the normative and cultural sphere.

The third major resource offered to Third Way politics by the discipline of sociology was, paradoxically enough, sociology's long-term engagement with 'modernisation', both as an explanatory theory and as a normative goal of social action. An historicist or neo-evolutionist view of progress is a joint Enlightenment inheritance of several social science disciplines. Classical economics, Marxism and sociology have a common root and share many assumptions in this respect. But the discipline of sociology, from the writings of its founding fathers (Durkheim, Weber et al.), through the functionalism of Talcott Parsons and his associates, to the present-day, has had a particular interest in theorising 'modernisation' as a systemic process, with effects on all spheres of social life, but exclusively determined by none (and in particular, *not* by the modes and relations of production).[3] This model of modernisation has been, like most large sociological conceptions, suggestive in its scope of application rather than precise in its factual referents. Modernisation theory has both historical and systemic dimensions. It attempts both to explain the direction of change, and the interdependence of the different elements of social structure upon each other. This provides advocates of 'the modern' with grounds for critique of apparently anachronistic or dysfunctional institutions or practices, what Tony Blair terms 'conservatism'.

A paradox is that sociologists like Giddens have been among the foremost critics of the historicism and holism of the 'rival sociology' of Marxism, insisting by contrast on the fluidity of modern societies, the autonomy of their sub-sectors, and the permeability of all previous boundaries of time and space. One of the main purposes of Giddens' *Contemporary Critique of Historical Materialism* (1981) was to refute the idea of a single grand historical narrative, criticising the one-dimensionality of Marxism and its reluctance to acknowledge the autonomy of separate domains of power.[4] His important idea of the duality of structures, developed in *The Constitution of Society (1984)*, substituted an interactive view of agency and structure for the determinist view of structures and roles upheld both by functionalist and Marxist sociologies. It thus insisted on an element of contingency in societal development, the converse of historicism.

Whilst methodologically Giddens has insisted on a pluralist and inter-actionist form of sociological analysis (one which can be characterised as neo-Weberianism enriched by later more sophisticated theories of agency, language and culture), theoretically he has contributed to a more generalised explanation of modern social transformation. This is the theory of globalisation and individualisation.[5] Its argument is that powers which could formerly be exerted only within fixed boundaries of space and time have now become capable of being exercised at a distance, and sometimes with almost instant effects. Limits to military power formerly bounded by the daily marching capacity of an army vanished to almost nothing with the arrival of nuclear missiles. Limits to economic power established by the dependence of manufacturing on natural resources located on a particular site, and on spatial communities of workers, can be overcome by corporations free to locate their plants wherever they wish. Most important of all, and fundamental to this conception, is the power of information, especially electronic information, to travel and pervade the globe in microseconds. The 'electronic herd', as Thomas Friedman (1999) calls it, by its flights of capital and currency across the world, can discipline actors in the world economy, whether they be corporations, trade unions, or governments, to behave according to the norms set by the market.

The other side of globalisation is the transformation of social structure and identities under the impact of these enhanced and speeded-up flows of capital, commodities, people (through migration and tourism), and especially information. Old solidarities are destroyed as the insulation of spatially and temporally isolated life-worlds is eroded. Collectivities based on communities of place and time (that is, shared histories) become weak in their capacity to stand up to broader forces, and at the same time lose their moral hold on members who find they have alternative options and aspirations put before them.

A substantial body of contemporary social theory has contributed to these reconceptualisations of modern society. Michael Mann's (1986) neo-Weberian reconceptualisation of social power; Manuel Castells' theory of the information society (1996–98); Ulrich Beck's concept (1992) of 'risk society' and his idea of 'reflexive modernity'; David Harvey's descriptions (1990) of the speeding-up of the devaluation and revaluation of capital brought about by new technologies; Scott Lash's and John Urry's work on 'disorganised capitalism' (1987), and the 'economy of signs and space' (1994) and Urry's advocacy (2000) of the substitution of a model of 'mobilities' for the key sociological idea of 'societies' are among the most influential of these recastings. Some of these writers (for example Harvey) remain avowedly Marxist, and in several others such as Castells the Marxist idea that the accumulation of capital remains the major driving force of change remains important. Modernisation theory in sociology thus does not easily dispense with the insights of the Marxist tradition. Giddens' own work intersects and overlaps in many ways with these contributions of his contemporaries.

THE THEORY OF GLOBALISATION

The broad if imprecise discourse of globalisation has legitimised New Labour's insistence on the fact of a changed world. It is held that the political options which were available to the left in the conditions of industrial society are no longer available to it in an increasingly post-industrial or information-driven society. It is pointed out that the industrial working class has been much diminished and dispersed. Collective class identities have been weakened.

A relationship of collectivistic dependence on standardised social services (public housing, for example), has been largely replaced by more individualised, consumer-oriented aspirations for greater choice and diversity. (In practice, this choice is often an illusion, for example for the poor in the housing market.) Meeting these aspirations, it is assumed, requires rejecting the idea of equality of outcomes, though New Labour continues to insist instead on its commitment to equality of opportunity.[6] People become less invested in their roles as producers, more in their roles as consumers. New Labour believes that a previously highly structured electorate has become fragmented, as class loses its saliency as the main organising principle of society. New dimensions of identity, for example gender, have become relatively more important. Giddens has given considerable emphasis to 'feminisation' as one source for the politics of reflexivity and identity.

There is plainly some truth in this description of contemporary society. New Labour has chosen to reposition itself in its light, seeking to define itself as the party of the upwardly mobile, those with a stake in modernisation and its benefits. It has abandoned the idea that it should principally represent those who are collectively disadvantaged by capitalism or the market society. New Labour has had some success in capturing this 'modernising' ground, leaving the Tories in danger of becoming the party of those mainly threatened by change and modernity. It is those threatened by change – those who are or who perceive themselves in danger of becoming downwardly mobile – who are the most susceptible to xenophobia, to fear of crime, to antagonism to refugees, asylum seekers and immigrants, and above all to Europe, precisely the issues which the Tories under Hague are now targeting. This repositioning has lost the Conservatives much of their natural support from the business sector.

Globalisation and individualisation are not, however, processes or forces external to economy and society, merely constituting its impinging external environment. There is a link to be made between Goldthorpe's earlier sociological interpretation of the economic phenomena of inflation, and how one can now conceptualise the processes of globalisation and individualisation. The common thread is to be found in the Weberian concept of social power, and the question of who gains and who loses it.

The principal argument of the information society thesis is that the power and cost-effectiveness of communication, both of information and of commodities and persons, have greatly increased. More communication of all kinds takes place, as we all know, and it takes place much more quickly. Hence the vast almost instantaneous trade in currencies and financial assets; the footloose corporations, able to locate or source their production where they want, since the cost of communication and transport, as a proportion of the total cost of marketed output, has fallen so much; and the global mass culture, transmitted by advertising, film and television, the internet, and by global consumer corporations like Coca-Cola, McDonald or Nike.

But the onset of the 'information society', and of globalisation, are not neutral regarding the distribution of different kinds of power. Changes in the relative costs of communication and information strike participants in economic activity unequally. The 'disembedding', as Giddens calls it, of activities from constraints of time and space enables those who control capital to become more powerful, relative to those whom they employ and who have to service capital's requirements. New technologies are deployed in order to redistribute power within organisations, and to increase their advantage *vis-à-vis* competitors. Technologies are often the instruments of power.

So far as the constraints of space are concerned, corporations have gained freedom to locate and relocate their activities at will, thus undermining the bargaining power of local producers. The reconfiguration of the United States away from the old 'rustbelt' of the north and east and towards the south and west, is an effect of this, and the troubles of Dagenham and Birmingham are examples closer to hand.

The greater and more continuous access to information by the managers of production processes reduces the leverage of those formerly employed to capture, process and transmit such information. Hierarchical bureaucratic organisation was a device to enable information flows to be managed in an orderly manner. The customer goes into the bank, fills in a form, the cashier reads the form and issues money, putting the form in a tray for subsequent processing in a back office. When the customer can find out what is in her account, and the bank can find out what it needs to know about the authenticity and specific requirements of the customer, on-line, this hierarchy of clerks becomes redundant, and we see the closure of hundreds of rural branches.

Thus both collective producers, given bargaining power in the past by the necessity for firms to undertake production processes in specific locations, and the intermediate grades of information-processors, managers, and professional staff, find their bargaining positions weakened or destroyed by the deployment of information technologies. These changes amount to a major redistribution of power towards capital, as a fully global market develops, squashing many local monopolies of labour, skill and information, and providing commensurable and instantly available measures, through balance sheets and ultimately stock values, of relative competitiveness.

'Individualisation', described sometimes as if it were an exogenous change in social character, even a beneficial one for its implication of greater individuality, depth, reflexiveness and agency, is also in part a product of this new economic situation. As systems of collective protection, whether provided by family, state, occupational community or trade union, weaken, individuals are constrained to rely more upon their own efforts and their own talents. Richard Sennett has recently provided a graphic description of the implications of such a change of identity across two generations in the United States. What is hailed by some as an unprecedented access of power and agency to individuals, can also be seen as a state of increased vulnerability.

'Individualisation' has become, in effect, a positive goal of public policy. It is deemed to be a functional requirement of a successful capitalist economy that citizens acquire the competences and mentalities to compete in the modern labour market. New Labour accepts that changing the mentalities of the citizen is a legitimate task of government. The doctrine of 'no rights without responsibilities', which Giddens presents as a cornerstone of the Third Way, signifies that individuals whether they like it or not must be constructed as self-reliant and responsible citizens, via schooling, the management of the welfare system, and a 'modernised' system of justice and penal policy. Hence the hatred of 'dependency' and its undermining in institutions providing care and education for children. In its objective of changing mentalities, New Labour seems to combine the morality of the 'modernising' Benthamite reformers of the nineteenth century, with an affinity for the apparatuses for the governance of souls theorised by Michel Foucault.[7]

Just as the process of globalisation appears to be redistributing power towards capital and away from other forms of social organisation, so the process of individualisation is far from simple in its meaning for individual subjects. Whilst some sociologists draw attention to the facts of increased individual autonomy and reflexivity, the 'social production' of contemporary subjectivity seems to have a less emancipatory direction. The New Labour project of 'education, education, education', is mainly driven by the perceived needs of the labour market. Its welfare programme is similarly shaped by the idea that employment is the only secure route to social inclusion. In its zeal to achieve these outputs, the practice of the education and welfare sectors is subjected to increased regulation, measurement and accountability. Individuals and occupational communities working in these sectors find their autonomy being reduced. A spirit of Taylorism is stalking the services sector (including the universities), as supposed proxies for the productive and competitive efficiency of the market are imposed upon it (Poynter, 2000).

If globalisation and individualisation are broad hypotheses which are held to justify the need for a Third Way distinct from classical social democracy, modernisation is its often-proclaimed goal. But modernisation is usually a narrative of the winning side. The 'modern' is what has supplanted, or is trying to supplant, the 'ancient', in some struggle of power, values, or generations, or all three. At this point, it is global capitalism that seems to be the victorious party, and the argument needs to be about how much of its victory should be contested and qualified, and how much has to be accepted as ultimately beneficial or unalterable.

A POSITIVE FORM OF PLURALISM?

I argued earlier that the pluralist sociological analysis on which Third Way formulations have obliquely drawn could be a useful theoretical resource. Its central idea is that state, market, and normative community are *all* essential forms of social organisation, and that a viable politics cannot be founded on any *one* of these dimensions alone. Drawing the appropriate boundaries between these different principles of social coordination is an essential task of politics. It is not difficult to see the problems that arise when these limits are not properly drawn, as in the failures of state socialism, the oppressions of theocracies and fundamentalisms, or the destruction brought about by unregulated markets.

The pluralist idea that some balance is necessary between competing forms of social coordination (state, market, moral solidarity) may also be a resource for the construction of the social coalitions on which political power depends. This is somewhat different if overlapping social constituencies are engaged by each structure of power and affinity. Larger numbers are employed by, and depend as service-users on the public sector, and have an interest in its resourcing and quality. Substantial and perhaps increasing numbers of citizens are engaged in voluntary social action, in pursuit of various ethical, cultural and environmental goals. Their attachment is also important to a reforming coalition. And of course there are various markets which governments ignore at their peril ('The economy, stupid', as Clinton put it). Markets also stratify and divide publics, by their relative resources and life-chances, and through people's different roles as consumers and producers. No political party can appeal to everyone, and judgements need to be made about which lines of antagonism can be drawn with best political effect. New Labour has been inclusive to a fault in this respect, though in the 1997 General Election campaign it did find the nerve to attack with effect the windfall profits of the privatised utilities. A pluralist theoretical model is a necessary resource for a party which can no longer assume that binary class divisions can bring it to power.

We can thus imagine a Third Way politics which seeks to arbitrate deliberately between these conflicting forms of power and value, turning these theoretical resources for the analysis of difference and complexity into a political asset. Informational capitalism, or globalisation, within this perspective should be seen not merely as the environment to which societies must adjust, but as the source of new inequalities of power and wealth which must be recognised and confronted.[8]

There are in fact signs that New Labour may be a more complex and pluralist formation than one might have expected from observing its 'branding' practices alone. It may after all be making something positive of its

tactical choice of the centre ground. It is interesting to note too that it is now
becoming more inclined to characterise its position as a 'renewal' of social
democracy, acknowledging its continuities with this tradition, rather than as an
alternative to it.[9] For example, the government's longer-term public expenditure plans indicate that it *does* believe in a positive role for government, and
does not share, despite early appearances, its predecessors' long-term project
of rolling back the frontiers of the state. Reluctant as it is to depart from
business-led agendas, there are issues (banking, competitive pricing in the
motor industry, the minimum wage) where the government has found itself
gingerly marking out the boundaries of a public interest distinguishable from
a corporate one. A similar line of division is sure to emerge soon in regard to
the powers of large landowners.

Constitutionally the changes it has initiated are also significant, establishing
some new public political spaces (in Scotland, Wales and London) within
which some countervailing powers to the market are likely to find a voice.
There is also momentum to the positive side of globalisation, in the
development of various forms of international regulation (proposals for debt
relief for the poorest countries are an example), though the pressures upon and
within the government to fall in with an American world hegemony are also
considerable.

The acknowledgement that a moral agenda is part of government also
provides a potential resource for contesting the norms of competitive
individualism. So far, however, the moral agenda pursued by the government
has been largely in the service of a new 'protestant ethic' of work and enforced
conformity to the requirements of the market, and has shown no willingness
to call this ethos into question. The weakening of social hierarchies and
solidarities, described by Goldthorpe as one source of 'inflationary' demands
in the 1970s, has consequences which are equally difficult to deal with today.
Aspirations are more likely to be experienced individually than collectively as
in the past, but a pervasive individualism generates anxieties about a decline
of moral boundaries and certainties. The insecurity (especially of employment) brought about by the modern market economy intensifies anxiety,
which then becomes an indirect source of pressure on the school system to
deliver outputs satisfactory to all parents, who know that their children's life-
chances depend on their educational success. Fear becomes displaced into a
volatile state of hostility, directed in turn towards asylum seekers and
refugees, child molesters, foreigners and Europe in particular, and towards the
football hooligans who have turned dislike of foreigners into street-fights. This
public opinion is orchestrated by conservative media motivated by another
kind of resentment, against the 'modernising elites' embodied in New Labour
itself. One reason for the virulence of conservative media in Britain, compared
with Continental Europe, and for the continuing influence of American styles

of social intolerance (the rhetoric of 'zero-tolerance', enthusiasm for incarceration and the recent persecution of sex-offenders are examples) is that Britain remains a more individualised and 'Americanised' society than the rest of the European Union.

Although the New Labour government is attempting to deal with some of the causes of this condition of social anxiety (through health, education, welfare, and employment policies) it appears to have little understanding of the dynamics of these problems of norms and values. Instead it flails about trying to avoid being characterised as unduly liberal, a term which its enemies use, both in Britain and the United States, to signify cultural privilege and protection from everyday realities. The right-wing populism which Thatcher mobilised so effectively against both social democrats and conservative paternalists thus remains a potent force today. The dilemma for New Labour is that 'right-wing populism' is an unintended consequence of the processes of 'modernisation' and individualisation that are in other respects central to its own project.

Progressive government could hardly be easy in an era of global market supremacy, when 'all that is solid melts into air'. While the Third Way has often seemed to be a meretricious and empty gesture towards an insubstantial theory, there seem grounds for hope that something better is in process. There is a vigorous social scientific debate going on about the transformation of the modern world, whose major driving force is once again being acknowledged to be capitalism. The Third Way, whatever its deficiencies, does contribute to that debate.

NOTES

1. This view of sociology has been best expounded by Goran Therborn (1976).
2. A view of Giddens' work which sees it as a sustained attempt to develop a critique of Marxism which nevertheless seeks to remain of the left is outlined in Rustin (1995).
3. Formulations of the modernisation process are reviewed in Allen et al., Bocock et al., Hall and Gieben, and Hall, Held et al., the four (1992) volumes of the Open University's Understanding Modern Societies series.
4. One way of reading the development of 'Western Marxism', in both its Althusserian and Gramscian traditions, is as a means of recognising the partial autonomy of different sub-sectors of society (the political, the ideological, and so on) whilst retaining the ultimate 'in the last instance' causal dominance of the mode and relations of production. See Laclau and Mouffe (1985) for a view of how the elastic of this stretched Marxist model finally snapped, clearing the way for Post-Marxism.
5. Globalisation and individualisation have a level of abstraction rather typical of sociological ideas. Open-ended in their factual referents, they are nevertheless highly suggestive and 'connective'. Esping-Andersen (2000) has described sociological concepts like this (he gives the examples of industrialism, welfare capitalism, Fordism) as 'leitmotifs', and calls them a 'workable substitute for strong theory'. They codify as ideal types recognisable features of the world, and set research agendas. Concepts such as globalisation and the network society are concepts of this variety, aiming to find order and coherence in current processes of transformation.

6. It is very difficult, however, to imagine a society which combines large inequalities of outcome with equality of opportunity. These values are not alternatives, but complements of each other. The steeper the gradient of inequalities, and thus the larger the costs of failure (in material terms, and in social respect), the more fearful people will be of giving up any competitive advantage they or their children may possess.
7. This argument is developed in Rustin (2000).
8. I argued earlier in similar terms (Rustin, 1989) that post-Fordist economic innovations had to be understood as a strategy of capital, not as a technology-driven inevitability, at a time when *Marxism Today* was writing some of what became the New Labour script.
9. Anthony Giddens' *The Third Way and its Critics* seeks a constructive debate with critics on the left. *On the Edge*, a collection jointly edited with Will Hutton, similarly seems to look for common ground despite many differences of view.

REFERENCES

Allen, J., Braham, P. and Lewis P. (eds) (1992), *Political and Economic Forms of Modernity*, Cambridge: Polity Press in association with the Open University Press.

Beck, U. (1992), *Risk Society: Towards a New Modernity*, London: Sage.

Blair, T. (1998), *The Third Way*, London: Fabian Society Pamphlet No. 588.

Bocock, R. and Thompson, K. (eds) (1992), *Social and Cultural Forms of Modernity*, Oxford: Polity Press in association with Blackwell and the Open University Press.

Castells, M. (1996–98) *The Information Age*. Vol. 1 *The Rise of the Network Society* (1996); Vol. 2 *The Power of Identity* (1997); Vol. 3 *End of Millennium* (1998), Oxford: Blackwell.

Esping-Andersen, G. (2000), 'Two societies, one sociology, and no theory', in *British Journal of Sociology. Special Issue: Sociology facing the millennium,* ed. John Urry, **50**(1), January–March.

Friedman, T. (1999), *The Lexus and the Olive Tree*.

Giddens, A. (1981), *A Contemporary Critique of Historical Materialism*, London: Macmillan.

Giddens, A. (1984), *The Constitution of Society: Outline of a Theory of Structuration*, Cambridge: Polity Press.

Giddens, A. (1985), *The Nation State and Violence*, Cambridge, UK: Polity.

Giddens, A. (1990), *The Consequences of Modernity*, Cambridge, UK: Polity.

Giddens, A. (1996), *Beyond Left and Right*, Cambridge: Polity Press.

Giddens, A. (1998), *The Third Way: The Renewal of Social Democracy*, Cambridge: Polity Press.

Giddens, A. (2000), *The Third Way and its Critics*, Cambridge: Polity Press.

Giddens, A. and Hutton, W. (eds) (2000), *On the Edge*, London: Jonathan Cape.

Goldthorpe, John H. (1978), 'The Current Inflation: Towards a Sociological Account', in Fred Hirsch and John H. Goldthorpe (eds), *The Political Economy of Inflation*, London: Martin Robertson.

Gould, P. (1998), *The Unfinished Revolution. How the Modernisers Saved the Labour Party*, London: Little, Brown.

Habermas, J. (1988, c. 1976), *Legitimation Crisis*, Cambridge: Polity Press Series: Understanding Modern Societies.

Hall, S. and Gieben, B. (eds) (1992), *Formations of Modernity*, Oxford: Polity Press in association with the Open University Press.

Hall, S., Held, D. and McGrew, T. (eds) (1992), *Modernity and its Futures*, Cambridge: Polity Press in association with the Open University Press.

Hall, S. and Jacques, M. (1983), *The Politics of Thatcherism*, London: Lawrence and Wishart.

Harvey, D. (1990), *The Condition of Post-Modernity*, Oxford: Blackwell.

Held, D., McGrew, A., Goldblatt, D. and Perraton, J. (1999), *Global Transformations: Politics, Economics and Culture*, Stanford: Stanford University Press.

Hirst, P. and Thompson, G. (1996), *Globalisation in Question*, Cambridge: Polity Press.

Laclau, E. and Mouffe, C. (1985), *Hegemony and Socialist Strategy*, London: Verso.

Lash, S. and Urry, J. (1987), *The End of Organised Capitalism*, Cambridge: Polity.

Lash, S. and Urry, J. (1994), *The Economy of Signs and Space*, London: Sage.

Mandelson, P. and Liddle, R. (1996), *The Blair Revolution. Can New Labour Deliver?*, London: Faber.

Mann, M. (1986), *The Sources of Social Power, Vols. 1 and 2*, Cambridge: Cambridge University Press.

Offe, C. (1984), *Contradictions of the Welfare State*, London: Hutchinson.

Poynter, G. (2000), *Restructuring in the Service Industries: Management Reform and Workplace*, London: Mansell.

Rustin, M.J. (1989), 'The Politics of Post-Fordism, or The Trouble with "New Times"', *New Left Review*, 175, June–July.

Rustin, M.J. (1995), 'The future of post-socialism', *Radical Philosophy*, **74**, Nov.–Dec., 17–27.

Rustin, M. (2000), 'The New Labour ethic and the spirit of capitalism', *Soundings*, **15**.

Therborn, G. (1976), *Science, Class and Society. On the Formation of Sociology and Historical Materialism*, London: New Left Books.

Urry, J. (2000), *Sociology beyond Societies*, London: Sage.

3. European employment policies: a new social democratic model for Europe?

Euclid Tsakalotos[1]

This chapter attempts to address the question of whether we are seeing the development of an overall EU employment strategy that can in some sense be seen as a continuation of social democratic policies at the European level. The signing of the European Employment Pact at the Cologne Council in June 1999 was heralded by many as a turning point in two respects. First, the EU was taking a more activist stance on the employment issue in part to increase its legitimacy by showing that monetary union was not just about monetary and financial stability. The Pact sought to bring together the various policies and measures that had been agreed since Amsterdam into a coherent whole. Second, it was hoped that, by upgrading the importance of employment, this would move the economic agenda of the EU in a more social democratic direction.

The argument of this chapter is three-fold. First, the EU has managed to upgrade the importance of employment policies. This has entailed both creating mechanisms and institutions to coordinate individual Member States' policies and, at least to some extent, pushing for certain EU priorities. Secondly, the strategy as a whole, which links macroeconomic and microeconomic aspects, has a certain coherence in which the macroeconomic aspects seek to promote a stable framework for the supply-side labour market policies to work. This chapter does not address the success of the approach, which is after all still at an early stage of development and implementation. But we do argue that, to the extent that it succeeds, this will be a rejection of most left-wing approaches (social democratic, democratic socialist, and so on) to how the market economy works. That is to say, the strategy relies to a large extent on the idea that the unemployed, and in particular the long-term unemployed, can be helped back into the labour market and that this can be achieved through various supply-side policies without proactive demand management. Indeed, the growth aspects of the strategy rest to a considerable degree on releasing entrepreneurship and the inherent dynamism of the market economy. Finally, we argue that this reliance on market forces suggests that the strategy, while not being a neoliberal one, is far from being a model of revamped social democracy. It is in fact far closer to the agenda of the Third Way which entails a considerable scaling down of traditional left-wing aspirations on such issues as equality and extending democracy to the economic sphere.

3.1 THE MACROECONOMIC FRAMEWORK

Macroeconomic policy in the run up to European monetary union (EMU) was severely constrained in individual member states because of the Maastricht Treaty's emphasis on disinflation, and deficit and debt reduction. This strait-jacket for macroeconomic policy also became the basic framework for macroeconomic policy after the creation of the euro area as can be seen by the institutional design of the European Central Bank (ECB) with its primary emphasis on price stability and the adoption of the Stability and Growth Pact (SGP).

The above reflected not only the desires of the mostly centre-right governments in the 1980s and early 1990s, but also the consensus of academic opinion. In terms of economic theory, the underlying rationale was that the economy was basically a stable entity and that inflation arising from government failure was the number one problem. Given this, the recipe of the new classical and credibility literature lay in tying the hands of government to ensure credibility, the latter becoming almost the be-all and end-all of macroeconomic policy. This was thought to be compatible with high employment and growth, in part through what might be called 'expansionary fiscal consolidation'. For instance, a reduction in budget deficits, allowing for a more balanced mix between monetary and fiscal policies, could lead to lower interest rates, higher investment and aggregate demand.[2]

For a time it seemed that this orthodoxy could be challenged in the second half of the 1990s because of three developments. First, there was a growing awareness that the previous policies, while leading to inflation convergence, had also led to, or at least were compatible with, very high levels of unemployment. Increasingly, it was felt that such levels were putting into question the process of European integration itself. Secondly, this was accompanied by an observable shift in academic opinion. Economists were now more willing to accept that Europe may have shifted from a regime where inflation was the number one problem to one where deflation was more likely. Economists such as Modigliani (1996), Fitoussi (1997) and others[3] were arguing that European policymakers were too obsessed with the fear that inflation could very easily return, that fiscal policy was too often procyclical (particularly in the face of the slowdown in the early 1990s)[4] and that aggregate demand policies were at least part of the answer to reducing

European unemployment. Finally, there was the election of centre-left governments in many EU countries (including Germany, France and the UK). This led to a number of debates about the extent to which the then current orthodoxy needed to be challenged. While there were clearly differences between politicians such as Lafontaine and Jospin, and Blair and Schröder, the debates centred on the extent to which centre-left governments should treat the existing monetary and financial framework more flexibly, on whether Europe needed an additional 'economic pole' to provide more active and coordinated policies to reduce unemployment, and on other issues such as the role of the EU in the world economy in providing exchange rate stability through some kind of a target zone system and financial stability by challenging the power of financial markets (Dyson, 1999).[5]

However, the basic argument of this chapter is that this window of opportunity represented by the above factors did not lead to any significant shift in the macroeconomic framework for reducing unemployment. There was some rhetorical shift in EU policy debates towards stressing the importance of coordinating European macroeconomic policy with other policies, but, on the whole, this entailed the same role for macroeconomic policy – a credible and stable framework rather than a proactive policy for demand management. Nor were any significant measures taken to develop an EU role to stabilise the world economy as mentioned above. This can be seen by a careful reading of the conclusions of the Council Meetings which have taken place since Amsterdam in June 1997, along with other documents published by the European Commission. Table 3.1 presents a chronology of developments in both macroeconomic and employment policies. Table 3.2 provides an outline of the basic components of economic policy.

The macroeconomic aspects of economic policy are laid out in the Broad Economic Policy Guidelines (BEPGs) and are discussed in the macroeconomic dialogue. An enhanced role for the BEPGs was first signalled at the Luxembourg Council in December 1997. Their aim is to allow for greater coordination of economic policies between EU, and more especially the euro area, countries.[6] The macroeconomic dialogue, agreed at the Cologne Council (June, 1999) seeks to ensure the appropriate macroeconomic mix through a dialogue between the various EU bodies responsible for policy formulation and the social partners.

The BEPGs for 1998 talk of three essential ingredients to 'a growth and stability-oriented macroeconomic policy mix'. It is worth quoting them in full since in subsequent years they change little:

- a monetary policy oriented to price stability;
- sustained efforts to achieve and maintain sound budgetary positions consistent with the Stability and Growth Pact;

Table 3.1 European Council Meetings – main conclusions in areas of macroeconomic and employment policies

Meeting	Main points	Details
Amsterdam, June 1997	– Stability and Growth Pact (SGP) – Resolution on Growth and Employment	– Emphasis on controlling fiscal positions of member states in 3rd stage of EMU. – A new title on employment (Employment Chapter) was introduced into the Treaty which placed emphasis on employment creation, considering it a matter for common concern, and stating that member states should draw up and implement their employment plans in a way that is consistent with the Broad Economic Policy Guidelines.
Luxembourg, Extraordinary Council Meeting, November 1997	– Topic of the meeting is employment – leads to Luxembourg process and National Employment Action Plans	– Emphasis given to active labour market policies to strengthen employment prospects within the EU. The plans are drawn up annually and evaluated both by the Commission and the Council. One of the principles is the identification of best practices within the EU which can be adopted by all Member States (see Table 3.3 for more details).
Luxembourg, December 1997	– Exchange rate policy for euro – Economic policy coordination in 3rd stage – role of Broad Economic Policy Guidelines (BEPGs)	– Agreed in general that exchange rate policy guidelines for euro will be formulated 'only in exceptional circumstances' (para. 45). – Need for closer surveillance of national economic policies is stressed since, even with single monetary policy and exchange rate, national policies will affect inflation. Emphasis placed on developing the Broad Economic Policy Guidelines (BEPGs) in accordance with article 103(2).
Cardiff, June 1998	– Economic reforms to promote 'growth, prosperity, jobs and social inclusion' – collectively known as Cardiff process – Improve functioning of single market in goods, services and finance – Promotion of entrepreneurship and competitiveness	– Liberalisation of markets in telecommunications, utilities and so on. Proposals to be made for Vienna Council on improving the single market in financial services. Identification of best practices and their adoption throughout the EU. – Emphasis is given to improving conditions for small businesses including making start-ups easier and improving access to risk (venture) capital.

Table 3.1 (continued)

Meeting	Main points	Details
Vienna, December 1998	– Development of economic policy coordination via the BEPGs	– Coordination of policy seen as necessary to get the appropriate policy mix. Focus of BEPGs is to be on exchange rate developments, strengthened fiscal surveillance within the SGP, monitoring of wages and labour market developments, monitoring of structural policies and the National Action Plans on Employment. In other words, the BEPGs provide an overview of all the policies agreed by EU Member States.
	– The development of a European Employment Pact	– The pact is seen as a development of the Luxembourg process and attempts at embedding employment policy 'into a comprehensive approach, encompassing macroeconomic policies directed towards growth and stability, economic reform promoting competitiveness, and the Employment Guidelines, which are designed to improve employability, adaptability, equal opportunities and job creation in existing and new enterprises' (para. 28).
Cologne, June 1999	– European Employment Pact adopted	– The pact brings together three main processes: (i) 'coordination of economic policy and improvement of mutually supportive interaction between wage developments and monetary, budget and fiscal policy through macroeconomic dialogue aimed at preserving a noninflationary growth dynamic' (Cologne process); (ii) Luxembourg process, that is improvement of labour market efficiency; (iii) Cardiff process, that is improving efficiency of goods, product and financial markets.
	– European investment initiative	– Package of measures agreed including a broadening of EIB activities with extra money to be released for risk capital, and credit for urban renewal, education, health, etc.
	– Introduction of macroeconomic dialogue to enhance macroeconomic cooperation (Cologne process)	– This new process is a dialogue between representatives of the Council, the Commission, the ECB and the social partners (business and trade unions), aiming at improving cooperation and ensuring the appropriate macroeconomic policy mix. Clearly stated that the process should not jeopardise ECB independence, the autonomy of the social partners in collective bargaining or the SGP.

Table 3.1 (continued)

Meeting	Main points	Details
Helsinki, December 1999	– Report accepted on economic policy coordination	– The emphasis of the report was on applying the existing structures, that is, it was not felt that there was any need for new institutions. Some emphasis given to trying to streamline existing procedures.
Lisbon, March 2000	– Various microeconomic initiatives aimed at improving education, growth and employment	– These include developing the information-based economy, better coordination of R&D, completion of the internal market and the integration of financial markets (through Financial Services Action Plan, Risk Capital Action Plan, and so on). On employment, some emphasis placed on education and training, modernising social protection and a call for the social partners to be more involved in formulating the National Employment Action Plans.
	– Macroeconomic policy – specific goals	– The macroeconomic dialogue should aim at creating trust between the parties; within the SGP, the tax pressure on labour should be reduced and government spending should be redirected to investment in human and physical capital; the long-run sustainability of public finance should be a priority (in light of ageing of population).
	– High Level Forum in June to take stock of Luxembourg, Cardiff and Cologne processes	

Source: European Council Meetings, *Presidency Conclusions*, various years; *Broad Economic Policy Guidelines*, various years.

Table 3.2 Basic components of economic policy

Broad Economic Policy Guidelines (BEPGs)	Produced in accordance with Article 103(2) of the Treaty, these define the main objectives and policy orientation of member state national policies. They form the centre of the annual policy coordination process. The reviews by the Commission of product and financial market plans, the review by the Council of employment plans and the review of budgetary policies through the Stability and Growth Pact all feed into the BEPGs. The policy recommendations cover everything from macroeconomic policy, appropriate wage developments to microeconomic policies in goods, services and financial markets. Individual chapters in each member state are also included with more specific policy recommendations in these areas. Recently, at the Lisbon summit, it was argued that the BEPGs should focus increasingly on the medium-term and long-term implications of structural policies and reforms aimed at promoting employment and growth.
Cardiff process	Here the emphasis is on a better functioning of product, services and financial markets. The general principle is that best practice among member states should be identified and then adopted by all others. The first annual review of the process occurred in early 1999 and was incorporated into the Broad Economic Policy Guidelines for 1999.
Cologne process macroeconomic dialogue	The aim of the macroeconomic dialogue (otherwise known as the Cologne process) is to improve the interaction between wage developments, monetary and fiscal policy. The ultimate goal is to improve the macroeconomic mix and ensure macroeconomic stability and hence the appropriate environment for improving growth and employment prospects. The Council argued that price stability and sustainable wage developments are of crucial importance to good and sustainable economic performance.
European Employment Pact	Agreed at the Cologne Council, it brings together the Luxembourg, Cardiff and Cologne processes, seeking to promote employability, entrepreneurship, adaptability and equal opportunities in the labour market (see Table 3.3 for more details).
Luxembourg process	Refers to the adoption of the employment guidelines and the drawing up of National Employment Action Plans by individual member states. The first plans were submitted in 1998.
Stability and Growth Pact	Rules adopted at the Amsterdam Council meeting relating to fiscal policy. It states that in the medium term member states should aim at a budget in balance or in surplus. Emphasis is now being given to sustainability of government budget positions over the long term in view of the ageing of the population. There is also some attempt to improve the quality of government expenditure, that is increase its capital and reduce its current component.

Source: European Council Meetings, *Presidency Conclusions*, various years.

32

– nominal wage trends consistent with the price stability objective; at the same time, real wage developments should be consistent with increases in productivity and should take into account the need to strengthen the profitability of investment in order to create more jobs. (European Council, *Broad Economic Policy Guidelines*, 1998, section 2, p. 3)

Thus, far from a new proactive demand management policy, the overall stance of fiscal policy in the 1998 BEPGs was envisaged to be tight and indeed tighter than in previous years since it was argued that consolidation had not been completed and some countries were still suffering from high debt/GDP ratios. Furthermore, there was a recommendation that consolidation occur via expenditure restraint rather than increases in taxes. Indeed, tax burdens were to be reduced to help promote efficiency and particularly to lower the burden on low-wage labour so as to encourage employment. The only element that was at least partly reminiscent of traditional demand management and Keynesian policy was the recommendation that the decline in government investment as a percentage of GDP should be reversed (although not at the expense of consolidation, but rather through a shift from current expenditure to capital expenditure).

What is interesting for our purposes is that in the subsequent two years (1999 and 2000) the guidelines have not altered much. Budgetary consolidation was again stressed in 1999, even though the European economies suffered a slowdown in economic growth in the wake of the international financial crises in Southeast Asia, Russia and Latin America. One discernible difference only is noteworthy. The document argues that if fiscal consolidation occurred and wage negotiations proceeded sensibly, then this would assist monetary policy in pursuing its primary objective of price stability without negatively affecting growth. However the statement was carefully worded and merely stated the responsibilities of the European Central Bank under the Treaty. Again there is little evidence here of a more flexible interpretation of the existing rules.

Neither does it appear that the role of the macroeconomic dialogue has signalled a change in the direction of macroeconomic policy. Rather, it is used for the EU bodies to communicate effectively their views on the course of the macroeconomy and hence what they believe might be the appropriate response of the social partners in their wage bargaining process.[7] We return to this issue below when we discuss this new form of 'credibility bargaining' in more detail.

Thus, by and large, it can be concluded that the new emphasis on growth and employment finds little support in macroeconomic policies beyond an emphasis on the importance of macroeconomic stability for creating conditions conducive to growth and employment creation. But this does not represent a shift away from the ideas of the centre-right governments which formulated the institutional structure of EMU.

3.2   THE EUROPEAN EMPLOYMENT STRATEGY

The EU's willingness to have an employment strategy and place increasing stress on it reflects, in part, the economic conditions of the 1990s with high European unemployment and diverging labour market performance. This was thought to bring into question the legitimacy of the EU integration process. Furthermore, that process was leading to nation-states losing economic policy tools that were traditionally employed to respond to these problems. The process by which Europe came to adopt an overall and more coherent European Employment Strategy (EES) is summarised in Tables 3.1 and 3.2. The underlying rationale of this strategy is to enhance the efficiency of national employment policies which would improve through their being brought into the public domain by the National Action Plans (NAPs) and through a learning process where the policies of individual Member States are examined thoroughly, best practices identified and then adopted throughout the EU.[8] It is for this reason that the buzzwords in EU fora became benchmarking and peer group review to adopt best practice.

The NAPs are supposed to present what each country is doing about numerous guidelines that have been categorised into four basic pillars: employability, entrepreneurship, adaptability and equal opportunities. Table 3.3 gives a flavour of some of the most important guidelines. In effect, the entrepreneurship and adaptability pillars are supposed to ensure the creation of a large number of new jobs - not only to reduce unemployment but also to increase labour force participation from 61 per cent to 70 per cent over the next few years - while the employability pillar seeks to ensure that the labour force is fit for these new jobs. The rationale for many of the measures seems to be based on New Keynesian ideas about the problem of long-term unemployment, youth unemployment and the inflexibility of the duration of unemployment benefits as well as more market liberal ideas associated with those who see the problem as one of Eurosclerosis.[9] The fourth pillar is seen as essentially linking the strategy to the idea of a social Europe.

It is beyond the scope of this chapter to provide an assessment of how these NAPs have been able to energise national employment policies through benchmarking and peer group pressure. Indeed, it is perhaps too early to undertake an empirical analysis of the success of the strategy, especially since some of the early criticism of the NAPs was that they simply reflected policies which were going to be undertaken anyway and that not enough new initiatives had been generated.[10]

Rather we seek to address two questions which have to do with the economic logic of a strategy which relies to a large extent on market forces to create an increase in employment in Europe. The first is whether there will be

Table 3.3 Employment Guidelines (Luxembourg process, incorporated into European Employment Pact)

Pillars	Goals and policies
• Employability	– Youth and long-term unemployed to be offered a new start (training, work experience, help with finding work, and so on). Emphasis is on the idea that the schemes are active and not passive. – Increased education and training and adoption of the principle of lifelong learning for all workers. Young people to be encouraged to stay on at school. The social partners are encouraged to agree arrangements for training and retraining, especially in areas of information technology. – Promotion of work rather than dependence: reform of tax and benefit systems to ensure that work is rewarded, including an assessment of duration of and eligibility for benefits systems and a reduction in the tax burden, especially on low-paid workers. – Specific attention to be given to needs of special groups, including, for example, ethnic minorities, the disabled.
• Entrepreneurship	– Reduction of bureaucracy for enterprises (especially SMEs). This includes making the formation of new enterprises more simple, reforming capital markets to make venture (risk) capital more easily available, allowing those who go bankrupt a second chance, and so on. – Improve tax and social security regimes to encourage self-employment and job creation. The aim is to reduce the tax burden on labour and other indirect labour costs which might hamper hiring and hence job creation. – Promote job creation at the local level: in this respect, the social partners are to help, agreeing to wage bargains which take into account regional differences in productivity and unemployment levels. Measures to increase labour mobility are also included. – Exploit the potential of the services sector, including the information technology sector, to provide good quality jobs.
• Adaptability	– Modernise work organisation and increase the flexibility of work. Flexibility can be encouraged by increasing the range of contracts available (including, for example, part-time work), by making working hours less rigid (even though overall hours should be reduced), by allowing individuals to take career breaks more easily, and so on. A review of job protection legislation and redundancy payments should also be conducted. – Remove obstacles to investment in human capital and also examine the possibility of providing tax relief for companies offering training.
• Equal opportunities	– Reduce the gap in both unemployment rates and wage rates between men and women. Improve the provision of childcare and, in general, help to reconcile work and family life. – Collect data to enable equal opportunity issues to be monitored.

Note: Some of the policies noted here may not be strictly part of the Luxembourg process and the Guidelines which were specified therein, but they are relevant to the employment strategy and hence we include them. Note that it is increasingly difficult to support the view that only the Luxembourg process deals with employment, as the Employment Pact itself (composed of the Luxembourg, Cardiff and Cologne processes) testifies.

Source: European Council Meetings, *Presidency Conclusions*, various years; *Broad Economic Policy Guidelines*, various years; Philpott (1999).

a significant employment effect and the second is whether such an increase will be accompanied by a rise in inequality. The argument presented below suggests that there is cause to worry on both counts.

The iniquitous dynamic of trying to get a large number of people off welfare into work has recently been explored by Solow (1998). While Solow's concern is with workfare in the US where the element of stick is considerably larger than that envisaged in the EES, we cannot ignore the possibility that a similar dynamic will hold in Europe. The unemployed who go through the various schemes envisaged by the EES are unlikely simply to fill existing vacancies, as if the European unemployment problem was one only of skill mismatch. On the contrary, they are likely to compete with low-skilled workers in employment and this may only imply a small wage cut to displace those already employed. But the fall in wages at the bottom of the skill ladder may well affect employers' choices in the direction of replacing those on the last but one skill rung with the now more competitive lowest skilled workers. It is not hard to see how this could have knock-on effects up the skill distribution ladder, even if with decreasing impact the further up we go. In short, there may be a small increase in employment as you need more workers with lower skills to do the jobs previously done by those with greater skills. But there will also be an increase in inequality as wages at the lower end of the scale are hit. The extent to which employment increases will depend on the responsiveness of labour demand to a decrease in the wage rate. However, as we know, the demand for labour is not very elastic and, even more significantly, given that the elasticity compares changes in average wages to changes in employment, this implies that for any large employment effects, the wages of the lowest paid will have to decrease significantly more than average wages (Solow, 1998, pp. 30–31).

Of course, it is easy to envisage counterarguments to this pessimistic scenario of the lowest paid, employed workers paying for the strategy. First, one could argue that the above analysis ignores the entrepreneurship and adaptability pillars of the Employment Guidelines. These could lead to an increase in dynamism of the European economy to such an extent that the demand for labour schedule shifts rightward, a result which would unambiguously increase employment and also mitigate any fall in real wages. It is difficult to be specific on the likelihood of this happening. For instance a similar dynamism was predicted as resulting from the creation of the Single Economic Market in 1992 and the first round of liberalisation of labour, financial and product markets. While there have been undoubtedly static gains from that programme, it is clear that the more optimistic arguments that the programme would put Europe on a higher growth path have not been vindicated. But to the extent that the argument has some credence, it relies on a belief in the inherent dynamism of the market economy – the argument is almost as the Austrian School of Economics would present it. It is difficult not to draw the conclusion from the entrepreneurship/adaptability pillars that capitalists in Europe, and especially small and medium-sized enterprises (SMEs), are being held back by distortionary taxes, regulations, bureaucracy, and so on. This seems a long way from traditional social democratic arguments about the need for both regulations and taxes, and the economic arguments for what Streeck (1997) has called 'beneficial constraints', and we return to this argument in the following section.

Secondly, it could be argued that the inequitable dynamic could be mitigated by the fact of having a more skilled workforce participating in the 'knowledge economy'. The argument here is that the demand for labour also shifts right as the marginal product of workers increases, thus raising both employment and wages. But it should also be remembered that, additionally, the supply of labour might shift to the right as people re-enter the labour force on acquiring these new skills, and the focus in the employment guidelines on increasing labour participation would simply reinforce this effect. In this case, there would still be an unambiguous increase in employment, but the effect on wages is again less certain.

However, there are a lot of 'ifs' and buts' to the above. First, it is difficult to exaggerate the costs involved in establishing and running good training and other programmes. Whether the EU is willing to put up the resources entailed can be doubted. Agreement on the Employment Guidelines was only possible on the condition that expensive programmes at the EU level were avoided (Goetschy, 1999, p. 125) and, of course, as we have already seen, national budgets are severely constrained by the requirements of the Stability and Growth Pact. This effectively implies that any increased expenditure on employment must be met by decreases in expenditure elsewhere. Secondly, even the best-run programmes have met with only limited success in getting people back to work (Solow, 1998, pp. 34–43) and, of course, to this we can add the debates about to what extent skills are actually learnt in these programmes, and whether the jobs created are genuine new jobs or whether they would have been established irrespective of the existence of the programmes. This is a difficult area and we cannot get into it here, but the consensus is that it is unwise to be too optimistic especially over the short to medium run.

Thus we can conclude here that, taking the macroeconomic and supply-side measures together, if the EES does succeed in increasing employment without too much inequality, this will be a vindication of arguments about the stability and dynamism of the capitalist economy that have traditionally been given short shrift by non-liberal economists.

3.3   THE EUROPEAN EMPLOYMENT STRATEGY AND THE THIRD WAY

Does the rejection of Keynesianism and the reliance on the market, and its associated inequalities, mean that the EES is a revamped neo-liberal strategy? There are three reasons to suggest that this might not be the case. First, there is no frontal attack on the welfare state nor are the welfare-to-work elements as radical as they are in the US and, increasingly, the UK. Furthermore, the emphasis on equal opportunities and protecting part-time workers, as well as the 'social learning' potential of benchmarking, discussed earlier, all suggest that 'the bottom has not fallen out of the social agenda in Europe' (Teague, 1999, p. 59). Secondly, the role of the social partners has not been abandoned in the search for the best way to improve European employment performance (see Tables 3.1 and 3.3), although as we shall see later it is much more limited. Thirdly, the state is not seen as inherently problematic as it is in neo-liberal approaches and there is an active role for the state in promoting labour market policies, in coordinating policies across different areas and in bringing together the different actors. In terms of economic theory, the underlying rationale of the employment strategy itself, rather than the macroeconomic aspects, seems to derive more from new Keynesian thinking than monetarist/ new classical.

Rather the relationship between the employment strategy and 'Third Way' theory, we would argue, is much stronger. In Le Grand's conception of the Third Way as lying somewhere been neo-liberalism and social democracy, emphasis is given to four components: community, accountability, responsibility and opportunity. Although each of these terms is highly contentious,[11] it is not difficult to see their relationship with the EES.

Much of the Third Way theory has been influenced by the work of Giddens. We cannot provide a full review of his approach here, but many of his themes find important echoes in the approach of the EU to employment: the decline of Keynesian social democracy and the disaffection with distant political institutions; globalisation, the passing away of the Fordist mode of production and its replacement by more dynamic fragmented post-Fordist production methods; the associated decline in the importance of class and the rise of the 'new individualism'; the increasing significance of flexibility and risk taking; the importance of the 'knowledge economy'; and the emphasis on technology and the service sector (see Giddens, 1994, 1998). Unlike neo-liberalism, this does not imply limiting the role of the state to an absolute minimum. But it does imply an important shift in direction from traditional social democracy in favour of decentralisation, a 'social investment state' and a concern for social inclusion rather than equality *per se*.

This shift is easily detectable in the EU's employment strategy. Consider the role of the social partners. At the macroeconomic level, the macro-economic dialogue might be considered a kind of corporatism at the European level and there have been important recent national developments in countries such as Portugal, Belgium, Ireland and Spain. But the content of this bargaining, as we have seen, is much more narrow than in traditional corporatist arrangements and the focus is on 'credibility bargaining' to produce a 'national institutional lock-in' – in this sense labour market structures are more for the single currency than for social Europe (Teague, 1999, p. 39). After EMU, the focus is on ensuring that the various economies do not lose their competitiveness,[12] becoming essentially backwaters within the euro area. All this is far removed from the broader agreements and 'political exchange' of the social corporatist model. The latter tends to be seen by centre-left politicians, as in Third Way theory, as too reliant on centralised control and thus incompatible with sociological developments such as the internationalisation and fragmentation of production, the decline in the importance of class and the 'new individualism'.[13]

At the microeconomic level, the departure from traditional social demo-cratic approaches is, if anything, more apparent. Teague (1999, pp. 56-9) shows the extent to which the emphasis on employability and supply-side measures has a strong individualistic bias which is very far from the old social democratic idea of economic citizenship as expressed in collective labour market institutions, including labour law. And with trade unions on the defensive, it is not surprising that the agenda for bargaining at the enterprise level has been set by the employers in terms of greater flexibility as suggested by the adaptability pillar of the Employment Guidelines (Teague, 1999, p. 43). Significantly for our purposes, such an emphasis was supported not only by the Commission's own analysis, but also by Blair's Third Way and Schröder's 'new centre' (Goetschy, 1999, p. 125; Dyson, 1999, p. 206). Here it is not that the state has no role, but that its role is one of the 'social investment state' which helps individuals cope with the various risks that they face. The emphasis is on getting people back into work,[14] thereby also contributing to one of the other main components of Third Way politics, preventing social exclusion. The centrality of work in this approach is difficult to overstate as it bears on some of the most significant themes of the Third Way, revolving around the nexus of autonomy – well-being – responsibility. Freeden (1999, p. 47), in discussing New Labour ideology, nicely captures the extent to which this conception departs from previous left ideas: 'work is seen not in the socialist terms of human creativity, not even in the social liberal terms of a *quid pro quo* for services granted by the community, with its sense of a common enterprise, but as the far starker assumption of individual responsibility for financial independence and an activity subservient to the economic and productivity goals established by market forces'.

However, this emphasis on individualism which is so characteristic of Third Way theory, and which we have argued is reflected in the EU strategy, has further consequences. One which we want to emphasise here is that it downplays the importance of power in political strategy. When power is discussed by Giddens it is in terms of individual empowerment to fit market needs.[15] What is left out in this conception are the highly unequal structures of power both in the international economy and in individual capitalist economies. This is also implicit in both the macroeconomic and micro-economic aspects of the EES. We have already seen the acceptance of the macroeconomic framework is based on the ideas of 'sound finance'. The Kaleckian argument that full employment and capitalism may be incompatible without major institutional reform, precisely because full employment strengthens labour and is thus likely to be opposed by capital, is particularly pertinent here.[16] In the postwar era social democratic Keynesianism and/or corporatist arrangements can be seen as providing an institutional basis for the accommodation between labour and capital.[17] On the other hand, the doctrine of 'sound finance' can only be seen as an *ex parte* intervention. Without a full-employment guarantee, labour faces the stark choice of 'pricing itself back into the market' or unemployment, something which clearly weakens its bargaining power.

Moreover, the macroeconomic framework of 'sound finance' confirms the power of financial markets to give a verdict on the appropriateness of economic policy and, given the extent to which such market actors represent the most liberal type of capitalism, social democrats and leftists of very differing positions have all traditionally been aware that these actors were hardly likely to look favourably on more institutional forms of capitalism (Crouch 1997, p. 358), let alone on more radical measures of redistribution, ideas of industrial democracy, and so on. While the international financial crisis in the late 1990s, with influential economists such as Krugman and Stiglitz arguing in favour of reform, together with the election of centre-left governments may have been a window of opportunity to change this situation, it did not in practice lead to any serious effort at reform. Here the responsibility lies more with Third Way politicians, such as Blair and Schröder, than Third Way theorists who have supported institutional changes such as a Tobin tax (Giddens, 1998, pp. 150–51).

But it is not just a question of the international market context. The emphasis of the EES on entrepreneurship and flexibility, as we noted above, suggests a picture of reducing unemployment and increasing employment through releasing market forces from regulations, taxation and bureaucratic control. However, this approach clearly sidelines measures, institutions and policies that capitalist entrepreneurs can claim hamper efficiency. It is no accident that New Labour, for instance, has abandoned its ideas on stakeholding. For the stakeholding idea fits in best with more 'institutional' economies – in the sense that the market and hierarchical firms are more integrated with other mechanisms of economic governance such as the state, associations and communities (Crouch and Streeck, 1997). While 'institutional' economies, such as Japan and Germany, were never socialist, they did include many policies that did accept the need, if not to limit, at least to mediate capitalist power which, as Crouch (1997, p. 36) argues, could sit 'alongside the essential core of labour-movement values: assertion of the collective interest; reduction of inequalities; preventing the concentration of power in the capitalist class'. However, at least three of the four pillars seem to rest on unleashing market forces through, for instance, encouraging entrepreneurship, reducing regulations on start-ups and integrating capital markets further to allow more capital for SMEs and R&D. In this context, the rise of 'credibility bargaining', workplace reforms based on the employer's terms and a hostility to reform based on the expansion of collective institutions, discussed above, are hardly surprising. As we argued in Section 3.2, to the extent that this strategy works, it will be a vindication of liberal – or Austrian – views on the dynamism of the market economy and a rejection of the view that such decentralised liberal economies are prone to short-termism, underinvestment and conflict.[18]

But a too-ready acceptance of the existing structure of power in a capitalist economy has many further implications. While we cannot go into all these here, it is perhaps worth mentioning two: the first is the issue of equality. We have already seen the inequitable dynamic involved in welfare-to-work programmes. Furthermore, the quality of the jobs created is often ignored:

> the development of precarious forms of employment, a more fragmented (because more 'flexible') workforce, the growth of private services and of SMEs (where employment protections and conditions are normally inferior to those in the rest of the economy) is integral to the EU strategy of job creation. These dimensions are no longer questioned in EU employment policy or in the guidelines. The demand for a disposable workforce and flexible labour markets is taken for granted; its ideological content is no longer perceived. (Goetschy, 1999, pp. 135–6)

Again this is in line with Third Way theory's demotion of the conception of equality *per se* in favour of preventing social exclusion. Giddens and other theorists do not conceive of the market itself as promoting structural inequality (see Finlayson, 1999, p. 76), rather the market itself is seen as a tool of egalitarian choice (Freeden, 1999, p. 44). To the extent that the Left has traditionally distinguished itself from other political currents by a belief in equality (Bobbio, 1996), then the move from equality to social exclusion is an important retreat.[19]

The second issue is the marginalisation of economic democracy. The very name social democracy has suggested in the past the idea of an extension of democracy to the social and economic domain. Given the continuing hostility of capitalists to this idea, it is not surprising that it is ignored in both Third Way theory and the EES. As Marquand (1997, pp. 336–8) points out, in terms of logic, this may not contradict the idea of empowering individuals in their roles as citizens, but in

> the first place, the vision of the human self implied by citizen empowerment, differs radically from the vision implied by employee subordination. The citizenship ideal is one of participation, activity and self-development and, by the same token, of accountability, transparency and scrutiny. Good citizens debate, argue and question; they don't simply accept what is handed out to them. And they cannot switch off their citizen selves when they go to work. That, of course, is what the early social democrats meant by social democracy. A democracy confined to the political sphere was no democracy; it had to embrace the social sphere as well. Citizenship was indivisible.

Once more, Third Way politics and the EES represent an important retreat.

What is most worrying in the above is that the justification for such retreats is not based on any new ethical or philosophical reasoning, for instance that equality and economic democracy are not in fact important values. And this brings us to a final question about the relationship between Third Way values and the policies being pursued. As Finlayson (1999) has argued convincingly, Third Way theory is derived from a sociological analysis not a philosophical one. The main sociologial trends delineated by Third Way theorists are also similar to those found in contemporary EU policy papers, government documents, and so on. The danger, of course, is that these trends discussed above are seen as economic developments which are in some sense natural and where the role of government is seen in ensuring that citizens are equipped to meet this new context[20] (see Finlayson, 1999. p. 278). But many of these developments are surely endogenous to the political system, to the power of various social classes and actors and so on. And if policies are based on these trends, it is not surprising that they will tend to replicate the structure of power as it exists in market economies.

So, finally, is the EES a neo-liberal strategy? Probably not for the reasons already outlined. Rather it has been argued it is very close to some of the main ideas and policies promoted by the Third Way. But the acceptance of 'sound finance' as a basis for macroeconomic policy and the rejection of Keynesian ideas, the individualistic bias and centrality of the market with respect to the supply-side employment strategy, the acceptance of the actual structure of power of enterprises and the reliance on those enterprises for providing the dynamism and growth that the strategy relies upon all suggest that the approach is not simply a renewal 'to adapt social democracy to a world which has fundamentally changed over the past two or three decades' (Giddens,

1998, p. 26) but an explicit rejection of many of the economic, political and philosophical ideas of social democracy, let alone democratic socialist ideas.

NOTES

1. For helpful comments, discussions, and so on, I would like to thank Vassilis Droukopoulos, Heather Gibson, Margarita Katsimi, Isaac Sambethai and participants at the conference on 'The Economics of the Third Way', University of East London, 26 May, 2000.
2. See, for instance, Giavazzi and Pagano (1990). Of course, the conditions for this operating are rather strict and one could easily imagine such consolidation leading to pessimistic expectations about the future, thereby worsening the recession. Again, assumptions about the stability of the economy are crucial.
3. See, for instance, the Economists' Manifesto on EU unemployment (Modigliani et al., 1998).
4. In particular, it was argued that German Monetary Unification had been mismanaged – that being obsessed with credibility, European policymakers did not treat it as a one-off shock thereby allowing for more flexible policy.
5. Dyson (1999) provides an excellent account of these political debates from the mid-1990s onwards. He concludes that on the whole centre-left politicians were more in favour of interpreting the existing institutional framework more flexibly than changing that framework or radically challenging the neo-liberal paradigm on which it was based.
6. The BEPGs contain two sections. First, there is a general account of recommended policies in all areas, including macroeconomic policy, structural policies in product and capital markets and labour market policy. The second section provides specific recommendations for each EU country.
7. Indeed, in official documents, emphasis is always placed on the independence of the various parties and the fact that that independence should not in any way be compromised (European Council, *Presidency Conclusions*, Cologne, pp. 5 and 8).
8. For a fuller account of how these processes came to be adopted and how the mechanisms work in practice, see Teague (1999), Goetschy (1999) and Philpott (1999).
9. For a flavour of the debate, see Nickell (1997) for New Keynesian ideas, Siebert (1997) for Eurosclerosis and Alogoskoufis et al. (1995) for a more eclectic view of the problem of European unemployment which, while placing some emphasis on the inflexibilities of European labour markets, does not suggest that Europe can follow the US path with respect to employment and unemployment policies. This latter approach seems particularly close to the Guidelines of Table 3.3.
10. For some preliminary assessment of the EES, see Goetschy (1999, pp. 129–30).
11. For a discussion of Le Grand's conception, see Freeden (1999).
12. Thus, in the BEPGs, there is an emphasis on the need for wage agreements not to imitate each other across countries and to take into account regional differences in productivity growth, skill levels and unemployment. The decentralising dynamic behind this is that the EU is promoting the idea that these differences are not just between countries within EMU but within regions themselves in the different countries.
13. On social corporatism, see, for instance, Henley and Tsakalotos (1993). On the link of Third Way theory to these sociological developments, see Finlayson (1999).
14. For radical critics, such as Habermas (1999, p. 54), it is this emphasis which ties Third Way thinkers to the 'ethical conceptions' of neo-liberalism, that is a willingness to be 'drawn into the ethos of a "lifestyle attuned to the world market", which expects every citizen to obtain the education he needs to become an "entrepreneur managing his own human capital" '.
15. For an insightful account of the way Giddens ignores such questions of power, see Anderson (1994).
16. On the continuing relevance of this argument, see Glyn (1995).
17. See Henley and Tsakalotos (1993). Eichengreen (1996) gives a more orthodox account of how social democratic institutions in the postwar era worked as commitment mechanisms

that overcame the problem of collective action and tried to ensure that the social interest groups were locked into the bargain.
18. For a number of articles which discuss these issues more fully, see Hollingsworth and Boyer (1997) and Crouch and Streeck (1997).
19. For more on this retreat, see Freeden (1999) and Finlayson (1999).
20. The technocratic or managerial slant in much of the EU discussions, for example the emphasis on benchmarking and adopting best practices that we have seen, is also understandable in this context. For the downplaying of ethics in favour of sociology entails, as Finlayson (1999, p. 274) also points out, that 'the critique of capitalism as such turned into a critique of the particular capitalism of Thatcherite neo-liberalism. It ceased being a *political* claim and became a *managerial* one about how to run things better. The understanding of the state of current social forces and the design of a political strategy to mobilise them turned into a desire to adapt to a pre-ordained future. The sociological analysis became a normative claim' (emphasis in the original).

REFERENCES

Alogoskoufis, G. et al. (1995), *Unemployment: Choices for Europe*, Monitoring European Integration Series, vol. 5, Centre for Economic Policy Research, London.
Anderson, P. (1994), 'Comment: Power, Politics and the Enlightenment', in D. Miliband (ed.), *Reinventing the Left*, Cambridge: Polity Press.
Bobbio, N. (1996), *Left and Right*, Cambridge: Cambridge University Press.
Crouch, C. (1997), 'The terms of the neoliberal consensus', *Political Quarterly*, **68**(4), 352–60.
Crouch, C. and Streeck, W. (eds) (1997), *Political Economy of Modern Capitalism*, London: Sage.
Dyson, K. (1999), 'Benign or malevolent Leviathan? Social democratic governments in a neo-liberal Euro area', *Political Quarterly*, 195–209.
Eichengreen, B. (1996), 'Institutions and Economic Growth: Europe after World War II', in N. Crafts and G. Toniolo (eds), *Economic Growth in Europe since 1945*, Cambridge: Cambridge University Press.
European Commission (2000), *2000 Broad Guidelines of the Economic Policies of the Member States and the Community*, Commission Recommendation, Brussels, available from Website, ue.eu.int/emu/broad.
European Council (various), *Presidency Conclusions*, Brussels, available from Website, europa.eu.int/council/off/conclu.
European Council (1998), *The Broad Economic Policy Guidelines*, Brussels, available from Website, ue.eu.int/emu/broad.
European Council (1999), 1999 *Broad Economic Policy Guidelines*, Brussels, published in *European Economy*, no. 68.
Finlayson, A. (1999), 'Third Way theory', *Political Quarterly*, 271–9.
Fitoussi, J.-P. (1997), 'Is restrictive macro-economic policy the only way to EMU?', mimeo, April.
Freeden, M. (1999), 'The ideology of New Labour', *Political Quarterly*, pp. 42–51.
Giavazzi, F. and Pagano, M. (1990), 'Can Severe Fiscal Contractions be Expansionary? Tales for two small European countries', in O.J. Blanchard and S. Fischer (eds), *NBER Macroeconomics Annual*, Cambridge, MA: MIT Press.
Giddens, A. (1994), 'Brave New World: The New Context of Politics', in D. Miliband (ed.), *Reinventing the Left*, Cambridge: Polity Press.

Giddens, A. (1998), *The Third Way*, Cambridge: Polity Press.

Glyn, A. (1995), 'Social democracy and full employment', *New Left Review*, May/June, 33–55.

Goetschy, J. (1999), 'The European Employment Strategy: genesis and development', *European Journal of Industrial Relations*, **5**(2), 117–37.

Habermas, J. (1999), 'The European nation-state and the pressures of globalisation', *New Left Review*, 235, May/June, 46–59.

Henley, A. and Tsakalotos, E. (1993), *Corporatism and Economic Performance: a comparative analysis of market economies*, Aldershot: Edward Elgar.

Hollingsworth, J. and Boyer, R. (eds) (1997), *Contemporary Capitalism: The Embeddedness of Institutions*, Cambridge: Cambridge University Press.

Marquand, D. (1997), 'After euphoria: the dilemmas of New Labour', *Political Quarterly*, 335–8.

Modigliani, F. (1996), 'The shameful rate of unemployment in the EMS: causes and cures', *De Economist*, **144**(3), 363–96.

Modigliani, F., Fitoussi, J.-P., Moro, B., Snower, D., Solow, R., Steinherr, A. and Labini, P.S. (1998), 'An economist's manifesto on unemployment in the European Union', *Banca Nazionale del Lavoro Quarterly Review*, 206, September, 1–35.

Nickell, S. (1997), 'Unemployment and labor market rigidities: Europe versus North America', *Journal of Economic Perspectives*, **11**(3), 55–74.

Philpott, J. (1999), 'Social Europe', *Economic Report*, Employment Policy Institute, **14**(5).

Siebert, H. (1997), 'Labor market rigidities: at the root of unemployment in Europe'. *Journal of Economic Perspectives*, **11**(3), 75–94.

Solow, R.M. (1998), *Work and Welfare*. Princeton: Princeton University Press.

Streeck, W. (1997), Beneficial Constraints: On the Economic Limits of Rational Voluntarism', in J. Hollingsworth and R. Boyer (eds).

Teague, P. (1999), 'Reshaping employment regimes in Europe: policy shifts alongside boundary changes', *Journal of Public Policy*, **19**(1), 33–62.

4. Economics of the British New Labour: an assessment

Philip Arestis and Malcolm Sawyer

INTRODUCTION

The Labour Party returned to office in May 1997 after 18 years in opposition (since May 1979) to the Conservative government, first of Margaret Thatcher (for 11 years) and then of John Major (for 7 years). This was the second time since World War II that the Labour Party had been in opposition for a long period of time. The years 1951 to 1964 had been years of opposition before returning to office in 1964 and being in government for much of the succeeding 15 years. But the changes in policies, especially economic policies, which took place during the most recent period of opposition (and particularly after 1990) have been much greater than any previous changes. On this occasion, the Labour Party sought to distance itself from the experience of the Labour government of 1974–79 and of its own policy proposals of the 1980s. It is not accidental that many in the leadership and elsewhere use the term New Labour to signify the changes in policy outlook.

We proceed by an attempt to draw out the macroeconomic policy implications of the analysis. Subsequent sections comment on taxation and social security, poverty and redistribution, employment and industrial policies before we summarise and conclude.

MACROECONOMIC POLICY

The macroeconomic policy appears to have been influenced by the requirements of the Maastricht Treaty and of the Stability and Growth Pact for euro membership.[1] Monetary policy is to be conducted by an 'independent' (of political and democratic control) Central Bank with an objective of low inflation. Monetary policy is not conducted through control over monetary aggregates such as monetary base or of any credit-based aggregate, but rather through the Central Bank discount rate. Monetary policy is seen to have the sole objective of low inflation but raises at least four objections.

First, and especially with the effective demise of active fiscal (and indeed regional) policy, macroeconomic policy comes close to being a 'one club' policy. It is now widely recognised that a level of interest rate which is appropriate (however that is defined) for economic conditions in one part of the country will generally not be appropriate for others. In particular, an interest rate level raised to combat 'overheating' in one region may cause the temperature to drop in an already cold (in an economic sense) region. Furthermore, changes in interest rates affect many economic variables, such as exchange rate and distribution of income, which are expected, in their turn, to have effects on the real economy, not just inflation.

Second, monetary policy is geared towards low inflation, without any mention of other objectives such as high employment or growth. The common defence is, of course, that monetary policy only influences nominal variables and the (equilibrium) level of (un)employment is set by supply-side factors and corresponds to the non-accelerating inflation rate of unemployment (NAIRU). The sole objective given to the Bank of England's Monetary Policy Committee (MPC) by the government has been an inflation rate of 2.5 per cent within a +/- 1 per cent tolerance margin with the interest rate as the sole policy instrument.

Third, the quasi-independence of the Bank of England and the introduction of the MPC has led to attempts to ultrafine-tune the economy: monthly decisions are made on interest rates with variations of 0.25 per cent being made frequently, in pursuit of an inflation rate target up to two years hence. Interest rates have been seen as politically sensitive through their effect on variable mortgage interest rates, and this device of a quasi-independence of the Bank of England serves to distance politicians and the government from those decisions. But in practice the course of interest rates is now a matter of considerable debate each month, and lobbying by relevant interest groups. It also has had the effect of de-coupling fiscal and monetary policy, and giving monetary policy the dominant role. The almost continuous adjustment of interest rates means that any change in taxation or public expenditure can be responded to.

Fourth, the mechanism by which interest rates are meant to influence the pace of inflation is rarely spelt out. The monetarist mechanism was clear: the demand for money had to adjust to the exogenously determined supply of money, and did so through a change in the price level. But when it is recognised that the stock of money is endogenously determined through first, the granting of credit, and second, the demand for money, matters are different. The channels through which interest rate changes are expected to influence inflation are rarely spelt out: however a recent document by the MPC (1999) attempts to throw some light on the matter. This views the MPC as setting the official short-term interest rate (the repo rate) which affects market rates, asset prices, expectations and the exchange rate. Both domestic demand and external demand are affected, so that total aggregate demand is affected, and with given supply which cannot be influenced by monetary policy, domestic inflationary pressures are thereby contained. The direct impact of a change in the official rate on inflation works through expectations and the exchange rate. Announcement of 'credible' changes in interest rates sends the 'right' signals to economic agents concerning the determination of the monetary authorities to fight inflation. Inflationary expectations are thus significantly affected. Changes in the exchange rate affect net external demand inflation directly via import prices. A sharp distinction must be made, however, between short-run and long-run impact. In the short run, changes in the official rate of interest will have an impact on both real activity and prices, but in the long run, monetary policy 'determines the nominal or money values of goods and services – that is, the general price level' (MPC, 1999, p. 3). It is the case, then, that 'inflation, in this sense, is a monetary phenomenon' (p. 4). In this context, interest rates are used to influence the level of demand which is then seen to influence inflationary pressures. It is notable that in their manifesto for the 1997 election, the Labour Party made no proposals for the control of inflation other than to set an inflation target of 2.5 per cent or less. This was followed by the reform of the Bank of England with operational independence being granted in the very early stages of the Labour government; the clear implication being that granting independence to the Bank was a signal that inflation can be controlled through manipulation of the interest rate.

Financial markets have always posed problems for governments, and especially Labour governments, and placed constraints, sometimes severe ones, on economic policy. The globalisation of financial markets and the very much greater flows across the exchanges have served to increase those constraints. But what is different about 'the third way' is the appearance of welcoming those constraints, or at least regarding them as benign. If the markets are all-knowing, then they serve the very useful purpose of keeping governments on the straight and narrow. This was expressed by Blair (1996) who argued that 'Errors in macroeconomic policy will be punished rapidly and without mercy', that is financial markets are right, governments can be wrong. Better to have the financial markets tell you that a policy is not credible than to implement the policy and find that it fails. More recently, Brown (1999) suggests that 'in the new open economy, subject to instantaneous and massive flows of capital the penalties for failure are ever more heavy and the rewards for success are even greater' (p. 7).

Fiscal policy has been cast in terms of a Code for Fiscal Stability. There is a so-called 'golden rule' of public finance,[2] which is taken to be that 'over the economic cycle the Government will borrow only to invest and not to fund current expenditure' (Treasury, 1997, p. 1), though capital consumption (depreciation) is regarded as current spending so that it is net capital formation which can be financed by borrowing. The 'public debt as a proportion of national income will be held over the economic cycle at a stable and prudent level' (ibid., p. 1). Furthermore, 'The fiscal rules focus on the whole of the public sector, because the debts of any part of the public sector could ultimately fall on the taxpayer. Looking at the whole public sector also removes incentives to reclassify activities simply to evade prudent constraints on borrowing' (ibid., p. 16). Thus the use of fiscal policy to regulate aggregate demand in the economy is much reduced, if not entirely removed, especially in the direction of stimulating the economy. It is thus argued that 'Discretionary fiscal changes should only be made if they are demonstrably consistent with achievement of the Government's fiscal rules over the economic cycle' (Treasury, 1997, p. 16).

To date, there has been a continuing fall in unemployment since Labour came back into office, and with some hiccups economic growth has largely continued. Fears of recession (particularly prevalent in late 1998) have appeared unjustified, and the British economy appears to have ridden out the effects of the East Asian crisis and the over-valuation of sterling, albeit with recession in the manufacturing sector (output in manufacturing has been broadly flat over the last three years, and fell in late 1998 and early 1999). The budget position has moved from deficit into surplus: a deficit of 3 per cent of GDP in 1996/97 has moved to a surplus of 0.5 per cent for 1998/99 and a forecast surplus of 0.3 per cent for 1999/2000. Investment has also been rising (relative to GDP) and in constant price terms has risen steadily from 16.3 per cent in 1994 and the same figure in 1995 to 18.6 per cent in 1998 and over 19 per cent in the first half of 1999. There has been an element of a consumer boom, with consumer expenditure rising faster than GDP, and also some clear hints have been given of a boom in house prices especially in the South East of England. A development of particular significance has been the decline of the personal savings ratio (though not as severe as that experienced in the United States and Canada). In 1996 the savings ratio was 9.5 per cent, and in 1997 9.3 per cent, falling to 6.4 per cent in 1998 and to 5.8 per cent in the first half of 1999.[3]

The trade on goods and services was roughly in balance in 1997, but went into deficit of £8.5 billion in 1998, but the current account remained roughly in balance through a large increase in income from abroad. In 1999, the trade deficit may reach £20 billion and with income from abroad expected to be lower than in 1998, a substantial current account deficit is likely this year. This has been in the face of a rising and overvalued exchange rate. But there is now evidence of the J-curve effect coming into operation. The behaviour of the exchange rate and that of exports are relevant considerations. In 1992, the pound sterling came down from DM2.95 after the events of 14 September and the suspension of Britain's membership of the Exchange Rate Mechanism (ERM). By the end of 1992 the pound was DM2.40 and continued to drop over the next two years reaching a low of DM2.20 during 1995. When Labour came into office in May 1997, the exchange rate was DM2.80 but with the control of interest rates being handed to the Bank of England and the consequent tightening of monetary policy, the price of sterling rose to just over DM3.00 by the end of summer 1997. Exports of services have not been much affected because they are usually priced in dollars and the pound/dollar exchange rate has not been affected as substantially as the pound/DM rate. But exports of manufacturing have been losing out. Indeed, had it not been for the recovery of the global economy, exports could have simply collapsed.

In comparison with previous Labour administrations, this New Labour government inherited a relatively healthy economy in that unemployment was falling, inflationary pressures were subdued and the foreign trade and government budget positions were relatively healthy. The continuing fall in unemployment has enabled the new Labour government to claim some success for its own economic policies and has underpinned the introduction of policies such as the 'New Deal'. The government's budget position has moved into surplus as growth has continued (and also associated with the declining savings ratio), which has also bolstered claims for fiscal prudence.

TAXATION AND SOCIAL SECURITY

The political success of the Conservative Party in establishing taxation as a major political issue and the association of the Labour Party as a 'high tax' party and the perception that at least the 1992 election may have been lost because of the 'tax issue', have had a strong impact on Labour's economic thinking. Any notion that the tax system should be used to redistribute income has virtually disappeared, apart from some mention that the tax system should be 'fair' (a favourite word in the lexicon of new Labour). There have been, for example, no proposals or ideas for a wealth tax nor for raising the higher rates of taxation. There may be some redistribution by stealth if, for example, the threshold for the higher 40 per cent tax rate continues to fall relative to earnings.

The manifesto (Labour Party, 1997) stated that 'the principles that will underpin Labour's tax policy are clear:

- a tax system that encourages employment opportunities and work incentives for all;
- a tax system that encourages more savings and investment;
- a tax system that is fair and seen to be fair.'

The level of taxation, and particularly 'headline' rates such as the standard rate of income tax, has been a standard battleground between the major political parties, albeit that the Liberal Democrats did enter the 1997 election with a declaration of a willingness to raise income tax by lp in the pound which would be earmarked for education expenditure. The charge of being a high-tax party was one which the Labour government has sought to avoid, and one element of that was a commitment that the basic rate of income tax would not be raised. With perhaps the exception of duty on petrol (where the Labour government initially continued with the pledge of the previous Conservative government to raise excise duty on fuel each year by 3p a litre over the rate of inflation but has announced that in future fuel duty will be set on a budget by budget basis), tax increases or new taxes have largely been relatively obscured, and 'headline' rates of taxation have been held or reduced.[4] There have been significant new taxes or changes in the tax system; for example a change in the taxation of pension funds that will raise several billion pounds annually, and which will surely have a substantial impact on future private pension levels.

In the 1999 budget the Treasury estimates were for substantial reduction of revenue resulting from that budget (many measures being pre-announced in that budget for future years) rising to over £3.5 billion in 2001/02 (on an indexed basis). Much of the decrease comes as a result of the introduction of a 10 per cent starting rate for income tax and a reduction of the base rate (these two generate a reduction of £4.6 billion in revenue), the introduction of Working Families Tax Credit and other tax credits (£2.7 billion), and a reduction in employers' national insurance contributions by 0.5 percentage points (£1.7 billion). Increases in tax come from the abolition of the married couple's allowance (£2.05 billion), abolition of mortgage interest relief (£1.4 billion) and a climate change levy on electricity, gas, coal and other solid fuels used by industry and commerce (£1.75 billion). Net taxes and social security contributions have so far continued to rise relative to GDP, despite the growth in GDP. It was 35.3 per cent in 1996/97 (the last year of Conservative government) and 36.5 per cent in 1997/98; in 1998/99 it was 37.4 per cent, but it is expected to decline to 37.0 per cent in 1999/2000 (Treasury, 1999).

There have been a number of major shifts in the arrangements for the provision and funding of old-age pensions in the UK over the past 40 years. It is likely that a further major change will be made by the Labour government if they continue in the office. So far, there have been a number of relatively small changes in the position of old-age pensioners: for example, a winter allowance raised from £20 per household to £100 and the restoration of free eye tests. A more significant change has, however, been the introduction of a minimum income guarantee which is to rise in line with average earnings (at least during the lifetime of this Parliament). This income guarantee is currently

£75 a week for a single pensioner and £116.60 for a couple (rising to £78.45 and £121.95 respectively in April 2000). This compares with the basic pension of £66.75 and £106.70 a week respectively.

Proposals advanced for discussion in the Green Paper *A New Contract for Welfare: Partnership in Pensions* involve a flat rate contributory pension for most, and some form of earnings related pension for many (whether from an occupational pension, private provision or State Earnings Related Pension Scheme, SERPS). The proposals would retain the flat rate contributory pension but make significant changes for the 'second' pension. For those earning less than £9000 a year and those off work who are caring for young children, ill or disabled relatives, or are ill or disabled themselves, there would be a new State Second Pension. For those earning £9000 a year or more, there would be 'low-cost and flexible stakeholder pension schemes backed by extra Government incentives to save'. For comparison, a person working a 40 hour week at the minimum wage would receive an annual income of just under £7500. Those earning between £9000 and £18 500 would receive incentives to contribute further to the stakeholder pension schemes (and for a transitional period also to the State Second Pension). These proposals represent a further shift away from public provision (through social security) to private provision (whether through occupational pension schemes or individual provision).

There is not space here to discuss the details of these proposals, but rather we seek to highlight some key features which we feel fit in with the general economic philosophy of New Labour. There is a belief, which we have not previously discussed, that there can be effective regulation of private pension schemes which would avoid scandals such as those of the Maxwell case and the mis-selling of personal pensions in the late 1980s. There appears also to be a belief that any failure of private pensions to deliver can be attributed to dishonesty rather than any inherent failures or inefficiencies of private provision. Public provision of pensions becomes much more of a 'safety net'. Private pension provision generates current savings which leads unproblematically to investment and higher future output.

POVERTY AND REDISTRIBUTION

At the beginning of the Labour government in 1974, Denis Healey (then Chancellor of the Exchequer) famously said that he would squeeze the rich 'until the pips squeak'. As part of its redistribution agenda that government established a Royal Commission of the Distribution of Income and Wealth and sought to evaluate new policy initiatives in part in terms of their distributive impacts. In the outturn there was little change in the distribution of income (and there is some indication that the distribution of earnings and of income may have started to worsen in 1977). It could be said that the redistributions of previous Labour governments were at least as much concerned with reducing high incomes as raising low incomes.[5] This new Labour government has not been interested in redistribution through, for example, raising income tax on higher incomes, but has made claims on its intentions to raise incomes at the lower end, specifically for households with children.

The government has set the target of cutting child poverty by half in the next ten years, and abolishing it in 20 years. There is a commitment to publishing an annual assessment on poverty, the first of which appeared in autumn 1999 under the title of *Opportunity for all: tackling poverty and social exclusion* (Cmnd. 4445). The government has viewed poverty and social exclusion as multi-dimensional and proposed 38 'success measures' against which to gauge their progress in the elimination of poverty. But in terms of income, a household income (adjusted for household size) of less than half of the median income is generally recognised as constituting poverty. On that relative measure, the proportion of the population in poverty rose from around 8 per cent in 1979 to 18 per cent in the mid 1990s.

It is perhaps surprising to find that one of the major policy initiatives of the Labour government has been the introduction of the national minimum wage. It could be seen as surprising in that it is a policy long advocated by many trade unions and particularly by the more left wing unions such as the public sector union UNISON (and its predecessors) though the hourly rate has been set considerably below that advocated by many unions. It is redistributive and it involves intervention in the 'free market'. However, a minimum wage involves some clear winners, but the losers are less clearly identified and income reduction is spread over many whilst the income gains are relatively concentrated. Further, efficiency wage type arguments are invoked (whereby an increase in wages invokes increases in productivity). Arguments based on discriminating monopsony models have also been invoked. This may be an example of where the implications of new Keynesian arguments (based on efficiency wages and insider–outsider models) coincide with those from arguments based on pursuit of equality and fairness to underpin a policy of national minimum wages. 'The National Minimum Wage will help underpin the Government's welfare reforms. Together with tax and benefit reforms, the minimum wage will help to promote work incentives. It will ensure greater fairness at work and remove the worst exploitation' (Treasury, 1999, p. 59; see, also, Hill, 1999).

Many of the policies which may have some significant impact on poverty such as the national minimum wage and the Working Families Tax Credit have only recently been introduced (in 1999). There has not been time for the effects of these policies to show up in the statistics on poverty (given the time

lags involved in the collection of the relevant statistics). A recent report of the
Joseph Rowntree Foundation[6] indicates the number of people with incomes
below half the national average income (before housing costs, adjusted for
household size) was little changed at 10.7 million in 1997/98, and that number
remained much the same in 1998/99.

Inequality of income rose sharply in the Thatcher years: for example the
Gini coefficient for disposable income (on an equivalised adult basis) rose
from 26 in 1978 to 36 in 1990, and for original income (that is before
transfers) from 43 to 52. In the Major years inequality of disposable income
fell (Gini coefficient fell to 33 in 1995/96) and of original income was broadly
flat. In the first two years of the new Labour government, inequality on the
basis of disposable income rose from 34 (in 1996/97) to 35 (in 1998/99), and
for original income was constant at 53.[7] It could be argued that little attention
should be given to year to year fluctuations of this magnitude (which could
represent sampling error) and that the effects of many measures such as the
national minimum wage would be captured in these figures.

The Institute of Fiscal Studies has sought to estimate the distributional
consequences of the tax changes since May 1997 including those that will
come into effect in April 2001.[8] Figure 4.1 summarises the cumulative effect

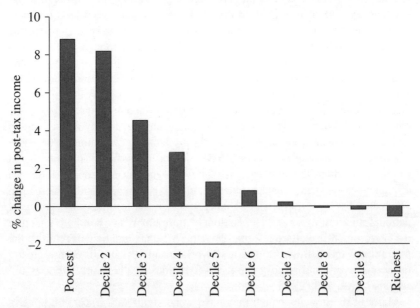

Source: Institute of Fiscal Studies.

*Figure 4.1   Distributional impact of major fiscal reforms announced since
July 1997, by decile*

of the New Labour government's four budgets since taking office in 1997. It can be seen that it is estimated that the two lowest income deciles would experience an increase of around 8 per cent in their post-tax income, whilst the richest decile experienced a decrease of around 0.5 per cent. In terms of family type (not shown in the chart) the largest (relative) gainers are no-earner and single-earner couples with children, single parents and single pensioners, whilst losers include no-earner and single-earner couples without children. However, although the income of the two lowest income deciles rose by some 8 per cent, it should be recalled that these two deciles receive around 8 per cent of total disposable income, and hence this represents a shift of around 0.65 per cent of total income. The income of decile 6 rises by 1 per cent but their income share is around 10 per cent, and their gain the equivalent of 0.1 per cent of total income.

A preliminary conclusion here would be that the tax system has shifted somewhat in the direction of reducing disparities of income but that these effects have yet to show up in the figures on inequality of disposable income.

EMPLOYMENT POLICIES

The incoming Labour government inherited a relatively buoyant economy, and measured unemployment has generally continued to decline to the time of writing in the first $2^1/2$ years of the government. Unemployment on the claimant count (numbers receiving unemployment benefit) has fallen from 1.636 million in May 1997 to 1.212 million in September 1999. Employment has risen with a rise of 542 000 between 1997Q2 and 1999Q2 of the total in employment (including self-employed).

The employment policy can be briefly summarised. Employment levels depend on the skills and work attitude of (potential) workers, and on the incentives and pressures to work. They have little to do with the level of aggregate demand or the demand for labour, or perhaps more than some form of Say's Law operates to ensure adequate demand. The level of employment is not seen as directly influenced by capacity. It could be said that the level of (un)employment is set by a form of NAIRU (Treasury, 1997).

The policy agenda towards employment and unemployment can be seen to be composed of two major elements. The first is to change the balance between net (after tax and benefits) 'in work' income and unemployment benefits. The national minimum wage and the Working Families Tax Credit (WFTC) have been the two major components of this, though continuing the previous government's practice of raising unemployment benefits only in line with prices and not with wages is a further element. The second is a significant shift towards a workfare approach. The Welfare to Work programme, often also called the New Deal (or New Deal relating to specific groups, for example New Deal for 18–25 year olds), was the most expensive initiative proposed by Labour whilst in opposition. Whilst other new spending had to be met from savings within existing budgets, this was to cost £5 billion and financed by a windfall tax levied on the privatised utilities. Labour Party (1997) describes the approach in the following terms: 'Because we believe that young people must play their part, there will be no fifth option of remaining permanently on full benefit. Where there is a suitable offer, people will be expected to take this up. We believe that is fair – rights and responsibilities must go together' (p. 17). The New Deal programme for 18–24 year olds and the long-term unemployed was financed by a windfall tax on the privatised utilities which yielded over £5.2 billions over two years, though the proceeds are to be spent over a five year period.

Under the Working Family Tax Credit (WFTC), which started in October 1999, there is a minimum income guarantee for a family with children with a full-time earner of £200 a week (£10 400 per annum: this can be compared with a minimum wage of £3.60 which for a 40 hour week would generate a gross weekly income of £144). The WFTC involves a lower withdrawal rate than the Family Credit which it replaces. The introduction of a 10 per cent starting rate of income tax and proposed changes to the national insurance contributions[9] significantly lower the marginal tax rate faced by low income earners. The Treasury's estimates are that 715 000 previously faced a marginal deduction rate of 70 per cent or more and this declines to 230 000, though nearly three-quarters of a million will now face a deduction rate of between 60 per cent and 70 per cent rather than only 15 000 previously (Treasury, 1999, p. 62).

INDUSTRIAL POLICY

Industrial policy in various guises had been a key element of previous Labour governments, including the nationalisation programme of the 1945/51 government, the National Plan and Industrial Reorganisation Commission of the 1964/70 government and the industrial strategy and National Enterprise Board of the 1974/79 government.[10] In each case, the industrial policy aimed at securing substantial structural and other changes which were intended to improve economic and industrial performance. It was also the case that there were underlying views on Britain's relatively poor economic performance and the causes of that poor performance which could be addressed, if not rectified, by government industrial policy. Although the identification of the causes was not always clearly articulated nor coherently expressed, nevertheless they were identified to include small scale of operation and/or fragmentation of an industry, poor management and underinvestment especially in research and development. There is a marked contrast with this new Labour government. This seems to be a combination of three factors. First, there is much less talk of relatively poor British economic performance. There is still some mention of this. For example, the 1997 election manifesto stated that

> the British economy is not stronger than its main competitors in Europe and elsewhere. We have fallen from 13th to 18th in the world league of national income. Our growth rate has lagged behind our main competitors over the 17 Tory years. People are having to work harder to stand still. We have the third highest inflation rate among the top seven industrial countries. We have had the worst job creation record of any major industrial economy since 1979. (Labour Party 1997, p. 11)

But this can be seen as focusing on the record of the previous government.

Second, in so far as there are perceived failings in the British economy, they now seem to be assigned to failures of education and training. Since education is largely provided by the public sector, this translates into a failure of the public sector rather than the private sector. If there is a mismatch between the demands of business in terms of skills and the supply of such skills, blame is attached to the supply side rather than to the demand (one aspect of this is summarised in the (in)famous quote from Blair that the priorities of his government were education, education, education). Third, there is a sense in which the thrust of policy has changed from seeking to make British industry competitive (or similar phrase) to one of making the British work force, tax system and regulatory regime welcoming to foreign direct investment. It is, of course, the case that in the era of globalisation it is increasingly difficult to say what is meant by a British firm or by British industry.

There have been few changes to industrial policy inherited from the Conservative government and it could be said that industrial policy fits into the 'correction of market failure' mode. There has been some change to the institutions of competition policy with the formation of the Competition Commission to replace the Monopolies and Mergers Commission, and some talk of an 'independent' body to decide on mergers, taking the final decision out of the hands of the government minister, a view that the structure of industry should be a technical rather than a political matter. There has been no attempt to promote public ownership or to reverse any of the privatisations of the Conservative government, and indeed there has been a continuation of privatisation (for example the prospect of the sale of air traffic control).

CONCLUSIONS

The macroeconomic policies so far pursued by the new Labour government can be seen as the final triumph of (new) monetarism and the defeat of Keynesian economic policies.[11] The central concern of government policy is with inflation and with the appeasement of the financial markets, whose judgement on economic policies is accepted. This thrust of policy has forgotten two essential requirements for full employment: sufficient aggregate demand and adequate productive capacity.

The microeconomic policies could be seen as correction of 'market failures' in the neoclassical sense. The stress on the provision of skills and training (and outside the scope of this chapter the attention on raising educational standards[12]) can be seen in that light. At another level, there is an absence of any policy measures designed to directly intervene in business and its decision making, or to change ownership.

NOTES

1. See Arestis et al. (2001) and Arestis and Sawyer (1999a, b) for our critical evaluation of the Stability and Growth Pact and proposals for an alternative.
2. We have tried to find any reference to such a 'golden rule' in books on public expenditure and the like, and asked many teachers of public economics, but to no avail.
3. This savings ratio is taken from *Economic Trends*, September 1999; savings and disposable income are defined here to include changes in net equity of households in pension funds, and hence influenced by the rising stock market prices.
4. Headline rates would include the standard rate of tax, value added tax and national insurance rates.
5. 'Labour Party General Elections manifestos always promise redistribution, but the commitments to increased benefits for the poor and to higher taxes on those most able to pay were unusually prominent in the February 1974 manifesto' (Gillie, 1991, p. 229). Gillie in his review of redistribution under the 1974/79 Labour government concludes that there was redistribution particularly through the tax and benefit system between 1973 and 1978, with the bottom decile gaining nearly one-fifth in relative income, that is their share rose from 2.92 per cent to 3.47 per cent.
6. Information taken from their web site: www.jrg.org.uk/social_policy.
7. All the figures in this paragraph are taken from *Economic Trends*, April 2000, Table 2 of Appendix 2.
8. Information taken from their web site: www.ifs.org.uk/budgets
9. These include raising the earnings level at which national insurance becomes payable in line with the starting point for payment of income tax, and by levying the excess of earnings over the starting point rather than on all earnings.
10. For the industrial policy of previous Labour governments see Graham (1972) (for the 1964/70 government), and Sawyer (1991) (for the 1974/79 government).
11. In Arestis and Sawyer (1998) we have outlined our views on what constitute Keynesian policies (for the new millennium). We can note here that our perception of Keynesian policies is much broader than (fine-tuning) demand management through fiscal policy. The defeat of Keynesian policies referred to in the text would apply both to a narrow definition of Keynesian policies and our broader definition.
12. Expressed by Tony Blair when he said the priorities of his government were 'education, education, education'.

REFERENCES

Arestis, P. and Sawyer, M. (1998), 'Keynesian policies for the new millennium', *Economic Journal*, **108**, 181-95.
Arestis, P. and Sawyer, M. (1999a), 'Prospects for the Single European Currency', in P. Davidson and J. Kregel (eds), *Full Employment and Price Stability*, Aldershot: Edward Elgar, pp. 57-75.
Arestis, P. and Sawyer, M. (1999b), 'The Economic and Monetary Union: current and future prospects', *Revista*, December.
Arestis, P., McCauley, K. and Sawyer, M. (2001), 'An alternative stability and growth pact for the European Union', *Cambridge Journal of Economics*, **25**(1), 113-30.
Blair, T. (1996), Speech to British American Chamber of Commerce, 11 April.
Blair, T. (1997), Introduction to Labour Party (1997).
Brown, G. (1999), 'The Conditions for Full Employment', Mais Lecture, City University London, 19 October.
Gillie, A. (1991), 'Redistribution', in M. Artis and D. Cobham (eds), *Labour's Economic Policies*, Manchester: Manchester University Press, pp. 229-47.
Graham, A. (1972), 'Industrial policy', in W. Beckerman (ed.), *The Labour Government's Economic Record: 1964-70*, London: Duckworth.
Hill, R. (1999), 'Social Democracy and Economic Strategy: the Labour Party in Opposition 1979-1992', Ph.D. thesis, Brunel University.
Labour Party (1997), *New Labour Because Britain Deserves Better*, London: Labour Party.
Monetary Policy Committee (MPC) (1999), *The Transmission Mechanism of Monetary Policy*, London: Bank of England.
Sawyer, M. (1991), 'Industrial policy', in M. Artis and D. Cobham (eds), *Labour's Economic Policies*, Manchester: Manchester University Press, pp. 158-75.
Treasury (1997), *Pre Budget Report*, Cmnd. 3804, London: HMSO.
Treasury (1999), *Budget 99*, HC298, London: HMSO.

5.   Anatomy of Clintonomics[1]

Robert Pollin

The performance of the US economy in the eight years of the Clinton presidency is widely regarded as having been an extraordinary success. There is no doubt that dramatic departures from past US economic trends have occurred under Clinton. Three, in particular, stand out: the attainment of balance, and then a surplus, in the federal budget; the simultaneous declines in unemployment and inflation, in direct contradiction to the predictions of mainstream economic theory; and the historically unprecedented stock market boom. The Clinton administration and its supporters tout these as the fruit of a new direction in economic policy – what Clinton himself terms a 'Third Way' between 'those who said government was the enemy and those who said government was the solution' – an 'information-age government' that 'must be smaller, must be less bureaucratic, must be fiscally disciplined, and focused on being a catalyst for new ideas'.[2]

Clintonites are not, of course, the only political force to boast of the discovery of a Third Way between the legacy of Reagan and Thatcher and that of traditional social democracy (or what used to be termed 'liberalism' in the United States). Over the past five years, regimes ranging from those of Blair in Britain to Cardoso in Brazil have invoked the same slogan. But if its main theoretical development has come from the UK, in the work of Anthony Giddens (for example 1998), it is the practical record of the US economy that is often held to offer the best evidence that there is substance to the claims for the Third Way.

The reality of both economic policies and performance under Clinton has been very different from this ideological image. In most respects, his policy initiatives represent a conventional centre-right agenda, akin – as Clinton himself once put it – to an 'Eisenhower Republican' stance updated to the post-Cold War epoch. Clinton's policy agenda has essentially been defined by across-the-board reductions in government spending, virtually unqualified enthusiasm for free trade, deregulation of financial markets, and only tepid, inconsistent efforts to regulate labour markets.

In terms of performance, the US economy under Clinton has also been far more mixed than is acknowledged by boosters of his Third Way. Considering the entire Clinton presidency, GDP growth and productivity gains have not exceeded the performance of previous presidential eras, even after official statisticians have revised national accounts upwards to reflect putative contributions to growth by computer technology, and after taking account of the strong acceleration of both productivity and GDP growth since 1996 according to these new statistical measures. Moreover, while unemployment and inflation have both fallen under Clinton, the drop has been in large measure due to the declining ability of workers to secure wage increases even in persistently tight labour markets. Finally, the real economic gains of the period have rested on a fragile foundation – a stock market in which prices have exploded beyond any previous historical experience, inducing an enormous expansion of private expenditure on consumption. But because household incomes have not risen to anywhere near the extent of financial asset values, the result has been unprecedented borrowing to pay for the spending spree. The springs of economic growth under Clinton have come from a levitating stock market setting off a debt-financed private consumption boom.

These developments within the US economy carry great significance for the performance of the world economy as well. However, for the present discussion, our primary focus will remain on the Clintonite policies and performance as these are reflected within the US domestic economy itself, even while recognizing that global integration is a central theme of Clinton's policy agenda. Finally, in referring thus far to the policies and agenda of the Clinton administration, I have written as if these had emerged fully formed from the President's head or the briefs of his advisors. In fact, of course, the initiatives implemented, or even floated, under Clinton were also shaped by Wall Street, a Republican-led Congress, and a host of other forces that converge in the lobbying vortex at Washington. Bill Clinton is a consummate 'consensus politician', to use Margaret Thatcher's term, rather than a 'conviction' politician. As such, the policies he has enacted reflect the general consensus inside the Washington beltway during his presidency more than any possible convictions of his own or of anyone else.

TAXATION AND FEDERAL EXPENDITURES

Taxation

Clinton's tax policies lessened the highly regressive effects of the Reagan–Bush years. However, the relative burden of taxation is now still more regressive than in 1977, prior to Reagan's 1980 election. Mishel et al. (1999) have compared the total impact of the Clinton programme with the Reagan record by analysing the federal tax rates of households at 1998 income levels, under the tax laws that prevailed in various years between 1977–98. Table 5.1 summarizes their main findings. As the table shows, between 1977–89, the bottom 80 per cent of households experienced a slight increase of 0.5 per cent in their tax obligations between 1977–89, and a somewhat bigger decline of 1.6 per cent between 1989–98. Most of the tax reductions were concentrated among the least well-off 20 per cent of households, who experienced a 4.6 per cent decline in their fiscal burden – a drop primarily due to the increased income supplements channelled through the Earned Income Tax Credit. Correspondingly, the richest 20 per cent of households experienced a small decline in their tax rates of 0.3 per cent between 1977–89 that was reversed between 1989–98 when their rates rose by 1.4 per cent. Here, by far the biggest swing was among the top 1 per cent, who experienced a 13.4 per cent tax cut between 1977–89 and a 7.7 per cent tax increase in the period 1989–98. Thus the Clinton Administration did restore part of the progressive dimension of the tax system that was lost in the 1980s, but not all of it.

What is not clear from the table is the extent to which the stock market boom, and consequent rise in revenues from capital gains tax, helped to swell government coffers and allow a balanced budget by 1997. Between 1992 and 1997, revenues from capital gains rose from \$126.7 to \$362 billion – jumping from 2.7 to 5.0 per cent of Treasury receipts. This is just one indicator of the extent to which Clinton's economic record has depended on the fortunes of Wall Street, a topic we consider in more detail below.

Table 5.1   Estimated effective federal tax rates on 1998 income under prevailing tax law, 1977–98

Income group	Percentage point change	
	1977–89	1989–98
Bottom four-fifths	+0.5	−1.6
First	+0.2	−4.6
Second	+1.3	−1.8
Third	+0.4	−0.3
Fourth	0.0	+0.4
Top fifth	−0.3	+1.4
81–95%	−0.3	+0.6
96–99%	−1.9	+2.8
Top 1%	−13.4	+7.7
All	+0.1	−1.0

Source: Mishel et al. (1999).

Expenditures

The overriding objective of the Clinton administration has been to bring government expenditures down, in line with its broader macroeconomic priority of deficit reduction. The extent of the spending cuts is set out in Table 5.2, which shows federal government expenditure patterns between 1992, the last year of the Bush Administration, and 1999. Total expenditures fell as a percentage of GDP from 21.9 to 18.6 per cent between these years, a decline of 14.9 per cent. The most significant reduction slashed military spending from 4.7 to 3.0 per cent of GDP, a drop of 36.7 per cent. But there have been large cuts in other areas as well, including support for education (–9.2 per cent), science (–19.1 per cent), transportation (–11.2 per cent) and income security (–16.0 per cent). The cuts in military spending, of course, reflect the end of the Cold War and consequent expectation of a widespread 'peace dividend'. While they have been substantial, what is more remarkable is that the annual military budget should have remained at $300 billion, after the Cold War justification for an exorbitant arms race evaporated. Spending on arms remains 4.6 times greater than federal outlays on education.

Table 5.2   Federal expenditures by function, 1992–99

	Percentage of GDP		Per cent change, 1992–99
	1992	1999	
Total expenditures	21.87	18.62	–14.9
Defence	4.72	2.99	–36.7
International	0.25	0.16	–36.1
Science	0.25	0.20	–19.1
Natural Resources	0.32	0.26	–18.3
Agriculture	0.24	0.23	–4.6
Transportation	0.52	0.46	–11.2
Education	0.71	0.65	–9.2
Health	1.41	1.54	9.4
Medicare	1.88	2.21	17.3
Income Security	3.12	2.62	–16.0
Social Security	4.56	4.24	–7.0
Veterans	0.54	0.47	–11.8
Justice	0.22	0.26	16.8
Interest	3.15	2.45	–22.3

Source: OMB, Budget of the United States, Historical Tables.

The Administration's extension of the Earned Income Tax Credit has been its most significant anti-poverty initiative. The EITC originated under Ford's Republican Administration in 1975, and expanded under Carter, Reagan and Bush alike. By 1992, the last year of the Bush administration, it covered 14.1 million families, who received an average income supplement of $1076 (in 1998 dollars). By 1997 Clinton's add-on had extended it to an estimated 19.5 million families for an average supplement of nearly $1600. But against this enlargement must be set the dismantling of welfare assistance programmes – these traditional 'family support' programmes falling by $2 billion under Clinton. Moreover, this was not the only area of poverty alleviation expenditures to contract under Clinton. Spending on Food Stamps and other Nutritional Assistance dropped by $4.3 billion, from $37.8 to $33.5 billion between 1992–98 – a decline reflecting an increase in the percentage of households who are not receiving food assistance even though their income level is low enough to qualify them to receive it. Overall, the Clinton administration's anti-poverty policies have not increased income transfers to the poor as a share of GDP. After allowing for the increased costs of child care, the overall conditions of life for America's poor families may have worsened during the Clinton administration.

ECONOMIC PERFORMANCE UNDER CLINTON

However the Clinton administration may have jiggered economic policy, economic performance in the United States under Clinton has been widely hailed as an unqualified success. But looking at some basic indicators in a comparative historical perspective, presented in Tables 5.3–5.6 below, we observe a much more mixed picture.

Macro Performance

Table 5.3 presents some basic macro statistics – GDP growth, productivity, unemployment, and inflation. In the upper panel of the table, the data are grouped by presidential eras – I have combined Kennedy/Johnson, Nixon/Ford, and Reagan/Bush, as well as showing the Carter and Clinton years separately. In the lower panel, I group the same data according to NBER business cycles, as a check on the reliability of presidential eras as a measure of economic trends.[3] These indicators make it clear that, at least through 1999, the Clinton years have not been unusually successful in historical terms. Most strikingly, the Clinton period has not approached the macro performance of the Kennedy/Johnson era, when both GDP (4.8 vs. 3.7 per cent) and productivity growth (3.4 vs. 1.8 per cent) increased much more rapidly, while average unemployment (4.8 vs. 5.6 per cent) was substantially lower. The figures for Clinton will improve when 2000 is included in these aggregates. Nevertheless, even allowing for an additional strong year, the Clinton performance will not match that of the Kennedy/Johnson era in GDP growth, productivity, or unemployment. On the other hand, the rate of inflation under Clinton has been kept down to the low range of the Kennedy/Johnson years,

Table 5.3   Macro performance indicators

(A) Performance by Presidential Terms

	1961–68 Kennedy–Johnson	1969–76 Nixon–Ford	1977–80 Carter	1981–92 Reagan–Bush	1993–99 Clinton
GDP real growth (%)	4.8	2.7	3.4	2.9	3.7
Productivity growth (% for non-farm business sector)	3.4	2.1	0.7	1.7	1.8
Unemployment rate (%)	4.8	5.8	6.5	7.1	5.6
Inflation rate (% measured by CPI)	2.3	6.5	10.3	4.3	2.5

(B) Performance by NBER Business Cycle Averages

	1960–69	1970–79	1980–90	1991–99
GDP real growth (%)	4.4	3.2	2.9	3.2
Productivity growth (% for non-farm business sector)	2.9	2.0	1.4	2.0
Unemployment rate (%)	4.8	6.2	7.1	5.8
Inflation rate (% measured by CPI)	2.5	7.5	5.3	2.7

Note: In the B panel, NBER cycles are grouped on a peak-to-peak basis. For brevity, two sets of cycles – 1970–73/1974–79 and 1980–81/1982–90 – have been merged.

Sources: National Income and Product Accounts (NIPA); Bureau of Labor Statistics.

and declined over time, whereas inflation took off towards the end of Johnson's presidency. Of course, a decline in inflation in itself does not tell us much about who gains or loses from it – it might indicate slack labour markets of no benefit to wage-earners.

Judged by less rigorous standards than the 1960s the macroeconomic record of the Clinton years compares favourably with those of Nixon/Ford, Carter and Reagan/Bush. GDP growth was higher and both unemployment and inflation were lower. Productivity growth was still slow, even relative to the Nixon/Ford years. But the overall performance of the American economy has been stronger, if not to a dramatic degree.

Changing Composition of GDP

Further perspective on the macroeconomic record of the Clinton years is offered by Table 5.4, showing the breakdown of GDP into component

Table 5.4   Components of GDP (in percentages)

(A) Performance by Presidential Terms

	1961–68 Kennedy– Johnson	1969–76 Nixon– Ford	1977–80 Carter	1981–92 Reagan– Bush	1993–99 Clinton
Consumption	61.7	62.2	62.6	64.9	67.0
Government	22.4	21.9	20.0	20.6	18.2
Investment	15.5	15.9	18.2	16.1	16.3
Net Exports	0.4	–0.05	–0.9	–1.6	–1.5

(B) Performance by NBER Business Cycle Averages

	1960–69	1970–79	1980–90	1991–99
Consumption	61.8	62.4	64.4	66.9
Government	22.4	21.2	20.6	18.7
Investment	15.5	16.7	16.7	15.7
Net Exports	0.3	–0.3	–1.7	–1.3

Notes: In the B panel, NBER cycles are grouped on a peak-to-peak basis. For brevity, two sets of cycles – 1970–73/1974–79 and 1980–81/1982–90 – have been merged.

Source: National Income and Product Accounts (NIPA); Economagic web page.

expenditure categories – consumption, government, investment, and net exports. Two sets of figures stand out here. The first we have already noted – the substantial contraction of government spending, which at 18.2 per cent of GDP is far below that of any of the previous presidential periods we are considering. What we also see in Table 5.4 is that the slack created by the fall in public expenditure has been taken up by private consumption, which at 67 per cent of GDP is more than five percentage points higher than during the Kennedy/Johnson boom. It is clear from these figures that the rise in consumer spending has been the driving force of aggregate demand under Clinton, allowing government expenditure to fall without generating a slowdown in overall growth. Thus, to understand what has sustained growth in these years, we need to look at the bases for the expansion of private consumption.

Financial Market Behaviour

The most dramatic economic change of the Clinton presidency has been the transformation of the country's financial structure by the stock market boom and shifts associated with it. Table 5.5 provides some indication of what has been involved. During the Kennedy/Johnson and Reagan/Bush periods, the Standard and Poor index of the stock prices of the top 500 companies in the economy (S&P 500) rose at a rapid annual rate of 6.2 per cent. During the Nixon/Ford and Carter years, the S&P 500 actually fell in real terms. Under Clinton, it has registered an annual growth rate of 17.6 per cent that has no historical precedent.

The performance of the stock market under Clinton becomes even more amazing when measured against GDP during the various presidential eras. In theory, fluctuations in stock prices over a full business cycle are supposed to reflect the underlying performance of the real economy. Thus, by measuring the difference between growth of the S&P 500 and GDP, we can observe the extent to which the stock market is responding to real economic developments. Here again, the Clinton experience is without precedent. Since 1993 the annual rise in stock prices has been 13.9 per cent above that of the real economy. Even in the Reagan and Bush years, during which economic policy overwhelmingly favoured the prerogatives of capital, and financial capital in particular, stock prices rose only 3.3 per cent faster than GDP.

Table 5.5 also presents some data on changes in household financial patterns during the Clinton boom. The third row of figures suggests the degree to which the consumption boom has been debt financed. Household debt – including mortgage and consumer debt – has ratcheted upward dramatically during Clinton's tenure, to reach 94.2 per cent of disposable income. This compares with a ratio of 77.8 per cent during the Reagan/Bush years, itself an

Table 5.5   Financial market indicators

(A) Performance by Presidential Terms

	1961–68 Kennedy– Johnson	1969–76 Nixon– Ford	1977–80 Carter	1981–92 Reagan– Bush	1993–99 Clinton
S&P 500 real average annual growth rate (%)	6.2	–3.6	–2.8	6.2	17.6
S&P 500 real growth – GDP real growth (% gap)	+1.4	–6.3	–6.2	+3.3	+13.9
Total household liabilities/disposable personal income (%)	65.8	64.3	70.0	77.8	94.2
Total household liabilities/financial assets (%)	17.1	19.1	22.2	23.0	21.8
Household bank deposits + govt. securities/total financial assets (%)	25.1	25.4	26.6	26.0	17.8
Real Interest Rate (10-year Treasury bond – CPI rate)	2.2	0.6	–1.2	5.5	3.7

(B) Performance by NBER Business Cycle Averages

	1960–69	1970–79	1980–90	1991–98
S&P 500 real average annual growth rate (%)	2.9	–3.5	5.7	15.9
S&P 500 real growth – GDP real growth (% gap)	–1.5	–6.7	+2.8	+12.7
Total household liabilities/disposable personal income (%)	65.1	65.8	75.7	92.3

	1960-69	1970-79	1980-90	1991-98
Total household liabilities/financial assets (%)	17.0	20.2	22.7	22.2
Household bank deposits + govt. securities/total financial assets (%)	23.2	26.1	26.6	18.5
Real Interest Rate (10-year Treasury bond – CPI rate)	2.1	0.0	5.1	3.9

Notes: Wage data for decile groupings begin in 1973. In the B panel, NBER cycles are grouped on a peak-to-peak basis. For brevity, two sets of cycles - 1970-73/1974-79 and 1980-81/1982-90 - have been merged.

Source: Economagic website; Flow-of-Funds Accounts.

unprecedented level compared with previous periods. The next column, showing household debt relative to total financial assets, indicates how this expansion of debt has been collateralized - by a rise in asset values rather than incomes. Thus, we see that the households' liability/asset ratio has actually fallen slightly during the Clinton presidency, even while the debt/income ratio was shooting up. But the composition of household assets has changed markedly. Traditionally, property-owners have maintained a steady share of their holdings in insured bank deposits and non-defaultable Treasury securities - prior to the Clinton period, somewhere between 25 and 27 per cent. Under Clinton, this 'safe asset' proportion has fallen to 17.8 per cent, a sharp departure from previous patterns.[4]

Finally Table 5.5 reports figures on real interest rates for 10-year Treasury bonds. It shows that rates did fall in the Clinton period relative to Reagan/Bush years, from an average of 5.5 to 3.7 per cent. But the 3.7 per cent rate under Clinton is still far higher than the level of any previous presidential era. Indeed, for the whole postwar period 1947-79, the average real Treasury rate was 1.2 per cent, less than a third of its level in the Clinton period.[5] These figures make it difficult to argue the sharp increase in household debt is a response to low interest rates. The reality is that these have been low only relative to the unprecedented peaks of the Reagan/Bush years: they are high by any other historical benchmark. Moreover, the basic justification of the Clinton administration for its drive to eliminate the federal deficit was that this alone could cut interest rates dramatically, by reducing total demand for credit and enabling the Federal Reserve to pursue a looser monetary policy. In practice, however, rates have fallen relative to the Reagan/Bush years, when federal deficits soared, but remain historically high despite the attainment of fiscal surplus.

Conditions for Workers and the Poor

Finally, Table 5.6 provides some measures of how working people and the poor have fared during Clinton's presidency. The patterns are highly unfavourable to Clinton. Despite the relatively strong macro performance – to say nothing of the stock market boom – both the average wages for non-supervisory workers and the earnings of those in the lowest 10 per cent decile of the wage distribution not only remain well below those of the Nixon–Ford and Carter administrations, but are actually lower even than those of the Reagan–Bush years. Moreover, wage inequality – as measured by the ratio of the 90th to 10th wage decile – has increased sharply during Clinton's tenure in office, even relative to the Republican heyday of the 1980s. Nor has there been any significant reduction in poverty under Clinton, relative even to the Reagan/Bush years, during which government anti-poverty efforts were sharply curtailed. If low rates of unemployment have been a positive feature of the 1990s, it is still quite possible that the overall condition of the poor will prove to have worsened in Clinton's final years of office, as the dismantling of federal welfare programmes proceeds.

EXTRAORDINARY DEVELOPMENTS UNDER CLINTON

What Happened to the Inflation/Unemployment Trade-off?

Whatever else may be said of macroeconomic performance under the Clinton presidency, the simultaneous fall of unemployment and inflation has defied the expectations of virtually all orthodox economists. In 1999, according to official figures, some 4.2 per cent of the workforce were jobless, while inflation was running at 2.4 per cent – higher than the 1.6 per cent rate for 1998, but otherwise lower than all but two other years since 1965. Most economists, adhering to the Natural Unemployment/Non-Accelerating Inflation Rate of Unemployment (NAIRU) doctrines dominant since the early 1970s, had long predicted that unemployment in the region of 4 per cent must lead to headlong inflation. They argued that policymakers were therefore obligated to maintain unemployment at or above its NAIRU rate – that is, above the unemployment rate at which inflation would take off. To this end, it was generally believed that unemployment needed to be perhaps as high as 6 per cent.

Table 5.6   Measures of well-being for workers and the poor

(A) Performance by Presidential Terms

	1961–68 Kennedy–Johnson	1969–76 Nixon–Ford	1977–80 Carter	1981–92 Reagan–Bush	1993–99 Clinton
Average wage for nonsupervisory workers (in 1998 dollars)	$11.53	$13.17	$13.51	$12.82	$12.37
Average wage for 10th percent decile	—	$6.14 (data begin in 1973)	$6.32	$5.68	$5.52
Ratio of 90th/10th percent decile wages	—	3.7 (data begin in 1973)	3.6	4.1	4.4
Individual poverty rate (%)	17.5	11.9	11.9	14.0	13.8

(B) Performance by NBER Business Cycle Averages

	1960–69	1970–79	1980–90	1991–98
Average wage for nonsupervisory workers (in 1998 dollars)	$11.54	$13.36	$12.95	$12.35
Average wage for 10th percent decile	—	$6.24 (data begin in 1973)	$5.73	$5.54
Ratio of 90th/10th percent decile wages	—	3.6 (data begin in 1973)	4.1	4.3
Individual poverty rate (%)	17.5	11.8	13.8	14.0

Notes: Wage data for decile groupings begin in 1973. Because of some gaps in the available data for 1999, all figures in the table end with 1998. In the B panel, NBER cycles are grouped on a peak-to-peak basis. For brevity, two sets of cycles – 1970–73/1974–79 and 1980–81/1982–90 – have been merged.

Source: Bureau of Labor Statistics; Mishel et al. (1999).

What caused the dramatic shift in the trade-off between unemployment and inflation, and to what extent has the Clinton administration been responsible for it? Some leading economists have begun to concede that the NAIRU is subject to change over time. Robert Gordon, for one, has concluded from an extensive econometric analysis of the past two decades that NAIRU is 'time-varying' – falling, for example, from 6.2 per cent in 1990 to 5.6 by mid-1996 (see Gordon, 1997). Staiger et al. (1997) concur, finding that NAIRU in 1997 was between 5.5 and 5.9 per cent, a full percentage point below its level for the early 1980s. They also admit that 'the most striking feature of these estimates is their lack of precision'. Their NAIRU estimate not only varies over time but also has the capacity to range widely at a given point in time.

The general thrust of these broad econometric findings appears solid enough. Indeed, they are difficult to dispute precisely because they are so broad. But in focusing exclusively on the details of how a NAIRU varies over time, they miss the fundamental question that leaps out from these results – namely, what makes a 'time-varying' NAIRU vary in the first place? It is remarkable that leading economists who have devoted so much time to estimating values for NAIRU almost completely neglect this question. Occasionally, however, a few revealing hints are dropped as asides. Gordon, for example writes:

> The two especially large changes in the NAIRU ... are the increase between the early and late 1960s and the decrease in the 1990s. The late 1960s were a time of labor militancy, relatively strong unions, a relatively high minimum wage and a marked increase in labor's share in national income. The 1990s have been a time of labor peace, relatively weak unions, a relatively low minimum wage and a slight decline in labor's income share. (Gordon, 1997, p. 30)

Gordon also casually refers to intensified world competition in product and labour markets, and increased flows of unskilled immigrant labour into the United States, as factors contributing to a declining NAIRU. Though again these observations are mere asides in Gordon's paper, the overall point is clear: it is changes in the balance of forces between capital and labour, and the growing integration of the US into the global economy – which has increased the difficulty of US firms raising prices and US workers getting wage increases – that have been the main forces driving the NAIRU down. Gordon's general hunch is consistent with the econometric results generated by Cara Lown and Robert Rich (1997) of the New York Federal Reserve Bank. They found that, between 1990 and 1995, the stagnation of wages and benefits by itself fully explains the lack of inflationary pressure at low levels of unemployment. Data for the Lown and Rich study end in 1995. Since then, additional factors have contributed to dampening inflation. For one, energy prices fell substantially over 1997–98. In addition, the East Asian financial crisis triggered currency devaluations throughout the region, making American imports cheaper.

The central fact remains, however, that wage gains during the Clinton boom have remained well below those of any other expansion, much less a period of near full employment. These facts provide the basis for the poll findings reported in *Business Week* (27 December 1999) that substantial majorities of US citizens expressed acute dissatisfaction with various features of their economic situation. For example, 51 per cent of American workers interviewed by the magazine declared that they 'felt cheated by their employer'. Such negative popular reactions are striking. Behind them lies the primary explanation for the collapse of the trade-off between unemployment and inflation, openly acknowledged by Alan Greenspan in his regular semi-annual testimony to Congress in July 1997. Saluting the economy's performance that year as 'extraordinary' and 'exceptional', he remarked that a major factor contributing to its outstanding achievement was 'a heightened sense of job insecurity and, as a consequence, subdued wages.'[6] This 'heightened sense of job insecurity' lies at the very foundation of the Clinton administration's economic legacy.

THE STOCK MARKET BOOM

Effects of the Stock Market Boom

The stock market boom has been the other extraordinary development associated with the Clinton presidency. From a perspective beyond that just of Wall Street itself, what makes it extraordinary is the effect it has had on the rest of the US and world economy. Foremost among these broader effects has been the way it has underwritten the debt-financed consumption boom. Dean Baker has summed up this effect as follows:

> The run-up in stock prices, in excess of GDP growth, has added more than $8 trillion in financial wealth over the last nine years. A conventional rule of thumb is that $1 of stock wealth increases consumption by 3 cents. This calculation would imply that the $8 trillion of excessive stock market accumulation over the last nine years has increased consumption by $240 billion compared with a situation where the stock market had only kept pace with GDP. This additional consumption corresponds almost exactly to 4.5 percentage point drop in the saving rate that the economy has experienced during this period. (Baker, 2000, p. 222)

The rise in debt-financed consumption has, in turn, maintained a buoyant level of aggregate demand in the US economy, despite the fact that government expenditures have declined and the trade deficit has grown. At the same time the federal government received nearly $50 billion more in revenue in 1997 relative to 1992 from capital gains tax – by far the largest proportional increase from any fiscal source. Thus the stock market boom has been central both to the creation of a fiscal surplus under Clinton, and – through wealth-driven increases in consumption – to counter the negative effects of that surplus on aggregate demand.

What Caused the Stock Market Boom?

Conventional explanations of the bubble give pride of place to the dramatic advances in computer and internet-related technology, which are held to have engendered formidable productivity gains. But we have seen that productivity has not registered exceptional growth through the full Clinton presidency, even after national accounts were revised upward to make special provision for computer-driven improvements. Still, we should note that productivity did accelerate between 1996 and 1999, to an average annual rate of 2.6 per cent, relative to the dismal 0.8 per cent figure for 1993–95, the first three years of Clinton's term. But such productivity figures are hardly a sufficient basis to underwrite the Clinton stock market boom. To begin with, assuming the new productivity figures are accurate, a 2.6 per cent growth figure is still well below the 3.4 per cent rate in the Kennedy/ Johnson period, during which time nothing close to the Clinton stock market boom ever occurred. In addition, much recent research suggests that the productivity statistics are indeed inflated, perhaps by a substantial amount.[7]

Of course, the promise of future internet-led leaps in productivity remains. But even if we allow that possibility, it still does not explain the magnitude of the current stock price inflation. As Doug Henwood notes:

> The Internet stocks that have headlined the mania over the last year are without known precedent in U.S. financial history. At its highs in early April, the market capitalization of Priceline.com, which sells airline tickets on the web and has microscopic revenues, was twice that of United Airlines and just a hair under American's. America Online was worth nearly as much as Disney and Time Warner combined, and more than GM and Ford combined. Oh yes, enthusiasts respond, but these are bets on a grand future. But previous world-transformative events have never been capitalized like this ... RCA peaked at a P/E of 73 in 1929. Xerox traded at a P/E of 123 in 1961. Apple maxed out at a P/E of 150 in 1980.[8]

Given the historically unique character of the bubble of the 1990s, it will be some time before we have a definitive account of its causes. But for the moment, and still to some extent groping in the dark, we may point to five significant factors:

1. *Financial deregulation.* Charles Kindleberger and others have amply documented the way in which speculative manias have historically recurred in financial markets (see, particularly, Kindleberger, 1977). After the Wall Street crash of 1929 and the slump of the 1930s, postwar governments in all major capitalist economies set in place far-reaching systems of financial regulation to prevent renewed bouts of destructive speculation. In consequence, for the first 25 years after the end of World War II, stock markets were relatively tranquil. This experience suggests one simple explanation for the Clinton boom: that in the absence of effective regulation, speculative excess will inevitably occur in financial markets, though exactly how bubbles will emerge and develop can never be known in advance.

2. *Increased inequality and profitability.* As we have seen, the rewards of economic growth under Clinton have been claimed increasingly by the wealthy. Wages have continued to stagnate or decline for most workers, even as GDP and productivity growth have risen. With wages held down as output and productivity rise, profits inevitably increase. Under Clinton they have reached a 30-year peak. In 1997 the share of total corporate income accruing to profits was 21.6 per cent, as opposed to cyclical highs under Nixon (1973) of 18.0 per cent, Carter (1979) of 17.4 per cent, and even Reagan (1989) of 18.4 per cent (see Mishel et al., 1999). If the strong measured productivity gains since 1996 end up being real and sustainable, this in turn will yield still higher profit shares, until the point at which US labour achieves increased bargaining power. But with labour remaining weak, the escalation of profits under the Clinton presidency in turn feeds expectations of further increases in profitability, in conditions where the political system continues to favour so heavily the interests of the rich, regardless of whether there are Democratic or Republican incumbents in the White House.

3. *Changes in US wealth-holding patterns.* We have seen the extent to which American households have moved their portfolios out of low-risk bank deposits and Treasury securities into riskier assets – above all equities. The rise of mutual funds and derivative markets, through which the risks associated with stock-ownership are spread, has certainly contributed to this shift. But it also suggests that property-owners have come to believe that equities are now less of a hazard than they have been at any prior point in history.[9] The Clinton administration alone is obviously not responsible for creating this state of mind among investors. In part, such thinking stems from the rise in profitability and especially the positive feedback effects of favourable returns on investor expectations. Alan Greenspan himself has repeatedly tried to dampen such 'irrational exuberance' among wealth-holders. But the enthusiasm with which the

Federal Reserve and the Clinton administration have pushed for the deregulation of financial markets has more than counterbalanced any downward jawboning efforts by Greenspan.

4. *Shifts in foreign wealth-holding patterns.* From 1989 onwards, the US has become a net debtor nation, as foreign-owned assets in the country have exceeded American-owned assets abroad. Through the 1990s, foreign wealth-holders have increasingly purchased dollar-denominated assets in US financial markets. By the end of 1998, the magnitude of the foreign debt had reached $1.5 trillion, equal to 18 per cent of GDP - tripling in size over the previous 24 months (see D'Arista, 1999). This inflow of foreign savings is the other side of the persistent American trade deficit. Indeed, it is the continued willingness of foreigners to accept payment in dollars and to invest in dollar-denominated assets that alone has made the trade deficit sustainable. Here the instability of stock markets across the rest of the world has been critical for making American assets so attractive. Independently of the Wall Street bubble, foreign investors prefer US bonds as well as stocks not because returns on them as such are always highest, but because they are perceived as the best risk-adjusted choice. At the same time, the main source of the rise in foreign-owned assets in the US in 1998 was not an increase in net new holdings, but rather price increases in the value of previously purchased foreign-held American assets relative to the prices of American-held foreign assets.

5. *Adept Federal Reserve policy.* The Federal Reserve has been praised for allowing unemployment to fall well below the level that inflation hawks had said was prudent. But, as we have seen, Greenspan understood that job insecurity would inhibit American workers from pressing for wage demands even in tight labour markets, as they had done in the past. Greenspan's real achievement during the Clinton presidency has lain elsewhere - in holding a balance between the need to keep financial markets liquid enough to sustain the stock market, and to keep interest rates high enough to ensure a continued flow of foreign savings into the US. Greenspan has certainly managed this well, even as the counter-vailing market pressures have mounted. Furthermore, had Greenspan and Rubin not conducted successful bail-out operations when the sequence of Mexican, East Asian and Long-Term Capital Management crises broke out, the US stock market would probably have dived as the cumulative effects of these shocks coursed through global financial markets.[10] By a 'successful' bail-out, I mean an operation that not only prevented a chain-reaction of debt defaults, but also protected the wealth of US investors - since substantial losses by American investors would almost certainly have burst the US bubble.

CONCLUSION

How does the record of Clintonomics sum up? It should be clear that the claim that his administration has pioneered a Third Way which renews the best traditions of social democracy is risible. This is not to say that Clinton's policies have been indistinguishable from those of Bush or Reagan. The general requirement of product differentiation in an electoral market means that at the margin any Democratic President will offer more social concessions than a Republican opponent of the same cohort. Viewed historically, as the centre of gravity of the system has shifted to the right over the past generation, a Republican incumbent of one period may well deliver a less pro-business agenda than a Democrat in the next. Such a pattern is suggested in the data we have reviewed – with Nixon-era wage levels substantially higher and poverty levels substantially lower than those under Clinton.

These structural coordinates set the parameters of the US political economy. But what specifics can we attach to the Clintonite Third Way? The core of Clinton's programme has been global economic integration on terms defined almost entirely by business, with minimum interventions to promote equity in labour markets or stability in financial markets. Gestures to the least well-off have been slight and back-handed, while wages for the majority have either stagnated or declined. Wealth has exploded at the top, of course. But with the stratospheric rise of stock prices and the corresponding debt-financed private spending boom being the economy's primary growth engine, Clinton hands over to his successor the most precarious financial pyramid of the postwar epoch.

NOTES

1. An earlier version of this paper was presented at the January 2000 AFEE/ASSA session organized by Philip Arestis and Malcolm Sawyer. I also thank Armagan Gezici and Josh Mason for their excellent research assistance and Perry Anderson, Bob Brenner, Jerry Epstein, Andrew Glyn, and Tom Mertes for their constructive comments. A longer version of this paper was published in the May/June 2000 issue of *New Left Review*.
2. See Clinton's address on Social Security, 9 February 1998, on the White House website.
3. The cyclical data are organised on a peak-to-peak basis, through reference dates established by the National Bureau of Economic Research (NBER). I have derived yearly peak dates from the NBER monthly peaks. When the NBER peak month falls between January and September of a given year, that year becomes the cyclical peak year. If the monthly peak falls between October and December, the following year becomes the peak year. In addition, I have merged two sets of cycles into a single cycle–those for 1970–73/1974–79 and 1980–81/1982–90.
4. Godley (1999) provides a detailed analysis as to why these financial patterns in the household sector cannot last.
5. For the historical figures on interest rates, see Pollin and Dymski (1994).
6. Greenspan's testimony can be found on the Federal Reserve site at www.bog.frb.fed.us.boarddocs/hh/1997/July/testimony.htm

7. Robert Gordon of Northwestern contends that since 1995, virtually all the increases in productivity have occurred in the manufacturing of computer hardware. Gordon claims that 'there has been no productivity acceleration in the 99 per cent of the economy located outside the sector which manufactures computer hardware', James Grant, 'Wired Office, Same Workers', *New York Times*, May 1, 2000, p. A27.
8. 'The United States', *Monthly Review*, July 1999, p. 129.
9. Recent business-book titles giving graphic expression of this state of mind include *Dow 36,000* by James Glassman and Kevin Hassert; *Dow 40,000: Strategies for Profiting from the Greatest Bull Market in History* by David Elias, and, not to be outdone, *Dow 100,000: Fact or Fiction* by Charles Kadlec and Ralph Acampora. An insightful antidote to this literature is Robert J. Shiller, *Irrational Exuberance*.
10. In saying 'probably', as opposed to 'certainly', I am acknowledging the countervailing possibility that worsening conditions in overseas markets might have driven foreign investment in the US upwards still further. But it is still difficult to imagine that a full-scale bankruptcy of Long-Term Capital Management would not have burst the bubble of 'irrational exuberance' in America.

REFERENCES

Baker, D. (2000), '"Something New in the Nineties?" Looking for Evidence of An Economic Transformation', in Jeff Madrick (ed.), *Unconventional Wisdom: Alternative Perspectives on the New Economy*, New York: Century Foundation.
D'Arista, J. (1999), 'International Capital Flows and the US Capital Account', *Capital Flows Monitor*, December 6.
Elias, D. (1999), *Dow 40,000: Strategies for Profiting from the Greatest Bull Market in History*, New York: McGraw Hill.
Giddens, A. (1998), *The Third Way: The Renewal of Social Democracy*, Cambridge, UK: Polity Press.
Glassman, J. and Hassert, K. (1999), *Dow 36,000*, New York: Times Books.
Godley, W. (1999), 'Seven Unsustainable Processes: Medium-Term Prospects and Policies for the United States and the World', Special Report, Levy Institute, Annandale.
Gordon, R. (1997), 'The time-varying NAIRU and its implications for economic policy', *Journal of Economic Perspectives*, **11**(1), 11–32.
Kadlec, C. and Acampora, R. (l999), *Dow 100,000: Fact or Fiction?*, New York: Prentice Hill.
Kindleberger, C. (1977), *Manias, Crashes and Panics: A History of Financial Crisis*, New York: Basic Books.
Lown, C. and Rich, R. (1997), 'Is there an inflation puzzle?', *Federal Reserve Bank of New York Economic Policy Review*, December, 51–69.
Mishel, L., Bernstein, J. and Schmitt, J. (1999), *The State of Working America 1998-1999*, Ithaca, NY: Cornell University Press.
Pollin, R. and Dymski, G. (1994), 'The Costs and Benefits of Financial Instability: Big Government and the Minsky Paradox', in Dymski and Pollin (eds), *New Perspectives in Monetary Macroeconomics*, Ann Arbor: University of Michigan Press, pp. 369–402.
Shiller, R.J. (2000), *Irrational Exuberance*, Princeton, NJ: Princeton University Press.
Staiger, D., Stock, J. and Watson, M. (1997), 'The NAIRU, unemployment and monetary policy', *Journal of Economic Perspectives*, **11**(l), 33–50.

6. Social democratic policy and economic reality: the Canadian experience

Jim Stanford[1]

6.1 OVERVIEW

This chapter reviews the economic policies of Canada's New Democratic Party (NDP) through the 1990s. To varying degrees during the decade, the federal and most provincial wings of the NDP have adopted more conservative, 'Third Way' style, economic policies. Canada's political economy was dominated during the decade by a historically significant scaling back of public-sector programmes, regulations, and economic activities, nominally motivated by the need to eliminate the chronic deficits which were experienced by the federal and provincial governments through most of the last quarter-century. In general, the NDP has accepted, and in some cases even advanced, this sea-change in Canada's economic and social policy, and the consequent downsizing of the public sphere. The NDP's present policy stance is one which explicitly accepts a smaller and more defensive economic and social role for the state, the leading role of private profit-seeking investment in motivating growth and job creation, and more 'disciplined', deregulated, and unequal outcomes in the labour market. The ways in which the NDP's economic policies differ from those of an increasingly conservative mainstream are becoming less evident. Indeed for the political strategists guiding the party's reorientation, the acceptance of that mainstream vision – lower taxes, smaller state programmes, an orientation of policy towards fostering international and business competitiveness – forms a key element in their effort to present the NDP as a less threatening political alternative.

The recent rightward shift in NDP economic policy is placed here in the context of the party's failure (hardly unique in the global social democratic movement) to develop a more far-reaching, structural critique of an economy that is dependent almost exclusively on the process of private capital accumulation. When capitalism is vibrant and growing, social democrats have shown a proven ability to argue for, and win, substantial concessions from both private employers (in the form of higher private labour incomes) and governments (in the form of an expanded social wage). But when the internal logic of private, profit-led capitalism starts to falter – as it clearly did in Canada in the 1990s – then the social democratic recipe is in trouble. The party needs to articulate a more radical critique of why the private, profit-led economic engine is sputtering, and to explore what types of structural reforms might help to reconstruct the economy on alternative grounds, leaving society less vulnerable to the mood swings of private investors and businesses. Without this structural analysis, social democratic policy seems more-or-less destined to accept the broad dictates of the neoliberal vision for resuscitating profit-led capitalism. Social democrats will then be relegated to proposing various measures which would attach a more 'human face' to that fundamentally oppressive project.

6.2   THE ECONOMIC AND POLITICAL CONTEXT

Canada is a federal state, with constitutional powers for economic and social policies divided between the federal government and ten provincial governments. The provincial governments have relatively extensive powers of taxation (including the levying of personal and corporate incomes taxes, and consumption taxes), and hold responsibility for the administration of most 'big-ticket' social programmes (including health care, education, and welfare). A portion of the cost of these programmes has traditionally been borne by the federal government through a network of transfer payments to the provincial level, although the generosity of these transfers was radically reduced during the late 1990s. Programme spending by provincial governments is significantly larger than equivalent programme spending by US states; lower-level government programme spending[2] was equivalent to 25 per cent of GDP in 1999, compared to about 12 per cent in the US. In contrast, programme spending at the federal level in Canada is now slightly smaller (in the wake of deep late-1990s spending cutbacks) than federal programme spending in the US, measured as a share of GDP.

Provincial governments in Canada thus possess relatively important economic and social powers, although control over the major macroeconomic levers (including monetary, trade, and exchange rate policies, and the largest portion of taxation) remains at the federal level. This has created both problems and opportunities for the NDP – which has never been elected at the federal level, but which has experienced periods of governance in four different provinces.[3] Provincial governments enjoy considerable leeway over the design and funding of important public-sector economic and social initiatives: at the same time, however, they are vulnerable to negative macroeconomic developments which are largely beyond their control. This vulnerability imposed a major constraint on NDP provincial governments during the 1990s.

Since the formation of the NDP in the 1930s,[4] Canadian federal elections have always featured at least three main contenders; in recent years, this has grown to five (including new Quebec nationalist and conservative parties). This is important to consider in evaluating the NDP's recent repositioning, for the following reason. Since the party has never ranked higher than third in federal politics (and currently ranks even lower), the strategic electoral arithmetic which has motivated Third Way political movements in the UK and US does not apply in Canada. Unlike New Labour, for example, the NDP cannot hope to win much 'middle ground' by adopting more conservative economic policies; the middle ground in Canada is already well-inhabited by much stronger political rivals (namely the Liberals). This casts considerable doubt on the electoral pay-off that could feasibly be expected to result from a Third Way repositioning – even if it were accepted that short-term electoral success would legitimate such a repositioning (a point which is obviously controversial in its own right).

In contrast to federal elections, the NDP has enjoyed relatively regular electoral success at the provincial level, particularly in three Western provinces: largely rural Saskatchewan (where the first-ever NDP government was elected after World War II, and where the party pioneered the introduction of socialised medical care – subsequently copied elsewhere in Canada – in the 1960s), equally rural Manitoba, and British Columbia. At the time of writing, the NDP forms the government in Saskatchewan and Manitoba (ruling in coalition with the Liberals in Saskatchewan). The NDP also served one ill-fated term as government of Ontario, Canada's most populous province, from 1990 to 1995. Currently, the party's electoral base is weak in most parts of Canada. Perhaps even more importantly, there is a historic lack of vision and enthusiasm regarding the party's prospects and direction, both among the rank-and-file activists in the party itself and those in various social movements and constituencies which have been traditional sources of NDP support.

Developments in Canada's economy have also exerted an important and obvious influence on the recent evolution of NDP economic policy. Canada's macroeconomic performance during the 1990s was disastrous, both in relation to previous historical periods and compared to the performance of other OECD countries during that time. Canada's economic performance was among the worst in the entire OECD during the 1990s. Three major factors account for this poor record. The implementation of the Canada–US Free

Trade Agreement (FTA) in 1989 resulted in a painful but largely one-time process of dislocation and restructuring, particularly focused in the manufacturing sector. The effects of this restructuring were considerably exacerbated by Canada's experiment between 1987 and 1993 with an ultra-tight monetary policy regime. Under the leadership of then-Governor John Crow, the Bank of Canada became one of the first in the OECD to adopt official inflation targets, drove up interest rates far above international or US levels, and even flirted publicly with the notion of a zero-inflation policy. The effects of this regime included a vastly overvalued exchange rate (which was probably more important than the FTA itself in the subsequent recession experienced in export industries) and a domestic recession that was far deeper than that experienced simultaneously in the US.[5]

Thirdly, Canada experienced a dramatic tightening of fiscal policy that dominated its macroeconomy through the latter half of the decade (see Figure 6.1). The watershed moment in this respect was the 1995 federal budget, implemented by Liberal Finance Minister Paul Martin, which outlined dramatic cuts in federal programme spending (which fell by about one-fifth, measured as a share of GDP, over the next three years). After years of chronic deficits, Canada's public debt (at the federal and provincial levels) exceeded 100 per cent of GDP by 1996, the second-highest in the G7; this alone hardly

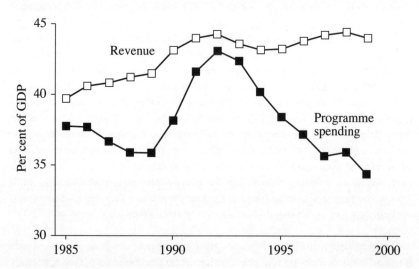

Note: Includes all levels of government.

Source: All figures are author's calculations from Statistics Canada, *Canadian Economic Observer*.

Figure 6.1   Canadian public finances, 1985–99

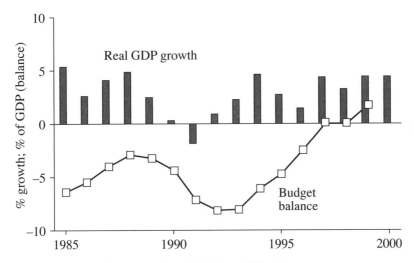

Figure 6.2   Canadian growth and deficits, 1985-99

justified the painful and one-sided measures which were taken to arrest this accumulation of debt, but the circumstances certainly contributed to public acceptance and even approval of this broadly painful fiscal restructuring. Most provincial governments matched this tightening with spending cutbacks of their own - motivated in large part by the trickle-down effects of steep reductions in federal transfer payments to provincial governments. This ultra-tight fiscal policy allowed Canada to become the first of the G7 economies to balance its overall public budget in 1997 (see Figure 6.2); but the macroeconomic price was steep (not to mention, of course, the social implications).

Economic circumstances were brightening considerably by the end of the decade, in the wake of the easing of first monetary and then fiscal policy. Canada's growth and job creation between 1998 and 2000 matched or exceeded that of the US, and governments at all levels reaped the fiscal benefits of this growth in the form of higher-than-expected tax revenues. The federal government and several provinces began to generate significant fiscal surpluses - the first in a generation. The fiscal dividends of renewed growth have sparked an important public debate over how the looming surpluses should be allocated, with conservatives supporting major tax cuts (especially reductions in personal income taxes), and social advocates calling for a rebuilding of tattered public programmes. The NDP's shifting position in this debate has provided an important barometer of changes in its overall economic policy outlook, as will be discussed in more detail in the following sections.

6.3   MISSED OPPORTUNITIES: THE FEDERAL NDP'S ECONOMIC POLICY OUTLOOK

The federal NDP has traditionally advocated a rather mainstream, Keynesian vision of economic and social policy. The government should play an important role in supplementing and moderating the growth of the private-sector economy, through redistributive taxes and transfers, investments in 'human capital', and public spending and investments in public services and infrastructure. In terms of deeper structural issues, the party's economic position has been largely defensive – opposing conservative-leaning structural changes to postwar institutions and policies which were implemented by earlier non-NDP governments. This would describe the party's opposition to the various neoliberal structural reforms which were implemented by the Conservative government which ruled from 1984 to 1993, and similar changes introduced by a remarkably conservative-looking Liberal government since then (including free trade with the US and Mexico; the deregulation of the energy, transportation, and communication industries; and the radical downsizing of Canada's unemployment insurance system). Apart from resisting these conservative policies, and defending the general economic and social role of the state which was inherited from earlier postwar decades, the NDP has not had much to say about how to reform and develop the structure of Canada's economy in a progressive way.[6]

Two areas of structural weakness in Canada s economy particularly seem conspicuous by their absence from this traditional Keynesian economic policy package. Canada has always been hampered by the disproportionately resource-based nature of its economy. Structural policies to promote investment and development in secondary manufacturing have long been identified by progressive economists as a crucial ingredient in any strategy to qualitatively advance the Canadian economy, but have not received wide attention in NDP policy statements.[7] While Canada's economy and exports have diversified in recent years, the structural underdevelopment of the economy (especially apparent in a very small high-technology electronics and computing sector) is still readily visible. Apart from vague supply-side prescriptions for public spending on education and training, the NDP's economic platform has not traditionally addressed this structural issue.

Secondly, Canada – like most other nations of Anglo-Saxon colonial heritage – has an overdeveloped and politically influential financial sector. The crucial features of this industry are a group of large banks which typically retain only arm's-length relationships with the real businesses they finance, and a large stock market. It has consistently been argued by progressives in

Canada[8] that the economic and political power of this financial sector distorts the processes of real capital accumulation and economic development in an unfavourable way. Once again, however, the NDP position on this subject has been largely defensive. The party still has an official policy resolution on its books (dating from the 1970s) calling for the nationalisation of a major bank, but this policy is no longer advanced publicly. Party policy calling for the establishment of a national public investment bank has been similarly downplayed in public fora. More recently, the party joined the widespread opposition to major proposed bank mergers that were announced in 1997 (and subsequently rejected by the Liberal Finance Minister), without providing much of a vision for progressive structural changes in the existing financial system. The party also supports the introduction of a US-style Community Reinvestment Act to force banks to finance mortgages and loans in low-income regions of the country; this is a good but limited initiative.[9]

Following the 1997 election there was a serious attempt to remake the federal NDP's policy outlook. On the face of it, this is somewhat surprising: the 1997 election was conducted on a very traditional Keynesian economic platform, and the party did reasonably well (tripling its number of seats, and regaining official party status after a disastrous showing in 1993). It is hard to argue that the more traditional approach – despite the aforementioned inadequacies – was an electoral liability. However, impressed by the electoral successes of New Labour and other European social democratic parties, and impatient with the limits of being an opposition 'social conscience', the professional strategists guiding the party launched a major makeover in 1998. A now famous cross-Canada train trip by the party's parliamentary caucus was the springboard for the reinvention of NDP economic policy. Then-Finance spokesperson Nelson Riis announced at the conclusion of that caucus retreat that the NDP would henceforth expound a more business-friendly economic strategy. At the same time, the traditional NDP view that future fiscal surpluses should be invested in the rebuilding of public and social programmes was abandoned, in favour of a simple 'balanced' formula: an NDP government would spend equal portions of the surplus on social programmes, tax cuts, and the repayment of some of the outstanding debt. This was the most shocking of the policy changes as it positioned the NDP (temporarily, in retrospect) to the right of the governing Liberals (who had conducted the 1997 election on a pledge to devote half of future surpluses to social programmes, and half to the combination of tax cuts and debt reduction). Under the NDP's formula, in fact, federal programme spending would actually continue to decline as a share of GDP.

These announcements of a Third Way-style policy shift for the federal NDP were premature, and occurred without sufficient party debate and consultation. After widespread criticism of the positions by many segments of the party faithful, some of the positions (such as the 'one-third' rule for allocating future surpluses) were withdrawn, pending the outcome of a more formal policy review which concluded with the party's 1999 federal convention. Publicity surrounding that convention described the meeting as a showdown between 'left-wing traditionalists' and the 'modernisers' who wanted to bring NDP policy into the modern era.

This showdown turned out to be mostly symbolic, since the resulting policy changes were surprisingly modest and rather inconclusive.[10] Two policy papers dealing with economic policy were passed at the convention – one dealing with fiscal policy, the other with job creation. The fiscal policy paper stated the generally non-controversial point that large fiscal deficits are not sustainable on a long-run basis, and hence budgets should be balanced (on average) over the course of the business cycle. As far as dividing future fiscal surpluses, the paper states vaguely that 'priority ... must be given to rebuilding and modernizing ... important public services and social programs'. [11] This leaves unspecified room for tax cuts which would in theory be targeted at lower- and middle-income Canadians (although some of the recommended measures would also deliver large benefits to high-income Canadians). This vague position allowed party publicists to argue that the NDP supports tax cuts, too – hence capitalising on (or at least being less injured by) the right-wing 'tax revolt' which was being stoked across Canada by conservative parties and business lobbyists. The 1999 job creation paper was even more muddled and symbolic, repeating traditional calls for public-sector job creation and the establishment of formal unemployment-reduction targets to guide monetary policy, while expressing support for additional vague measures to assist the job-creating activities of private business (especially small business). Both papers were heralded by the party's modernisers as proof of a new era for the NDP – as if the party had ever 'supported' deficits, or 'opposed' private-sector job creation.

In the wake of the 1999 federal convention, the federal NDP's economic policy, in formal terms, has not much changed despite all the public relations hype about a major shift in the party's thinking. A close reading of the party's policy documents does not yet support the conclusion that the NDP has adopted a Third Way approach – although the continued emphasis of some party leaders on tax cuts and other conserative measures (an emphasis which is technically legitimated by the loose wording of the policy papers) provides grounds for concern. The deeper problem is that the NDP's 1999 policy statements are so vague that they leave no clear impression whatsoever about the party's ideological direction.

The confusion over the federal NDP's policy direction only deepened during the November 2000 federal election. The federal party's election programme stayed remarkably true to its traditional mainstream Keynesian roots – advocating significant increases in programme spending in several key areas. The one exception to this trend was a high-profile emphasis on 'targeted' tax cuts. This represented a concession to the seeming power of right-wing anti-tax ideology, even though opinion polls ironically showed that Canadians consistently ranked social programme spending far above tax cuts in their ordering of fiscal priorities. Despite a status-quo election programme, party strategists and spin-doctors continued their efforts to portray the NDP as having 'modernised' and broken from its traditional 'free-spending' ways. The party's popular support declined even further in the 2000 election, to just 8 per cent of the national vote, and commentators on all sides agree that the party's future is in doubt.

A Third Way remaking of Canada's federal NDP has thus been announced, but is a long way from being fully enacted. Large segments of the party membership (including segments of the politically and financially important labour movement) are clearly opposed to this direction. Professional strategists view it as essential to the resuscitation of the party's flagging electoral fortunes (despite the glaring lack of any electoral dividend to date from the repositioning). Party leaders are influenced by the strategists, but are not yet determined or confident enough in their direction to push through policies which would clearly qualify as Third Way in nature. Such an effort would necessitate a more open and genuine struggle to defeat the influence of party 'traditionalists' (in the same manner, for instance, as New Labour had to rout the political and structural base of its opponents within the Labour Party). A veneer of vague consensus is preserved within the party, but as a consequence its economic policies seem to say little of substance about anything – hardly a recipe for rebuilding the NDP's public profile and appeal. Canada's left is now weaker at the level of federal electoral politics than at any time in the last four decades. This is an astounding setback, given the immense political opportunities which should have existed. Canada's economic policies shifted dramatically to the right in the 1990s, with huge human and social costs. The rightward move of the ruling Liberals, combined with disunity and disarray among the more conservative parties, could have presented the NDP with significant opportunity. Historically significant mobilisations among Canadian social movements protesting free trade, social cutbacks, and other negative developments would have supported any electoral initiative which captured their imagination and their energy. But the federal NDP's preoccupation with modernising its economic image has repeatedly led it to emphasize as much what is 'necessary' or 'inevitable' about these neoliberal changes, as how they could be opposed and ultimately defeated.

88 *The economics of the Third Way*

6.4 FROM THEORY TO PRACTICE: THE NDP IN PROVINCIAL POWER

NDP economic policies have been put into practice in four different provinces in Canada during the 1990s.[12] The NDP governed for most of the decade in BC and Saskatchewan. It was elected at the end of the decade in Manitoba (where it also governed for a period during the 1980s). The NDP governed Ontario for one term, from 1990 to 1995. The NDP also constituted a serious electoral challenge in Nova Scotia later in the decade. NDP policies in each of these provinces will be considered briefly below, in the context of overall economic developments.

As will be seen, official NDP policy positions – hardly radical or visionary to begin with – were substantially watered down or even negated entirely in many, if not most, attempts to attain their real-world application at the provincial level. Figures 6.3 to 6.12 provide summary illustrations of the fiscal and economic performance of each province considered, while Table 6.1 provides an interprovincial comparison of three key indicators of labour market regulation: minimum wages, trade union density, and welfare rates.

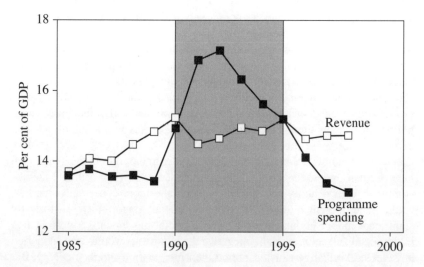

Note: In this and the following figures, the shaded areas indicate periods of social democratic administration.

Figure 6.3 Ontario public finances, 1985–98

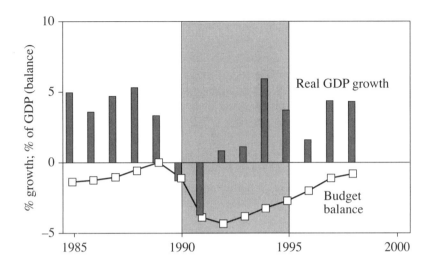

Figure 6.4   Ontario growth and deficits, 1985-98

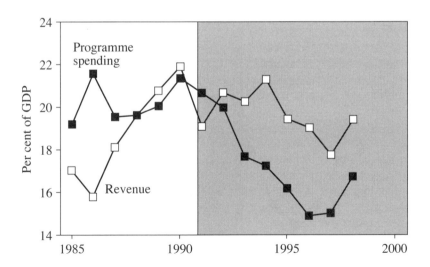

Figure 6.5   Saskatchewan public finances, 1985-98

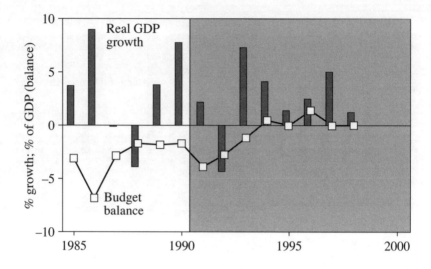

Figure 6.6   Saskatchewan growth and deficits, 1985-98

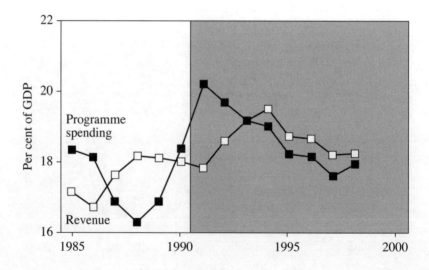

Figure 6.7   British Columbia public finances, 1985-98

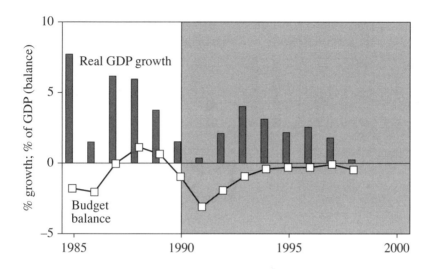

Figure 6.8   British Columbia growth and deficits, 1985-98

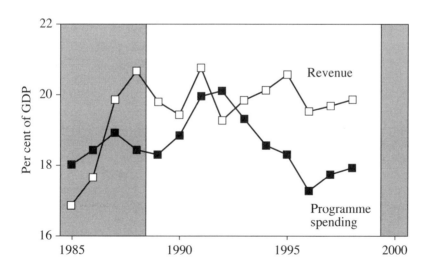

Figure 6.9   Manitoba public finances, 1985-98

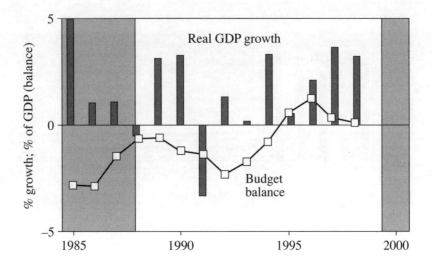

Figure 6.10   Manitoba growth and deficits, 1985-98

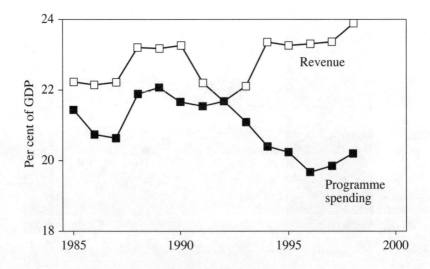

Figure 6.11   Nova Scotia public finances, 1985-98

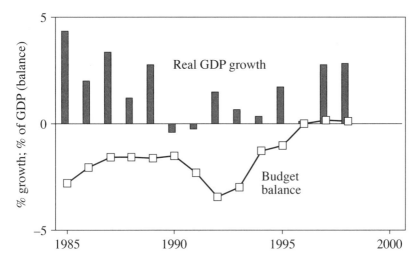

Figure 6.12 Nova Scotia growth and deficits, 1985-98

Table 6.1 Indices of labour market regulation, Canadian Provinces

Minimum wage[1]		Trade union density[2]		Social assistance[3]	
Province and rank	Level	Province and rank	Level (%)	Province and rank	Level
BC (1)	$7.15	Newfoundland (1)	40.2	Ontario (1)	$11 659
Quebec (2)	$6.90	Quebec (2)	40.0	BC (2)	$11 611
Ontario (3)	$6.85	BC (3)	36.6	Newfoundland (3)	$11 436
Manitoba (4)	$6.00	Saskatchewan (3)	36.6	Quebec (4)	$10 823
Saskatchewan (4)	$6.00	Manitoba (5)	36.3	Nova Scotia (5)	$10 382
Alberta (6)	$5.90	Nova Scotia (6)	30.6	New Brunswick (6)	$9 924
Nova Scotia (7)	$5.60	Ontario (7)	29.4	PEI (7)	$9 669
New Brunswick (8)	$5.50	PEI (8)	29.3	Manitoba (8)	$9 333
Newfoundland (8)	$5.50	New Brunswick (9)	29.2	Saskatchewan (9)	$9 288
PEI (10)	$5.40	Alberta (10)	25.8	Alberta (10)	$9 184

Notes
Shaded areas indicate provinces with social democratic governments as of end-1999 (although the NDP government in Manitoba had been in power only a few months).
1. Dollars per hour, adult workers, end-1999; source, *CCH Canadian Labour Law Reports.*
2. Per cent of non-agricultural employees covered by union contracts, 1998; source, 'Unionization – an update', by Ernest B. Akyeampong, *Perspectives on Labour and Income* (Statistics Canada Catalogue 75-001), Autumn 1999, pp. 45–65.
3. Annual income for single parent and one child, 1998; source, National Council on Welfare, *Welfare Incomes 1997-1998* (Ottawa, 2000).

Ontario

No province better symbolises the stumbling of social democracy in Canada than Ontario. The NDP gained an almost-accidental majority in that province's 1990 election, despite receiving well under 40 per cent of the total vote. The province, Canada's manufacturing heartland, was already slipping into a major recession – induced by free trade restructuring and very high interest rates – even as the ballots were being counted. What supporters viewed as an historic opportunity on election night, turned into a painful and historically destructive effort by the NDP merely to manage the fiscal fall-out of that recession. The NDP government was crushed in 1995 by a resurgent. aggressive Conservative party which has since overseen radical cutbacks to provincial social programmes and deep cuts to personal income taxes. This right-wing administration was re-elected in 1999, while the NDP slipped even further – losing its official party status, and failing to win even the official support of many traditional allies who quite understandably became more concerned with defeating Conservatives (by voting for the Liberals in some strategic ridings) than with electing NDP candidates.

Trends in Ontario's overall economic and fiscal indicators are summarised in Figures 6.3 and 6.4.[13] Programme spending rose sharply in the first two years of NDP rule, although hardly at all because of new spending initiatives. Rather, it was the escalating cost of existing programmes in the face of a brutal recession (Ontario was hardest hit by the 1990–92 downturn) which drove the budget deeply into the red. The provincial deficit reached 5 per cent of GDP in 1992, which is a large deficit by any definition – particularly for a sub-national jurisdiction. The rest of the NDP administration was then preoccupied with efforts to reduce spending. These culminated in the decision to impose forcible wage concessions on the province's unionised public sector workforce. This destroyed the relationship between the party and most of the labour movement, which refused to support the NDP in the next election campaign.

By the end of the NDP's short stay in power, programme spending had declined most of the way back to its pre-1990 levels; spending (and taxes) have continued to decline under the subsequent Conservative regime. The NDP succeeded in arresting an emerging fiscal crisis, but at huge cost to its own political base, and to its long-term political fortunes.

The NDP did implement a set of relatively modest reforms in various legislative areas, including pro-union changes in labour law and strong employment equity and pay equity laws. These were all reversed by the subsequent Conservative government. One interesting experiment in the economic policy field was the NDP's establishment of a series of sectoral partnership initiatives, which brought together labour, business, and academics to develop sectoral development strategies for a series of key industries in the province. These initiatives, however, were underfunded and possessed no real decision-making authority; they, too, were dissolved by the Conservatives in 1995. Other initiatives in the area of industrial strategy included a series of rescue efforts involving public funds and (in many instances) wage concessions by unionised workers, aimed at saving several troubled firms in the steel, paper, and aerospace industries.

Clearly the Ontario NDP inherited a terrible economic situation that was not of its own making. But even if real constraints were imposed on its ability to implement new programmes, one would have at least expected the party to put more effort into strengthening the ideological and institutional position of its traditional supporters – rather than turning on them when they refused to go along with the NDP's strategy for 'managing' the crisis. If ever there was a case in which a political party should have declined an opportunity to govern, this was it.

Saskatchewan

Saskatchewan is a largely rural province in Western Canada which has been the longstanding 'cradle' of the NDP's electoral base. After close to a decade in opposition, the NDP was returned to office in 1991 under the leadership of self-defined moderate Roy Romanow. The NDP inherited a large deficit from the previous Conservative regime, and made its top priority the balancing of the provincial budget. This was achieved in 1994 – in fact, Saskatchewan was the first province in Canada to balance its budget in the 1990s – partly thanks to tax increases (the government temporarily increased its sales tax to help fund the deficit-reduction effort) but mostly due to major reductions in programme spending (most controversially including the closure of dozens of hospitals in rural Saskatchewan). As indicated in Figure 6.5, provincial programme spending declined by over 7 points of GDP during the first seven years of the NDP's current reign – among the steepest declines in any Canadian province.

After the attainment of a balanced provincial budget, the Saskatchewan NDP pledged to devote equal one-third slices of future fiscal surpluses to tax reduction, programme spending, and debt repayment.[14] This implies that programme spending will continue to decline as a share of GDP under the NDP administration (as indeed it has). The first major tax cut implemented under this formula was the reversal of the temporary deficit-related increase in sales taxes; this seems sensible, given the linkage of the earlier sales tax increase to the deficit-reduction exercise. Subsequent tax cuts, however, are taking the form of across-the-board reductions in personal income taxes which will disproportionately benefit high-income residents. Following the restructuring of the province's personal income tax system, which will be completed in 2001, Saskatchewan will be one of the lowest-tax jurisdictions in Canada. In a bizarre case of a race-to-the-bottom among social democratic administrations, Saskatchewan's tax cuts have added important pressure on the new NDP government in neighbouring Manitoba to follow suit. All of this has earned the Saskatchewan NDP a reputation among journalists and financial analysts as one of the most fiscally conservative regimes in Canada.

In other policy areas, the Saskatchewan NDP's record is mixed. It has been one of the first jurisdictions to experiment with legislation requiring the compulsory provision by private-sector employers of pro-rated non-wage benefits to part-time employees. This is an important policy initiative, although the government has been criticised by the labour movement for moving too tentatively in this area. The government earned the further wrath of its labour supporters by legislating striking nurses back to work in 1999 before their strike even began; as with other NDP regimes, collective bargaining freedoms seem politically contingent in Saskatchewan whenever they become fiscally inconvenient. Saskatchewan has also introduced a unique programme (partly funded with federal child support monies) to subsidise the incomes of low-wage workers. These wage subsidy schemes are popular with market-oriented economists because of their effect in enhancing the 'incentive to work' among welfare recipients and other poor people. Yet the programme is controversial with social advocates because it denies benefits to non-working poor people, and may serve to perpetuate low (pre-subsidy) wages paid in the private labour market. As indicated in Table 6.1, minimum wages and welfare rates in Saskatchewan are not high by Canadian standards, despite the NDP's long time in office there; the traditional tools of progressive labour market regulation also seem to have fallen out of favour with these most ambitious Canadian advocates of Third Way policies. Saskatchewan's government continues to operate a number of important Crown corporations in a number of resource and utility industries.

The NDP was re-elected with a majority government in Saskatchewan in 1995 but then suffered a surprising electoral setback in 1999. Despite a divided and corruption-ridden opposition, the NDP squeaked back to power with a minority position, and subsequently formed a formal coalition government with the Liberal party. This is likely to enhance the rightward direction of the province's economic policies. The 1999 election raises further questions about whether the NDP can indeed expect to attain significant electoral benefits from the adoption of more conservative economic policies, even in jurisdictions (like Saskatchewan) where a largely 'two-party' political tradition would seem most amenable to efforts to position the NDP in the political middle. Centrist Premier Roy Romanow resigned his position in

September, 2000, and promptly suggested that the NDP should merge with the Liberals – a notion also being touted by Ontario's one-term former NDP Premier, Bob Rae.

British Columbia

Of all of the NDP governments which held power during the 1990s, the BC government was by far the most consistently committed to progressive economic and social policies. In contrast to other NDP administrations which oversaw significant reductions in programme spending, the BC government increased provincial programme spending on a modest but sustained basis, by about 2.5 percentage points of GDP (see Figures 6.7 and 6.8). This clearly went against the stream of restraint which dominated Canadian politics during the decade, and occurred in the face of fierce opposition from the government's critics. The government was helped earlier in its mandate by a provincial economy that was the fastest-growing in Canada (in fact, the province escaped the 1990–92 recession altogether), but then was hurt later in its mandate by relatively weak economic conditions. Resource- and export-dependent BC was the part of Canada hardest-hit by the economic side-effects of the 1997–98 financial crisis in Asia. Unfairly but unsurprisingly, the provincial government received most of the blame for this set of circumstances which was clearly beyond its control.

The BC government was also the most ambitious in terms of pro-active economic interventions aimed at improving the structure and performance of the economy and the labour market. Some of these experiences were highly successful, and should serve as models for similar measures elsewhere. The construction of a new highway on rugged Vancouver Island, for example, incorporated a pioneering effort to impose public-sector labour regulations (including very ambitious affirmative action hiring of women and aboriginal workers) on privately-contracted work activity, and was largely successful. More of these experiments, unfortunately, were not successful. These would include failed efforts to stimulate value-added and alternative forms of employment in BC's troubled forestry sector, and a programme to finance the construction of new high-technology passenger ferries in BC shipyards; both programmes experienced difficulty meeting performance targets (including budget targets), and contributed to the public perception of the government as wasteful and inefficient. Bail-outs of failing private firms (especially in the forestry products sector) constituted another unsuccessful component of the government's overall economic strategy.

The government was also plagued by several non-economic scandals, largely of its own making (two successive premiers were forced to resign by public pressure associated with investigations into separate gambling-related concerns). And to some extent, the NDP in BC failed to sufficiently challenge the right-wing ideology that now has it so much on the defensive. For example, the party aggressively promoted its claim to have balanced the provincial budget during the 1996 election; this backfired when economic circumstances deteriorated and the province turned out to have incurred an (economically trivial) deficit. BC is one of Canada's least-indebted provinces. and recent provincial deficits (none of which exceeded a single point of GDP in public accounts terms and which were near-zero in national accounts terms) did not add significantly to that low debt burden. Yet these deficits were highly damaging politically to a government which was reluctant to argue publicly that deficits of this magnitude are simply not worth worrying about. Making matters worse, in 2000 the NDP under new Premier Ujal Dosanjh even implemented token 'balanced budget' legislation to force future governments to balance the books – a completely symbolic gesture to the ideology of fiscal restraint that only strengthened the government's opponents.

Unlike other provinces, this was an NDP government that – for the most part and despite many difficulties – stayed true to the broadly progressive platform on which it was elected. Yet it faced seemingly overwhelming opposition from an aggressive business community, an incredibly partisan media, and other forces. The NDP was crushed in the May 2001 provincial election, almost wiped out by the right-wing provincial Liberal party. The BC experience seems to indicate that the NDP needs much more than just principled and reliable leaders if it is to effect real progressive change. A successful socialist movement will also require the long-run development of structures which allow it to challenge the ideological power of pro-business media and intellectual institutions. Even more dauntingly, it will also need measures which would insulate to some degree the overall economy against negative trends in private investment spending and job creation (such as public investment projects, public-sector job creation, and non-profit or cooperative economic undertakings).

Manitoba

The NDP was elected to the government of Manitoba during the fall of 1999, after over a decade in opposition. It is too early to judge the direction of economic and social policy that this newest provincial administration will pursue; the previous NDP government of Premier Howard Pawley, which governed during the mid-1980s, was certainly one of the more principled NDP provincial administrations that Canada has experienced. The provincial NDP's election platform, however, did not give cause for too much optimism. It emphasised balanced budgets and sound management; it criticised the then-ruling Conservative party for promising to spend an extra $500 million each on tax cuts and improved health care, claiming that neither was fiscally responsible. Importantly, the only tax cut promised by the NDP was a relatively modest property tax credit for homeowners. Incoming Premier Gary Doer certainly seemed to endorse a Third Way vision, stating, 'I really believe that [the NDP] cuts across both left and right to be the party of education and training and skill development'.[15] Provincial programme spending declined in the wake of the previous Conservative government's deficit-reduction efforts (see Figures 6.9 and 6.10), although not as quickly as in neighbouring NDP-ruled Saskatchewan. The NDP government's first budget, in May 2000, adopted an essentially stand-pat approach. Taxes (including personal income taxes) were cut, but not as aggressively as in other jurisdictions: programme spending increased slightly in some areas, but will continue to decline as a share of provincial GDP.

Nova Scotia

The NDP has never held power in Nova Scotia, a relatively poor province in Eastern Canada. But the party's near brush with power in the 1998 provincial election (when it tied the ruling Liberals in number of seats),[16] and its subsequent setback in the follow-up 1999 election (which returned a majority Conservative government promising radical action to eliminate the provincial deficit) is sufficiently instructive that it is considered here. Nova Scotia already endured one round of steep provincial spending cuts, engineered in the mid-1990s by a right-wing Liberal government, whose unpopular leader then stepped down prior to the 1998 election (see Figures 6.11 and 6.12). The post-1998 minority Liberal government made a solemn promise that it would maintain the newfound balance in the provincial budget. The budget which it brought down in 1999, however, contained a thinly-disguised but moderate deficit incurred to finance badly-needed health care investments. Surprisingly, the NDP opposition joined with the Conservatives to defeat this budget (and hence the government) on the grounds that it broke the balanced-budget promise made by the Liberals in the 1998 election. Running chronic deficits to pay for essential public services, in the long run, is hardly a sustainable fiscal strategy, so there were some grounds to criticise the transparently manipulative strategy adopted by the Liberal minority government. At the same time, however, it is strange indeed to see a left party taking the rhetoric of balanced budgets so far as to actually defeat a government on grounds that it was spending too much on human services.

The NDP contested the follow-up 1999 election with an extremely moderate election platform, stressing its commitment to fiscal responsibility, balanced budgets, and support for small business. The central goal was to emphasise that voting for the NDP did not mean voting for deficits, inefficiency, and turmoil. Third Way party strategists and even conservative newspaper columnists heralded the Nova Scotia NDP, under popular leader Robert Chisholm, as representing an energetic new wave for the party. When the ballots were counted, however, the party had failed in its jump for power: it lost eight seats, 5 percentage points of voter support, and ended up tied with the Liberals for second place. Meanwhile, the new Conservative government pledged to cut already-emaciated public programmes with a vengeance. This has sparked an outpouring of public opposition to the spending cuts. Ironically, the strategic focus of the NDP's overall political and electoral strategy can only have undermined these grass-roots efforts to preserve public services. By bringing down a government on the grounds that it failed to balance the budget, and making 'fiscal prudence' a centrepiece of its own campaign, the NDP clearly contributed to the emergence of the current regressive trend in Nova Scotia politics.

6.5   SOCIAL DEMOCRACY IN QUEBEC

Quebec is currently governed by the nationalist Parti Québecois (PQ), a party that is committed to the goal of national independence for the province. The nationalist movement in Quebec has long enjoyed strong support from the labour movement and other progressive social constituencies in the province, and hence the PQ has tended to espouse a rather shaky commitment to social democratic principles. After a decade in opposition, the PQ was elected to provincial government in 1994, and re-elected again in 1999. Ironically, the PQ was led back to power by Lucien Bouchard, a former cabinet minister in the much-hated federal Conservative government of Brian Mulroney. This in itself is reflective of the extent to which ideological concerns in Quebec are often fluidly subjugated to the ultimate goal of national independence. Nevertheless, in many important respects the PQ government reflects a social democratic outlook (certainly more so, say, than the NDP government of Saskatchewan).

Indeed, to some extent the experience of Quebec under the PQ illustrates both the worst and the best of what Canadians can expect from social democratic governments. On the one hand, the Quebec government has repeatedly shown itself rather shamelessly willing to sacrifice important principles of progressive economic and social policy to the imperative of building support for the nationalist project. Fiscal policy under the current PQ administration, for example, has been dominated by a major downsizing of provincial programme spending (among the deepest spending cuts in all of Canada – see Figures 6.13 and 6.14). These cutbacks were explicitly justified with the argument that Quebec could never achieve independence without first

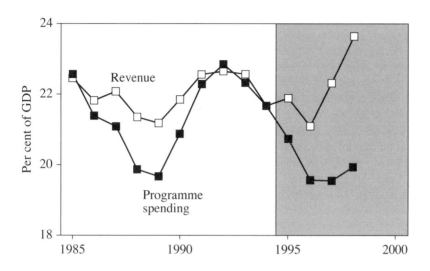

Figure 6.13   Quebec public finances, 1985-98

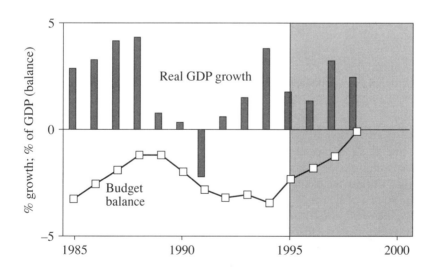

Figure 6.14   Quebec growth and deficits, 1985-98

balancing its budget; the acquiescence of public-sector unions and other important social constituencies was largely attained on the basis of the shared desire for internal solidarity within the broader nationalist movement.

At the same time, however, the Quebec government has also demonstrated its commitment to a vision of fundamental structural and social change – also integrally connected with the nationalist project – that far surpasses anything espoused by the NDP in English Canada. A whole range of alternatives, largely non-profit economic, financial, and social institutions have been built over the last three decades in Quebec, and these have collectively come to be known as the 'Quebec model' of social and economic development.[17] These include a large provincial pension funding agency (with assets exceeding $100 billion Cdn by end-1999), which pro-actively places its investments in companies and projects of strategic importance to Quebec. Labour markets are also relatively regulated in Quebec (see Table 6.1); workers' incomes and living standards in Quebec are clearly higher than in other provinces with equally or even more affluent economies. Despite the harsh fiscal constraints experienced through most of the 1990s, the PQ government found the funds (and the political fortitude) to implement what has become the single most important innovation in Canadian social policy during the decade: a wide-ranging family policy, the centrepiece of which is the provision of nearly-free child care services to families with working parents. This programme, while initially highly controversial, has since become extremely popular, and serves as an inspiration to activists in English Canada fighting for similar measures. One only wishes that provincial NDP administrations could show similar courage and creativity in fighting for advances in public services and programmes.

6.6   ANALYSIS: SOCIAL DEMOCRACY AND THE LOGIC OF CAPITALISM

The recent rightward shift within most (but not all) sections of Canada's NDP is not at all untypical in light of similar developments in other social democratic parties around the industrialised world. And it would be quite wrong to place the blame for this shift solely at the feet of opportunistic, short-sighted political leaders and strategists more concerned with grasping for electoral success than with being able to do anything with that success should it ever be attained (although in many instances the regressive role played by leaders of this sort is undeniable). The difficulties faced by the NDP government in British Columbia provide a difficult and challenging lesson in exactly how daunting the current economic and political obstacles to progressive social and economic change in an advanced industrial economy have become. It is hardly surprising that many otherwise sincere progressives would prefer to follow an easier and seemingly more feasible path of accepting the fundamental constraints of the lean, mean neo-liberal economy while attempting to put (where it is fiscally responsible to do so!) a somewhat more human face on those features.

The welfare state of postwar Canada was not built by NDP governments (although the NDP played a supporting role). It was built by mainstream political parties responding to popular pressure (expressed in many ways, not just at the ballot box), within an environment of vibrant accumulation and economic expansion in which the cost of those programmes and services could be borne by businesses and taxpayers relatively painlessly. All of this changed when the regime of private-sector accumulation which fuelled the postwar boom began to sputter – as it did in Canada, like most other OECD economies, beginning in the late 1970s. In the context of macroeconomic stagnation, poor business profitability, slower growth, and constant vigilance against inflation, the costs to capitalism of providing services and entitlements which once were widely taken for granted, became unacceptably high. To restore a regime of profitable business-led growth, business now demands lower taxes and a more 'disciplined' labour market – one in which workers are less protected by income security measures and other forms of regulation, and more subject to the raw dollars-and-sense logic of private labour commodification.

How ironic, then, that the NDP should enjoy its moment of greatest electoral success in the early 1990s – the precise time in which the underlying economic conditions so vital to the fiscal health of welfare-state capitalism were more in question than at any time in the postwar era.[18] As of 1992 the NDP held power in provinces accounting for a majority of Canada's population, and held a record number of seats in the federal Parliament. Yet the economic underpinnings of Canada's existing social programmes and institutions were crumbling – along with popular hopes of improving those institutions under newly-elected NDP governments. At best, the NDP would have to fight vigorously just to defend programmes designed and implemented by earlier mainstream parties. At worst (as in Saskatchewan, Ontario, and under the PQ in Quebec) it would position itself explicitly as a party which was best able (by virtue of its support and credibility amongst the very elements of society most likely to forcefully resist the dismantling of the welfare state) to smoothly facilitate the necessary 'adjustments' in public programmes and public finance. The longer-run failure (or perhaps refusal) of the NDP to consider and fight for alternative economic structures which might reduce society's overall reliance on the private profit-led business sector, compromised its ability to respond to the crisis of the 1990s. Apart from defending a welfare state status quo which the most powerful elements in society wanted to substantially roll back, the NDP had little in the way of alternative visions of growth, capital accumulation, and job creation.

Canada's economy was radically restructured along neo-liberal lines in the 1990s, perhaps more dramatically than any other OECD country. This imposes clear constraints on the ability of future progressive governments to restore past levels of equality and security for Canadians, unless they are prepared to challenge the underlying features of that neo-liberal regime – in particular, the dominant role of private investment in generating growth and employment, and the largely unregulated power of private finance. The task of developing a more far-reaching critique of these structural constraints is not likely one that social democrats will undertake, given past experience. Others will have to take on this responsibility.

At the same time, however, there is clearly some discretionary room even within a neo-liberal regime to offer higher or lower degrees of economic well-being and security for working people. In other words, even under global neo-liberalism, there is still some 'choice of capitalisms' possible – as evidenced, for example, by the seeming sustainability of corporatist socioeconomic arrangements in some European countries (like Denmark, Austria, or the Netherlands). This may leave some political space for a party which explicitly accepts the dictates of the neo-liberal project, while arguing for limited reforms and protections within that project. Particularly in the event that private investment and job creation regain some of their lost vitality in the wake of the pro-business structural changes of the 1990s (as may be occurring in Canada), then resources will be available to both corporations and governments to fund improvements in private incomes and social programmes – without impeding (not immediately, at least) the underlying profit-driven dynamic of accumulation. But even within this very limited political horizon, recent policy debates within Canada's NDP have been disappointing. With the party's 'pragmatic' political professionals pushing for tax cuts, balanced budget laws, and other token gestures of conservatism in the interests of a questionable shorter-run electoral dividend, it seems that the vision of social democrats has been circumscribed even more narrowly than the grim realities of modern capitalism would require.

NOTES

1. Views expressed are those of the author and should not be attributed to the CAW.
2. Including programme spending by local governments and school boards, which are constitutionally accountable to the provincial governments.
3. This does not include Quebec, which would bring to five the number of Canadian provinces which have experienced social democratic rule at some time.
4. The original social democratic party was the Cooperative Commonwealth Federation (CCF), which was reconstituted as the NDP in the 1960s.

5. A new Bank of Canada Governor was appointed by the new Liberal government in 1993, and Canadian monetary policy has been considerably more balanced since then.

6. The most recent significant exception to this general rule was the NDP's support in the mid-1970s for a very interventionist approach to energy policy in Canada. While it was supporting a minority Liberal government between 1972 and 1974, the NDP extracted a promise to form a state petroleum company, subsequently called Petro-Canada (and subsequently re-privatised by the Conservative government in the early 1990s). The NDP also supported many elements of the Liberals' interventionist National Energy Programme which was introduced after the 1979 OPEC oil shock.

7. A left oppositional movement within the NDP, known as the 'Waffle', advocated a more nationalist economic strategy along these lines, but its leaders were expelled from the party in the early 1970s.

8. See *Paper Boom*, by Jim Stanford (Ottawa: Canadian Centre for Policy Alternatives and James Lorimer & Co., 1999) for a recent statement of this view.

9. Also deserving of honourable mention in this regard is the effort of NDP MP Lorne Nystrom in 1999 to have the House of Commons approve a resolution calling for the multilateral implementation of a Tobin Tax on international currency transactions – making Canada the first country to have such a resolution passed by its national parliament. However, the fact that the ruling Liberals supported the resolution, with no intention of acting to try to implement it, is ample testimony to its largely symbolic importance.

10. In a strange twist, the party leadership joined with dissidents in supporting a motion denouncing UK-style Third Way policies, with party leaders saying they wanted to find their own way, not a 'Third Way'. Thus the debate over policy direction dissolved into a dispute over semantics.

11. 'Social democratic fiscal framework in a global environment', NDP Discussion Paper, August 1999.

12. Social democratic policies in a fifth province, Quebec, are considered separately below.

13. In all of the Figures 6.3-6.12, periods during which NDP governments were in power are indicated with grey shading.

14. It was following this model that the federal NDP temporarily adopted a similar formula in 1998.

15. 'Doer declares health number one priority', by Lori Cuthbert, *National Post*, 23 September, 1999.

16. The Liberals were allowed to form a minority government by virtue of their status as the incumbent administration.

17. Not all of these innovations were implemented by PQ governments; the provincial Liberal party has also traditionally advanced a rather statist model of economic development, although it has shifted markedly to the right in recent years.

18. This point is made in 'The NDP in power: illusion and reality', by Leo Panitch, *Studies in Political Economy*, **37**, Spring 1992, 173–88.

7. The Third Way: Italian experiments

Augusto Graziani

7.1 INTRODUCTION

The following brief background will clarify the succession of political events in Italy. In 1992 a number of judicial cases were brought which demonstrated the extensive corruption of the two main political parties, the Christian Democratic Party and the Socialist Party. Craxi, the head of the government, was forced to resign and was replaced by a close follower of his, Amato. In 1993, Amato resigned and a totally new government was formed under Ciampi, former Governor of the Bank of Italy who did not belong to any political party.

In 1994 new elections were held. Right-wing parties gained a majority and a new government was formed under Berlusconi. The neo-fascist party National Alliance was part of the majority and was represented within the government, which shook public opinion throughout Europe. However, the government was short-lived. Among its opponents it counted the left-wing parties, the unions, and also, to a certain extent, major industry (authoritative daily newspapers such as *Il Corriere della Sera* or *La Stampa*, both owned by the Fiat group, never lost an opportunity to demonstrate their distance from the Premier and his government). The Berlusconi Government lost its majority in parliament and was finally forced to resign as a consequence of popular movements against a proposed reform of old-age pensions. In 1995, a new technical government was appointed under Dini, a former officer of the Bank of Italy and more recently Secretary for Foreign Affairs under Berlusconi, but who did not belong to any political party.

In 1996 new elections were held and the first centre-left government came into power under Prodi. Most commentators considered this to be a stable government. However, in October 1998, the left-wing party PRC refused to approve the Financial Law for the following year, which contained a severe reduction in social expenditure. Prodi was forced to resign and was replaced by D'Alema, Secretary of the DS Party (a descendant of the former Italian Communist Party). This new government faced serious problems. In 1999, the euro was created as an accounting currency and the Italian lira was brought into a regime of fixed exchange rates. In April 1999, the government had to make the difficult decision of joining NATO in the Kosovo operation. Two political defeats followed: in June 1999, the administration of the city of Bologna, an old and traditional stronghold of the Communist Party, was lost and a new mayor, belonging to the right-wing parties, was elected. In April 2000, local elections were held in various regions of the country, and resulted in a clear victory for the right-wing parties. The main regions of Northern Italy were now administered by right-wing local governments who all claimed greater independence on matters concerning security, hospitals and education. D'Alema was forced to resign and was succeeded by Amato, a former member of the Socialist Party who was politically close to Craxi. His government remained in power until the political elections of 2001.

7.2   THE ECONOMIC POLICY OF THE ITALIAN GOVERNMENT. PHASE ONE

As already said, in April 2000 the local elections gave a clear victory to the right-wing coalition. In eight regions, with a total of over 32 million inhabitants, the right-wing parties gained a clear majority, while the centre-left coalition gained seven regions having a total of only 16 million inhabitants. D'Alema resigned and a new government was appointed under Amato, who had led the government in 1992–93. A large number of former members of the now no longer existing Socialist Party entered the government, giving rise to a widespread feeling that, after eight years, the Socialist Party might again be in power.

The first task of the new government was to make it possible for Italy to be accepted into the European Monetary Union. Two main targets were selected as overruling any other possible accomplishment, namely reducing the current government deficit and bringing the inflation rate into line with the remaining European countries. Both targets made it necessary to follow a policy of extreme austerity, a policy deemed unavoidable in order to modify the image of the country.

Three lines of attack were chosen: (a) reducing current expenditure in any possible way, first of all by modifying the regime of old-age pensions; (b) fighting inflation by means of greater flexibility in the labour market; (c) reducing government involvement in industry and banking by a radical policy of privatisation.

The Attack on Pensions

The official interpretation is that, owing to a sharp decrease in the birth rate, Italy has an overwhelming number of elderly in its population structure. The consequence is that a radical reform of the pension system is necessary to avoid financial collapse. Opposing arguments suggest that the forecast of a financial collapse is exceedingly pessimistic. The budget of INPS (the national institute taking care of workers' pensions) is made unduly heavy by the number of payments pertaining more to charity than to social welfare proper. In addition to that, if, as it is to be hoped, unemployment rates decrease over the next few years, the revenue of INPS should increase, thus reducing the annual deficit. The same would be true if, as should happen, the extension of the black economy is reduced.

It has been suggested more than once that the so-called 'seniority pensions', paid to those who have served for a certain number of years independently of their age, should be totally eliminated. In addition to that, a fundamental reform is being introduced. In Italy, the annual payments for pensions are financed by means of the contributions paid by the employed workers during the same year. It is clear that when employment is growing the annual yields more than cover the needs, while when employment declines payments exceed current contributions and taxpayers have to cover the difference. Any worker, when reaching retirement age, gets a pension provided he has been working for a minimum number of years. The system is therefore based on a sort of solidarity among generations.

The reform called for by the centre-left governments gradually introduces the opposite system, according to which the pension of each worker will be paid in proportion to the amount of yearly contributions paid during his working life. In principle this seems to be fair, in that it introduces a sort of market system very similar to a private insurance. In practice, the system is perhaps even too fair, since it is widely felt that old-age pensions should not be the exact equivalent of insurance, something that the market, properly controlled, could provide for. It is easy to forecast that the new system will be one of increasing inequalities.

It is estimated that, as a consequence of the reforms already enacted or to be introduced in the system, the average amount of an old-age pension will no longer be equal, as it is now, to 80 per cent of the salary before taxes, but only to some 50 per cent of it (in most countries having a compulsory pension scheme, coverage reaches 80–90 per cent of the salary). As a consequence, measures are being taken in order to encourage workers to supplement the pension provided by law with additional voluntary savings. New legislation is being passed in order to encourage the establishment of pension funds, enjoying some sort of tax privilege so as to make them attractive. In order to make the working of the new pension funds easier, new rules have been introduced concerning the management of the retirement bonus.

A typical feature of the Italian system is that Italian workers when leaving a job get a retirement bonus, which is part and parcel of their pay, except that it is deferred until the day when the worker is dismissed or resigns, or reaches retirement age. In the past, so long as the worker was at work, the retirement fund was kept by the employer and a conventional yield was acknowledged on it. Now, in connection with the general reform of old-age pensions, workers will be able to freely dispose of the yearly appropriations made by the employers for the retirement bonus. This means that they can leave the sum as before, administered by their employer, or they can withdraw it and invest it in a pension fund. In this case, when reaching retirement age, the worker would no longer be credited with a flat sum but would enjoy an annuity, or supplementary pension, for the rest of his life. This would of course reduce the range of his possible choices as compared to the old system of paying the worker a retirement bonus.

The government is attempting to attract as much saving as possible to the newly created pension funds. Since the new system will sound less attractive to workers than the old one, for this operation to be successful pension funds have to be able to offer higher rewards. This means that higher tax exemptions are needed than the government so far has been inclined to grant. At the same time, it is widely recognised that for a fund to have a reasonably diversified portfolio and a low incidence of administration costs, a large flow of savings is vital. This is why most commentators agree on the fact that there should be some sort of compulsory scheme according to which workers would not be totally free to ask for their retirement bonus to be paid to them year-in-year-out in the form of a higher wage. The workers' choice should rather be restricted to leaving the fund with the employer, or using it in order to subscribe to a pension fund.

A further problem is that the government has been concentrating on the so-called 'Closed Pension Funds', administered by single firms or by groups of firms belonging to a single sector and open only to employees belonging to the same sector. The development of similar funds would of course make the operation more palatable to firms (or at least to big firms, able to manage a pension fund). On the other hand, in the view of more than one expert, it would seriously limit mobility in the labour market.

Health care

The administration of health care has long been the responsibility of regional governments. The new provisions of the centre-left governments have, however, considerably altered the situation. Three main policy lines can be indicated as relevant.

The orientation towards privatisation has been applied to hospitals as well as other institutions. The aim is to create a more rational administration and avoid a waste of resources. Doctors currently have to choose between working in a hospital or practising as private doctors. The aim is to force doctors to spend all of their time inside the hospital where they belong and where they are allowed to treat private patients. The patients will pay the hospital for the treatment they get and the doctor will get a given sum according to the treatment administered. In principle this is a most reasonable arrangement. A possible drawback is that the best doctors may prefer, and in more than one case they have in fact preferred, to be private practitioners since this grants them much higher incomes. In addition the new system might well be a source of increasing disparities in health care.

Hospitals are now financially independent, and the primary target of the governing bodies is reaching a balanced budget. Each patient's case is now dealt with from a cost-benefits perspective and in each case the profit or loss margin (namely the difference between the actual cost of the treatment and what will be covered by regional funds) is carefully computed. Patients are accepted or rejected according to the results of such computations.

A second policy line is to reduce expenditures by limiting the number of drugs distributed free (or at a fixed cost paid by the patient on each prescription). The reduction in the issue of free drugs is constantly increasing and it has become so severe that even seriously ill persons have to pay for the treatment they need.

The final policy line is an indirect one. The newly elected regional councils can now proceed to draw up their own statutes. This means that each region will now enjoy a larger autonomy than before. The tendency to grant greater autonomy to local authorities was a deliberate decision by the centre-left governments in an attempt, or rather in the illusion, of gaining the favour of the right-wing electorate. The response was that the regions of Northern Italy, all of which are now in the hands of right-wing local governments, have already decided to adopt similar statutes stressing the autonomy of each region in at least three fields, namely health care, school systems and local police. The general presumption is that health care provided by hospitals, now open in principle to all residents of Italy, will be gradually restricted to residents of the region.

7.3   THE ECONOMIC POLICY OF THE ITALIAN GOVERNMENT. PHASE TWO

On the political level, the centre-left government had to face equally serious kinds of problems in both internal policy and in foreign relationships.

Internal policy was dominated by the debate between centralisation and decentralisation. The regions of North Italy, by far the most prosperous of the country, have been requesting greater autonomy for a long time. In their view, an exceedingly high amount of government expenditure has been channelled to the South of the country where no productive capacity has been created. In contrast to that, the regions of Northern Italy have shown themselves able to set up competitive economies and efficient administrations. Therefore, the time has come to grant them as much autonomy as the political unity of the country can support (in some cases, politicians have also requested the complete political independence of North Italy). At the same time, a different but convergent movement has been developing in South Italy. Here the argument has been put forward that the administration of single big cities can do much more than the national government for the improvement of local situations. There was a certain moment in which the creation of a Party of the Mayors, bypassing the single political parties, was suggested. In an attempt to gain the favour of similar movements, the centre-left governments have approved new legislation granting a higher autonomy to each region of the country (Fausto and Pica, 2000).

In the field of foreign policy, the centre-left governments thought it necessary to give formal proof of being tied to the Western bloc. This was especially true of the two governments headed by D'Alema, a former member of the now dissolved Italian Communist Party. When the Kosovo war broke out, serious doubts were raised in various circles. The participation of Italy in the war was the subject of a hot debate in the cabinet and some authoritative secretaries of State spoke against it (an interpretation of the Kosovo war under a more general viewpoint is supplied in Chesnais, 1999).

The majority of the government (including the Premier, Amato), however, decided to let the NATO bases located in the Italian territory be used for air attacks against Serbia and to send military forces to join the NATO troops. The Italian presence was mainly used for assistance to refugees and only a reduced number of air attacks were actually performed by the Italian aircraft (or at least only a few of them were made public).

When the Kosovo war was over, the Italian Government declared that since the financial situation of the country had improved, new targets could be pursued and that the time had come to take care of employment and development. On the political level, the government took a clear stand in favour of giving greater power to local regional governments, handing over to regions a number of responsibilities now belonging to the national government. The single regions are now entitled to chose their own statutes and bylaws as well as their own electoral systems.

Flexibility in the Labour Market

On the economic level, employment policy was based on three main instruments: modernisation, wage flexibility and self-employment.

The debate on the possible effects of wage flexibility was intense. Employers claimed that on the one hand the cost of labour was too high as compared to international standards; and that, on the other hand, a number of constraints concerning freedom of hiring and dismissing had to be dropped. In January 1999, D'Alema himself, addressing in his capacity of Prime Minister a group of industry people gathered at the Bocconi University in Milan, declared that firms of large and average size should be made free from any constraint on the labour market (small firms are already free from any constraint). In fact, unions made a number of concessions concerning conditions of employment. As a consequence, new hiring was largely performed under what came to be called 'atypical contracts'. This meant that workers were hired for a limited number of weekly hours, or for a limited time, or under various kinds of specified arrangements. In practice, such part-time workers are used for replacing the old overtime work, something strictly forbidden by the law.

The argument put forward by employers, and supported by sympathetic independent scholars, was the typical neoclassical one of bringing real wages in line with the marginal productivity of labour. In this view, the wide increase in black economy employment would be a proof of the fact that a reduction in the cost of labour brings about an increase in employment. The circles close to industry do not deny that the growth of the underground sector, where labour is deprived of any sort of guarantee, is a sad characteristic of any industrial take-off. But they claim that this is only a temporary phase, a sort of initial cost to be met if industry has to gain competitiveness and enter the world market. The industrial development of the north-eastern regions of Italy over the last fifty years would supply historical proof of their argument.

The response by the unions, equally supported by other groups of commentators, was that no proof can be supplied of the fact that the productivity of labour is technically determined and that the cost of labour has to be made equal to it. The productivity of labour is in fact dependent on technology and a regime of low wages may induce employers to make use of more primitive technologies or to delay the introduction of technical progress. A greater flexibility might well result in higher employment but it would also produce a downgrading of national industry, thus slowing down long-term growth.

In some cases the introduction of greater flexibility also meant a retreat from previous social conquests. For instance the general prohibition of night shifts for female workers, introduced by law in 1977, has been greatly limited.

The debate on flexibility leads us to comment on the industrial policy of the left-wing governments.

Industrial Policy

In fact, it has been widely recognised that, over the last twenty years, Italian industry has withdrawn from the few advanced sectors where it was present (Guerrieri and Pianta, 1998). In the past, attempts were made to develop new initiatives in three advanced sectors, nuclear power, electronics and the pharmaceutical industry. The first and third sectors were in the hands of government-owned industry; the second one was being developed by the Olivetti group. Owing to reasons that were never made totally clear, each of these attempts was a failure and Italian industry gradually concentrated in the more traditional sectors; the same sectors in which it has to face the competition of the newly industrialised countries (NICs) of the Far East.

So long as the European Common Market was a protected area this was no great disadvantage. In fact Italian industry had found a convenient space of survival in the group of the six countries forming the initial Common Market. Some sort of division of labour had been put into practice, according to which the more advanced countries (Germany, the Netherlands, France) developed the more technologically advanced sectors, leaving market space to Italian industry in the more traditional sectors. All indexes of trade specialisation indicate as typical Italian export industries: food and beverages, textiles, clothing, leather and footwear, wood and furniture, ceramics, household appliances and cars. At the time, it could reasonably be maintained that inside the European Common Market trade diversion bypassed trade creation. But it was also clear that Italian industry was drawing an advantage from that.

In the following years, three groups of events radically altered the trade position of Italy. The first event was the appearance on the world market of the NICs of the Far East, all of which were mainly specialized in the same sectors in which Italian industry was having the greater success. The second factor was the gradual enlargement of the European Community, which from the initial six countries grew to include nine, twelve and finally fifteen countries. The enlargement of the Community has brought into the common market such countries as Spain, Greece and Portugal, all of which can count on far lower production costs. Finally, the downfall of the Soviet Union has opened the European market to imports from the former socialist countries which has encouraged a number of Italian industries to relocate their activities in locations where the cost of labour is lower and provisions against pollution less stringent. Initially, Italian entrepreneurs experimented with distant locations (such as the Philippines or Hong Kong). More recently much closer and more convenient locations have become accessible (East European countries, Albania).

The decline in large firms has been a general characteristic of Italian industry all over the country. In fact, the drive towards small- and medium-sized industry has been one of the few permanent criteria of industrial policy enacted by the national government. The leading idea has been that in a small-sized industry the cost of labour is lower and competitiveness consequently higher. The consequence has been fewer workers in the so-called guaranteed sector and an increasing number confined to precarious jobs, in small concerns, or working as self-employed or even in the underground economy (Bellofiore, 1998). The official creed is that the self-employed enjoy a much greater freedom since they are no longer held to obey the rigid rules of the big factory. While this may be true, it is also true that the self-employed are exposed to violent fluctuations in work and earnings, that in periods of high demand there are no limits to hours worked, and that in practice they have no welfare of any sort (Bologna and Fumagalli, 1997).

The practice of delegating a number of segments of production, once called decentralisation, now called outsourcing, has continued to increase. When outsourcing is applied to material production, the supplying firms live as separate entities, even if often located in the vicinity of the bigger firm. When applied to services, outsourcing often means that employees of the smaller suppliers work inside the main factory along with employees of the main firm. This gives rise not only to social frictions among workers, given the disparities in wage rates and fringe benefits, but also to frictions in management since it is always doubtful whether a problem in production is the responsibility of the main firm or of smaller suppliers.

A leading factor in the disappearance of large firms has been the policy of privatisation followed by the Italian Government (Berti, 1998). The official reason for government disengagement from the industrial sector was that since most government-owned firms were in the red, handing them over to the private sector would help reduce the government debt. In fact, ever since 1993, it was decided that any return coming from sales of government-owned concerns would be used for reducing government debt and not for financing new expenditure. The opposition parties put forward the idea that a second, more subtle, reason might have pushed the government to accelerate privatisation. In more than one case, the stock of former large companies (the main banks, the oil concern ENI, the electric agency ENEL) were bought by a multitude of small savers, suddenly turned from the status of wage earners to that of financial capitalists. As such, they were no longer interested in fighting for higher wages but more keenly interested in the behaviour of the stock exchange. All this, in the view of the government, might work for higher social stability.

In fact, behind the decision to privatise public industry, a deeper belief was present, namely that private industry is always more efficient than public industry. In fact, the government-owned industry had become an illegal source of revenue for practically all political parties. Of the two great centres of government industry, the great industrial holding IRI was controlled by the

Christian Democratic Party, while the oil concern ENI was under the control of the Socialist Party. Neither of the two parties exist any longer, at least not in their former structure.

The industries belonging to the IRI holding have almost completely been sold to private financial groups and the holding itself was dissolved in the year 2000. The oil concern ENI has been partially sold to private stockholders. The public firm ENEL, originally a monopoly for the production and distribution of electric energy, already transformed into a joint stock company, is in the process of being offered to private savers. The Italian Telecom was bought by a private group exceedingly indebted towards the banking system and forced to sell segments of the Italian communications industry to a German group. In the view of the Italian Government, that explicitly and enthusiastically approved the operation, this was proof of there being in Italy new courageous entrepreneurs ready to replace the old ones, clearly tired and demotivated.

Prodi, the present President of the Commission of the European Union, while being a President of IRI, declared that in his opinion, in an open and competitive economy, no industrial sector could be viewed as strategic or vital to a country. As a consequence firms belonging to any sector can be dismissed or privatized. In this philosophy, groups active in widely different sectors were sold to private financial groups: the steel concern, ILVA; the great national banks; INA, the national institute for life insurance; the Italian Telecom; the food concern Cirio; the firm for high-tech mechanics, Pignone. At least the latter two are examples of advanced and efficient firms, fully competitive on the world market. In addition to this, no barrier was ever raised by the Italian Government against sales of private concerns to foreign financial groups. As a result a number of efficient firms, active in various sectors (food, pharmaceutical, metals, mechanical, cars, motorcycles, shipping, publishing houses) are now under the control of foreign financial groups.

Two remarks cannot be avoided in connection with the policy of privatisation. The first is that in most cases the decline of large industry and its replacement by a multitude of small concerns implies a decline in research activities as well as in technological standing. The second, equally important remark is that in a number of cases the sale of government industry has been coupled with the entrance of foreign capital.

In principle, no objection can be raised against the presence of foreign capital in a national industry. In fact this was and still is the official position of the Italian Government. However, experience shows that things are different. The entrance of foreign capital never means further growth of the firms. More often than not foreign capital buys national firms either in order to enter the market by acquiring an already developed commercial network, or in order to eliminate a competitor. Even if the national factories are kept in business, it so happens that the richer segments of the firm (such as research, finance, marketing) are concentrated in the headquarters in some other country, while only the poorer segments, namely the process of material production, is kept where it used to be.

The list of firms sold to foreign capital is impressive. As already mentioned, it includes firms from the following sectors: food, pharmaceutical, metals, mechanical, cars, motorcycles, shipping, publishing houses, maritime transport, construction, chemicals, communications, domestic appliances. Even the Fiat group, practically the only big firm still in existence, has sold 20 per cent of the stock to General Motors, that is supposed to be gradually increasing its participation over the coming years. The result is that the country now has no longer, under Italian control, a food or steel or pharmaceutical industry to speak of.

Development by Modernisation

A backbone of the Italian social and political system has always been what in Italy is called the 'public school' and is in fact a school run by the State, open to everybody, accessible at nominal fees. In the past, the State schools were known for their high cultural standing and were able to attract the best teachers and pupils. The country used to be proud of a school system coupling the requirements of democracy and efficiency. A basic principle, clearly written in the Italian Constitution of 1948, ensures that anybody is free to set up a private schooling institution, provided it does not impose a financial burden on the State.

Over the last thirty years or so, the State school has been losing ground in favour of privately-owned schools, many of which are religious schools connected to the Catholic church. It is debatable whether the decay of State schools has been a consequence of the political movements of the late 1960s and 1970s, or whether the Italian governments have gradually yielded to pressures from Catholic circles and have no longer taken care of the government schooling system as was customary in the past.

Be it as it may, the centre-left governments have radically altered the system in favour of private schools, to which *de facto* subsidies have been granted. According to the new rules, the school system of the country is made up of State-owned and privately-owned schools. Both kinds of schools must meet the same educational and cultural requirements. Pupils attending private schools can get a subsidy in view of the higher fees they are bound to pay. The subsidy is clearly given to schools, and it is paid to pupils only in order to avoid a clear conflict with the text of the Constitution. It is a widespread opinion that the new school system is going to destroy one of the strongholds of the Italian democratic system.

In an attempt to answer the two questions of unemployment and of the inadequate technological advancement of Italian industry, the centre-left government announced a new industrial policy in the name of the modernisation of the country. Since most new jobs turn out to be created in sectors connected with electronics, communications and the like, it seemed clear that by increasing the education of the younger generations in the same fields this would give them greater employment opportunities. This might be true if the lack of trained manpower were the only bottleneck of electronic and similar industries, which is by no means evident. Be it as it may, the government launched a campaign for 'a computer in each class-room, a computer in each family' – to the clear satisfaction of the computer industry. It seems evident that new industries always have a good performance in terms of employment. This, however, does not mean that the new industries alone can solve the problem of unemployment in its entirety (Ciocca, 1997). The suspicion remains that modernisation (alongside partnership, new technology, new responsibilities) belongs to the 'lot of empty formulas' generated by the left-wing governments in a number of different countries (Nuti, 1999, p. 60).

Regional Income Disparities

The reduction of income disparities has always been a fundamental issue for Italian left-wing parties. However, over the last years, under the centre-left governments, regional disparities, an old tradition of the Italian economy, have continued to increase. It must be recognised that the policy line of the left was never adequately strong or well conceived. In 1950, the Communist Party opposed the establishment of the special Fund for Southern Italy (Cassa per il Mezzogiorno), on the grounds that what the region needed was not so much a flow of government expenditure as a radical change in the structure of land ownership. 'All the land to the peasants' was the programme of the left. In the 1960s, industrialisation was started by creating a number of big plants mainly, but not only, in heavy industry. With the birth of the first groups of organised wage earners in big plants, the unions, that so far had been almost absent, were forced to increase their presence in South Italy. At the time, the Communist Party seemed convinced of the fact that a greater local autonomy would bring about a more efficient development policy. The presence of a special authority for investment in South Italy was viewed as a source of corruption and waste and the return to a development policy run by the ordinary departments of the government was considered with favour. The special Fund for South Italy went through various transformations and in 1992 the so-called 'extraordinary measures for Southern Italy' were finally cancelled. The centre-left governments, whose main preoccupation was with reducing the government deficit and having Italy accepted in the European Monetary Union, did not place the problem of South Italy high on their agenda.

In the years 1973–75, per capita GNP in Southern Italy was roughly 60 per cent of the equivalent of the North-Central regions; in 1998 it had declined to less than 56 per cent. The same can be said of total regional income, which was almost 33.5 per cent of the North-Central regions in 1973–75 and had declined to 31.5 per cent in 1998. The decline in relative income of the Southern regions has been largely a consequence of the disappearance of the large firms that had been set up during the policy of industrialisation being carried out during the 1960s and early 1970s.

Recently a new agency, 'Development Italy' (Sviluppo Italia) was set up in the form of a joint stock agency, the stock being owned by the Italian Treasury. The agency results from the merger of eight former different companies, all of them owned by the Treasury, and variously connected with the development of South Italy (agriculture, research, big construction works, promoting young entrepreneurs). Its aim has been more than once defined and modified and its officers appointed and removed. The agency has two different and largely independent branches, the one supposed to promote entrepreneurship, the other to provide long-term co-finance for industrial investment. The two branches are supposed to act on the two different sides of the problem, stimulating local initiatives and attracting foreign investment, especially in high-tech sectors. The general philosophy leading to the establishment of the agency is that of no longer having a policy based on transfers and assistance and moving to measures aimed at increasing the productive capacity. So far the new agency does not seem to have taken precise actions.

7.4   CONCLUDING REMARKS

It seems clear that the centre-left governments have placed the problems of financial and monetary equilibrium high on their scale of priorities, leaving in second place the problems of a high level of activity and employment. The justification for the choice has been that Italy had to comply with the Maastricht Treaty and with the subsequent Amsterdam Agreement for Stability and Growth. As a consequence of both international agreements, Italy was pledged to reduce its own internal debt and to bring down inflation to European standards. A policy of financial constraint was therefore unavoidable, at the cost of reducing employment and running the economy below its capacity level.

It is also unquestionable that centre-left governments have shown an unlimited confidence in the virtues of the market, going far beyond what is theoretically justified or confirmed by empirical experience. In fact it has been taken for granted that the free market provides an allocation of resources which is by definition more efficient than any planned allocation could be. The trouble is that a similar belief has been directly applied without inquiring whether the market concerned is a competitive market or whether it is distorted by monopolistic or oligopolistic practices. An even more serious flaw is that the same faith in the operation of the market has been applied to the labour market, to the distribution of income and to the provision of social services, fields in which anybody would admit that the market needs to be corrected by some sort of government policy.

The centre-left governments have dismantled the structure of State-owned industry regardless of its efficiency, and at the same time reduced the weight of big industry. The industrial structure of the country has been downgraded and the employment possibilities of high level manpower have been greatly reduced. The country suffers from mass long-term unemployment in the less industrialised regions, while at the same time in the more advanced regions unemployment strikes the better-qualified workers and youngsters having acquired a scientific background.

This complex operation has been made palatable to public opinion and to voters in general because it is supported by a tireless campaign supporting the values of individualism and playing down the values of mutual solidarity. The practice of charity has been left to *ad hoc* charitable institutions, mostly run by religious orders and therefore lying beyond the rights and expectations of a regular citizen. The increasing inequalities in income distribution and the appearance of areas of real misery cannot be a surprise.

BIBLIOGRAPHY

Bellofiore, R. (ed.) (1998), *Il lavoro di domani*, Pisa: Biblioteca Serantini.

Berti, L. (1998), *Affari di fine secolo. Le privatizzazioni in Italia*, Roma: Ediesse.

Bologna, S. and Fumagalli, A. (1997), *Il lavoro autonomo di seconda generazione*, Milano: Feltrinelli.

Chesnais, F. (1999), *Réflexions sur la guerre en Yougoslavie*, Paris: Editions L'Esprit Frappeur.

Ciocca, P. (1997), *Disoccupazione di fine secolo. Studi e proposte per l'Europa*, Torino: Bollati Boringhieri.

Graziani, A. (1996), 'L'Italia e il suo inserimento internazionale', *Storia dell'Italia Repubblicana*, 3rd volume, Turin: Einaudi.

Guerrieri, P. and Pianta, M. (1998), *Tecnologia, crescita, occupazione*, Napoli: Cuen.

Fausto, D. and Pica, F. (2000), *Teoria e fatti del federalismo fiscale*, Bologna: Il Mulino.

Nuti, D.M. (1999), 'Making sense of the Third Way', *Business Strategy Review*, **X**(3), autumn, 57-67.

Padoa Schioppa, F. (ed.) (1996), *Pensioni e risanamento della finanza pubblica*, Bologna: Il Mulino.

Pizzuti, R. (1996), 'Nota sulla riforma delle pensioni', *Economia e lavoro*, 4.

8. Distribution and growth: can the New Left deal with the neo-Schumpeterian 'accord'? Some comments on the French experience

Pascal Petit

8.1 INTRODUCTION

The sense of modernity, for example the combination of reasons, principles and representations on which a society forges its notion of social and technical progress, seems to have changed considerably since the golden age of capitalism. The Fordist growth that most western economies enjoyed more or less in the decades that followed World War II, did not result purely from the combined effects of the diffusion of a scientific Taylorist organisation of work with a sustained expansion in wages which expanded demand and led to cumulative growth. Alongside the other components of this growth process (of which monetary social transfers to households and public services were important parts), the quasi deal, balancing a more productive organisation of work with an increasing standard of living of the wage earners, was part of a more general 'accord' defining the broad guidelines of policies. What has been called the 'conventions' on full employment were major parts of this general accord. Within each country political parties, though part of the consensus, did not have the same view on its implementation. Right and left thus took opposing positions on the relative coverage and intensity of public services and transfers. Some more radical political parties did not share this consensus and took a revolutionary stance. The broad consensus led to the development of various welfare states, in the midst of conflicts of interest and harsh wage bargaining. But these social conflicts were somehow part of the growth dynamics and the accord remained central to the social debate providing a common view that extended the Taylorist organisation of production and developed the wage labour nexus that represented the modern view.

Times seem to have changed and the old accord has been eroded on many grounds (the power of large Taylorist productive organisations, the growth of employment in number and quality, the rise in wage income). Modernity is now centred on the development of entrepreneurial spirit and the dynamics of markets. An accord has emerged in the past decade around a neo-Schumpeterian view of economic dynamism. However, the basis of this 'new' accord is not as clear as the previous one now seems to be. There are many reasons for this. First, the Fordist accord established itself in the aftermath of dramatic events when consensus and conventions were easier to establish.[1] Second, we may not yet have reached any kind of final workable neo-Schumpeterian consensus. There is a widespread feeling that a new 'spirit of capitalism' is emerging (Boltanski and Chiapello, 1999), but its political expression, that is how right and left parties adjust to this change, remains to be seen. This is a key issue for this chapter when looking at the challenge for the left, and the type of answer which the Third Way represents. What is clear, and follows from the change of environment itself, is the increased pragmatism in finding ways to serve broad democratic values. The Third Way is certainly part of this *tâtonnement* searching process,[2] but it follows that there are many brands. And it is interesting that left parties in power at the end of the 1990s saw their *aggiornamento* (updating) as types of common objectives (as in the case of the UK and France in the late 1990s). The diversity indicates that the field of the accord is intrinsically much broader, depending on how markets are viewed: to what extent they are a fixed element, more or less deeply socially embedded, and how they can be monitored. Large structural changes occurring worldwide, namely the internationalisation of economies and increasing technological advances are giving mixed experiences on these issues and the challenge of the new modernity is to find ways to manage these developments which are radically modifying the old pattern of modernity.

The fact that political parties on the right (the neo-liberal stream and affiliates) and on the left (the Third Way labour and affiliates) are working on their own political expression of this new accord indicates development, but the outcome remains open (how long, how broad, how viable). More specifically the question for this chapter is how the left can deal with such an accord and define Third Ways according to its traditional values of solidarity and welfare improvement.

In order to address this issue we shall start in Section 8.2 with a brief comparative assessment of the growth achievements of some countries over the last two decades of generally slow growth. Because it is more of a transition period we shall focus in particular on the late 1990s, when labour governments have been in power and have established their Third Way policies, for example, working out roughly the dynamism of markets, the entrepreneurial spirit and the necessity for individual incentives at the expense of less solidarity, because of the challenges of internationalisation and technological advances.

In Section 8.3 we shall briefly survey the achievements of the same subset of countries in terms of income distribution. It is a crucial issue in this assessment as the new accord seems also to have been accompanied by rising inequalities, not only in income but also in finding a proper job or in accessing knowledge.

These two sections will set the macroeconomic scenes within which what we called the neo-Schumpeterian accord is developing, charting the social and technical progress of the economies.

On this basis we can investigate how parties on the left have accommodated this new accord with their own heritage and values. We shall focus on the case of the French left, and particularly on the Jospin government in the late 1990s.

8.2   A PERIOD OF SLOW GROWTH

We can start the new period from the early 1980s with the active liberalisation policies of Reagan and Thatcher. We shall confine our comparison to a few large countries who all went through such liberalisation changes and ended the late 1990s with left-of-centre governments, namely the UK, France, Germany, Italy and the US.

Overall the growth rates (see Figure 8.1) are really low for these five large countries if one uses the 1960s as a benchmark. Only for the UK and the US do we see comparable achievements before and after the 1980s. Chiefly this

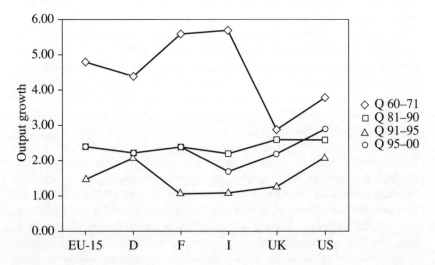

Figure 8.1   Output growth

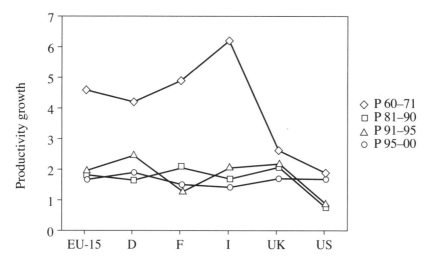

Figure 8.2   Productivity growth

slow growth was accompanied by slow productivity growth (productivity here is simply measured as real output per person employed) for all countries (and especially so in the US and the UK) in the last two decades (see Figure 8.2). This feature of low productivity gains lasted until the end of the 1990s. Somehow the Solow paradox of low productivity gains despite the increasing spread of computers (and all the information and communication technologies that go with them) was a central issue for the 'new accord'. Only in the late 1990s did we see the beginning of a steady economic growth in some countries. So far the noticeable productivity increases in some manufacturing industries or in some successful firms (see Brynjolfsson and Hitt, 1996; OECD, 1998) have not spread to the rest of the economy, nor to other economies. Furthermore manufacturing has been slimmed down and is wide open to worldwide or regional organisation and as such it is no longer the only engine of growth that it was in the past. It has at least to be combined or considered together with the bunch of complex business services that have emerged in the last decades and are also part of the dynamism activities closely linked with the diffusion of ICTs (information and communication technologies).

Intermediate services (which are not new and have not so much expanded in terms of employment in the last two decades but have been thoroughly transformed in the process) should also be considered in this exercise in growth accounting. Still the bulk of employment is within the set of social and personal services which have been continuously expanding from the postwar period onwards and the large share of business services which are not complex activities but rather menial jobs. These compromise the aggregate figure of productivity growth. They reflect two things which are crucial for the new accord: first, regarding the technology of the provision of all the menial, non-qualified jobs being considered, what is the norm? should they be changed, elaborated, upgraded? does it matter in the long run for those who do these jobs? and second, on the distribution of wages (and of wage incomes among other sources of income), is its widening fair? is it transitory and does it accompany the upgrading of qualifications required in good jobs? can it be countered or softened by means of redistribution? The new accord is unclear on these issues, as we shall see, except that both liberals and the new left praise rewarding the individual as a crucial incentive for 'entrepreneurial action' (competence, ability to respond to external challenges) at all levels and therefore are ready to approve, some increases in inequality in income distribution (a trend observed in all countries, see Atkinson et al., 1995; Gottschalk and Smeeding, 1997; Oxley et al., 1997). Still there are big differences among political parties and even within political parties on where is the borderline and whether the dynamics of these inequalities are transitory or durable.

Something which is less obvious is that the technologies under consideration may be deprived of part of their potential, particularly since sizeable parts of the population would be excluded both at work and at home (and in this process the two are more closely related than ever) from the kind of culture and practices, autonomy and responsiveness, that the 'new accord' praises so much.

To comment on France more especially, the figures on growth (Figure 8.1) and productivity (Figure 8.2) are indicative of poor records over the 1980s and early 1990s in relative terms when compared with the successes of the 1960s. In that respect the end of the 1990s seems more promising. The Jospin government thus benefits from a much better record, for many external reasons but also through some of its actions, as we shall suggest later.

Let us now turn to the crucial distributional issue.

8.3   DISTRIBUTION: THE WAGES UNDER UNEVEN STRAIN

Before looking at the distribution of incomes, it is interesting to look at the distribution of jobs as a follow up of our assessment on growth and productivity. We place it under the heading of job distribution since in the new accord employment seems to have become a highly differentiable product (with a whole range of good jobs and bad jobs). To speak of a wage earner job has not, on average, the simple meaning that it had in the old accord of

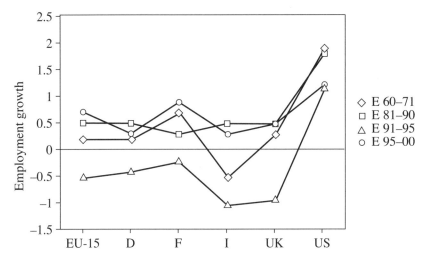

Figure 8.3   Employment growth

full-time employment with an unlimited duration labour contract and a fair wage. It may not have been true on all occasions, but it was certainly part of the appeal of the old accord, for instance for a young person entering the labour market with a basic qualification, while in the new accord the expectations of the same young entrant would be a temporary, part-time, low-paid job for a hazardous period of probation.

Figure 8.3 gives the growth rates of employment in the same five countries. While their productivity growth was similar (especially in the late 1990s), employment growth appears clearly to be divided between European countries on the one side and the US on the other, reflecting strong differences in the nature of employment. In that respect the profile of the end of the 1990s, after the recession in Europe of the early 1990s, shows some catching up with the US model. France is showing signs of precisely this kind, consistent with the recent rise in the number of temporary jobs (see Figure 8.4 and Table 8.1). This high increase in temporary jobs may stem from youth employment schemes, necessitated by a lasting high unemployment (see Figure 8.5), having a severe impact on young people (see Table 8.2).

These features of employment growth and unemployment have to be seen in the context of very different types of wage-earner societies if only we take into account the employment ratios, for example the percentage of an age group who are employed or looking for jobs (thus participating in the labour force). Employment ratios basically differ for three reasons between developed economies: (a) the length of the initial training period, (b) the average age of retirement and, chiefly, (c) the participation of women in their

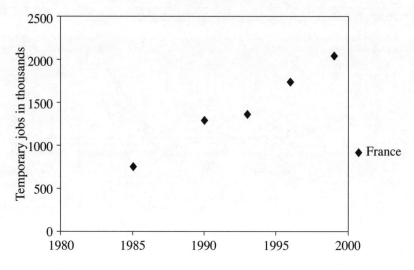

Figure 8.4   Temporary jobs

30s, 40s and 50s. We will not go too deeply into these structural explanations
but one should keep in mind that societies based on wage earners with large
differences in employment ratios may not be on the same trajectories with
respect to the new accord; a matter that should be considered when looking at
the opportunities of various policies. In effect overall the participation rates
which were relatively close in Europe (as a whole), the US and Japan in the
mid 1960s, decreased in Europe while they increased in the US and Japan (see
Figure 8.6). Europe itself has a mixture of countries following the US pattern,
such as the UK and the Scandinavian countries, with countries like France,

Table 8.1   Share of temporary jobs in employment in 1997

	Full-time jobs		Part-time jobs	
	Men	Women	Men	Women
France	10	11	48	22
Germany	11	15	24	7
Denmark	10	13	16	8
NL	5	10	28	17
UK	5	6	25	11
Italy	6	7	56	27

Source: OECD, *Employment Outlook*, June 1999.

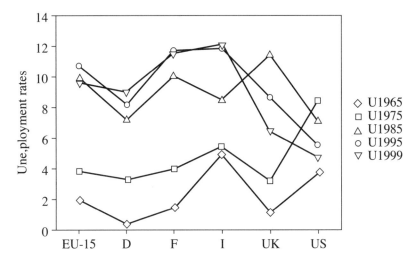

Figure 8.5   Unemployment rates

Germany and Italy where participation rates decreased (see Table 8.3). Early retirement and late entries are the main causes of these differences, while the overall trend for middle-aged women to increase their participation rate is universal. It raises two types of issues. Difficulties in entering employment may have detrimental effects on the attitudes of the youth towards work and society, depending on their expectations on the outcome of this poor entry experience. The importance of pensioners also raises questions, depending on their income and the use of their time. To have a lot of people out of work, not

Table 8.2   Unemployment rates by age group (in percentages)

	1990			1995			1998		
Age groups	15–24	25–54	55–64	15–24	25–54	55–64	15–24	25–54	55–64
EU	15.4	6.3	5.2	20.8	9.3	8.4	19.1	8.6	8.1
Germany	4.6	4.7	7.5	8.5	7.7	11.6	9.4	7.7	12.7
France	19.1	8.0	6.7	25.9	10.5	7.2	25.4	10.8	8.7
Italy	28.9	6.6	1.8	32.8	8.9	4.3	32.1	9.6	4.7
UK	10.1	5.8	7.2	15.3	7.4	7.5	12.3	5.0	5.3
US	11.2	4.6	3.3	12.1	4.5	3.6	10.4	3.5	2.6
Japan	4.3	1.6	2.7	6.1	2.6	3.7	7.7	3.4	5.0

Source: OECD, *Employment Outlook*, June 1999.

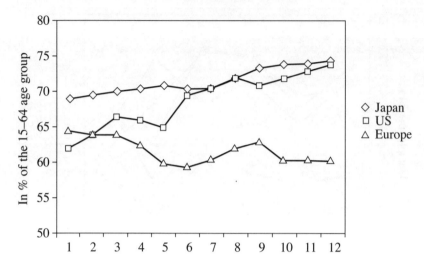

Figure 8.6   Employment ratios

unemployed, but training or occupied in socially useful and personally
rewarding tasks may be a good thing for a society. The room for manoeuvre
is wider in such cases and the need for a fully-fledged distribution side for the
accord much more imperative.

Let us now turn to the distribution of income, and first of all towards its
aggregate figures as given by the wage share in national income (see Figure
8.7). Here again the figures are clearly different between the countries of
continental Europe where the wage shares fell strongly in the 1980s and the

Table 8.3   Employment ratios by age group (in percentages)

	1990			1995			1998		
Age groups	15–24	25–54	55–64	15–24	25–54	55–64	15–24	25–54	55–64
EU	46	74	39	38	74	36	38	74	37
Germany	58	76	39	48	77	38	45	77	39
France	30	77	36	22	77	34	21	77	33
Italy	33	68	32	26	65	27	25	66	27
UK	70	79	49	59	77	48	61	79	48
US	60	80	54	58	80	55	59	81	58
Japan	42	80	63	45	79	64	45	79	64

Source: OECD, *Employment Outlook*, June 1999.

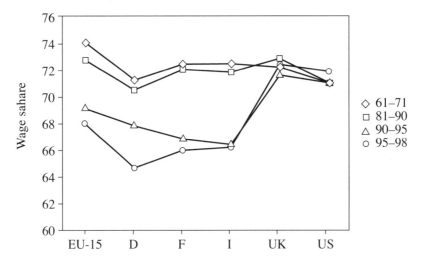

Figure 8.7   Wage share in national income

UK and the US where they kept up to their levels of the 1960s. This suggests that the share of income attributed to taxes and profits has increased in continental Europe. It may stem from an increased redistribution due to a rise in the number of unemployment benefits issued (a point we return to in the next section).

   The wage structure itself has become more unequal in most countries with the distance between the lower and upper quartiles increasing markedly. This polarisation is noticeably more marked in the US and the UK than in the other countries; a common trend largely due to a relative decline in the wages of non-qualified workers (and much less to a symmetric appreciation in the wages of the highly qualified, see Mishel et al., 1997). Only the upper decile of the wage distribution experienced a significant increase in real terms. The neo-Schumpeterian philosophy of the new accord, keen on entrepreneurship and individual initiatives, naturally favours individual incentives. However, the opportunities for such incentives are not uniformly distributed among the jobs, and new schemes are mainly concerned with the wages of highly qualified workers and professionals. Moreover incentives are more likely to take the form of extra wage benefits (from premiums to stock options and other profit-sharing schemes). In fact a great deal of the increased dispersion in wages has also occurred through a widening of the wage gap between sectors. In France the polarisation of the wage structure has been relatively modest so far compared with other countries, and the practices of profit-sharing schemes (and of stock options) are being debated. This prima facie feature of distribution in the new accord is important, but even more important is the redistribution feature where politicians can more directly put into practice their own views of the accord.[3]

8.4   NEW LEFT AND THE REDISTRIBUTION

Let us first consider the tax levy. There is a certain credo in the new accord which says that the tax levy in some European countries has reached levels where it could threaten individual initiatives, hence the number of programmes to lower the tax rates. Still looking at the broad figures, the global fiscal levy as a share of GDP has not declined since the end of the 1960s but has increased in the 1970s and 1980s (see Figure 8.8). Only in the UK do we see a remarkable stability in the tax levy over the whole period. France and Italy show on the contrary a marked and sustained increase in the tax ratio. This may follow from the rise in transfers to households linked with the rise in unemployment as well as with the increase in low-wage jobs.

In effect the share of transfers to households in GDP (Figure 8.9) in all countries has been steadily increasing over time, even in the US and the UK. This may come from increasing unemployment and from a rise in the share of poor jobs or it may stress new efforts to redistribute under the new accord.[4] It may thus stem from a mechanical application (or even a restrained one) of the past rules of transfer in a context of unemployment and rising poverty or indicate quality improvement in transfers. The general trend in the new accord has been to transform to a greater or lesser extent the rules of transfers in order

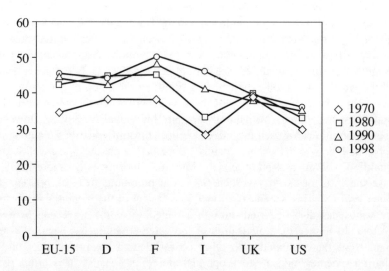

Figure 8.8   Fiscal levy/GDP

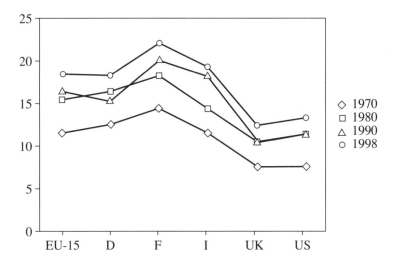

Figure 8.9   Transfers to households

to increase their incentive dimension.[5] By and large the share of transfers increased everywhere.

The new schemes that have been developed everywhere to cope with rising unemployment and/or poverty, such as a negative income tax system, a minimum guaranteed income and so on, have certainly contributed to this trend. Surveys show that these schemes have been insufficient to counter the rising trend in inequality, which was still strongly manifest in the US and in the UK in the mid 1990s but much weaker in countries like France or Germany (see Oxley et al., 1997).[6]

The issue does not end with the comparison between rich and poor quartiles or deciles. It is also interesting, in political and economic terms, as to what has become of the lower middle class and to what extent schemes of negative income tax can prevent them from falling into a poverty trap. There are hints, for instance, that such transfer mechanisms have relatively limited effects in the US on the detrimental effects of very low wages (the working poor phenomenon, see Ellwood, 1999). Certainly more information is needed on this aspect of redistribution to appreciate the political viability of the various areas of the distributive dimension of the 'accord'.

By comparison, France has suffered less from this trend, even if the rise in unemployment and poverty has been a shocking experience which led in the 1990s to the development of a minimum guaranteed income and more recently to the extension by Jospin of free access to health care for those not covered by the social security system. But looking at money transfers to households is not the only figure to consider when assessing redistribution. Subsidies to public services and even public spending on education and health, not considered above, should also be included in the discussion on redistribution. Beyond a common will from all parties in the accord to develop incentives and set conditions on subsidies, the overall public spending in fields like health and education did not recede.[7]

However, one should also go beyond these standard perspectives on redistribution and incorporate in the assessment policies which aim at remodelling markets and making the structural adjustments which they feel are required by the new economic context. The new accord is in itself open to such a comprehensive policy; it has often been read as a drive towards deregulation. But the issue is more tricky and cannot be reduced to the dismantling of the past regulations. New rules have to be set down, objectives have to be discussed as well as the level of monitoring required, if only to give similar opportunities to everyone as it is widely claimed in 'modern politics'.[8] Can the New Left in France be active in the broadening of this accord is the question we address hereafter.

8.5 A NEW LABOUR *À LA FRANÇAISE*

Although the socialists took over in 1981 in France and have been in office since then, with two interruptions in 1986–88 and 1993–97, the presidential nature of the system makes it difficult to appreciate who exactly is in charge and on which mandate. Mitterand won in 1981 (some may say that Giscard D'Estaing lost) and brought the socialists to government in the aftermath of his own election, but with a narrow mandate as it turned out in 1983 when the government wanted to launch more radical politics and was confronted by external constraints (with the pursuit of the construction of the European Union and competition at the world level) and an internal constraint (with the lack of support for a large redistribution[9]). The socialist government lost the elections in 1986, but the president remained in office (the first cohabitation) and was re-elected in 1988, repeating the move of 1981 by bringing back into office a socialist government with a weak majority and an even lower-key programme in order to win the elections. Little was done in such a context, also poised by the uncertainty in the east after the fall of the Berlin Wall and a worldwide recession in the early 1990s. Not surprisingly the socialists lost the elections to parliament in 1993 and to the presidency in 1995 which was won by Chirac (with an incredibly anti-liberal programme, dividing the right from then onwards) against Jospin. In this specific context the large and combative movement initiated in the railways during the winter of 1995 and spreading to most public services with its surprisingly wide popular support (when the situation created was difficult to bear for the public) represented a turning point in the construction of the new accord *à la française* as we shall see. It also directly contributed to the political shift that was manifested in the early parliamentary elections held by Chirac in June 1997 with a victory for the socialists headed by Jospin (who had gained this primacy in the socialist party after his gallant presidential campaign) on a programme of their own. It opened a new era where the socialists were in power for the first time in their own party right and not in the wake of a highly personalised presidential election. More precisely as stressed in Jospin (1999),[10] the victory in 1997 was the victory of an alliance, 'la gauche plurielle', including the green party and the communist party.

The Third Way à la Française

As we look to various brands of New Left in the context of a 'new accord', which praises individual initiatives and markets; a specificity of the French setting, also referred to in Jospin (1999) is worth recalling which underlines the political more than social nature of the social democracy in France. There is no mass party, no formal links with unions, which are themselves weak and divided, and a weak tradition of negotiation and dialogue.[11] It has largely moulded the way in which individualism has developed in France, without many intermediaries between individuals and the State (see Läidi, 1999). Developing such mediations may then be all the more important to ensure that the new accord is strongly based on the long-term rise of individualism in our societies and may not therefore offer spontaneous opportunities to develop such collective links. Some political voluntarism is therefore crucial to palliate this initial bias of the French social democracy. Market forces are quite different in such a context from what they are in countries where associations and organised intermediary institutions are more strongly implemented. In other words the distance pointed at by Giddens may be stronger than elsewhere when the State retreats (see Callinicos, 1999). The question is therefore two-handed: how to keep an active State, not contradicting the entrepreneurial spirit of the accord, and how to develop at the same time these intermediations which in France are not cushioning the extension of markets. Jospin has a phrase which is related to the above problem: he says 'yes to the market economy and no to the market society'. The characteristics of social democracy in France seem to imply that the balance will be hard to maintain. It requires an exceptionally clear and well publicised policy line in order to convince internally (easing the development of intermediaries) and externally (towards trade and regional partners). The existence of a political alliance may help in that respect in avoiding a too crude top-down approach of such policy definition.

So far the will to go forward with an active State is undeniable. We can see three fields of action for such an active State, which point at the discourse of the government in very different levels of strategic elaboration. They represent interesting challenges, the list of which could be extended but the cases chosen give a comprehensive idea of the issues that an active State strategy can address in the new context.

The first concerns the policy promoting the 35-hour week, which is already largely implemented and which we can refer to for the method, the objectives and the results. The second is looking at the future of large network services, a key issue in the new economic environment as they constitute the logistics of all markets, issues at the core of a major national debate in France (see Bourdieu, 1998; Jospin, 1999) largely brought to the forefront by the long and popular railways strike of December 1995. The third is on globalisation and finance markets and concerns the means of collective action by the New Left at the international level.

Let us briefly survey the issues raised in these three fields.

1.	*The reduction in working time* (RWT) has been promoted by the government as a key action against unemployment. It should not be seen as a simple arithmetical operation dividing a fixed stock of working hours to increase employment. The strategy was less naive but may be too ambitious in aiming at a major reshuffling of the work organisation of firms, hoping to generate innovative structures, new projects and in turn, employment. Some positive feedback occurred but first, in too few places initially and second, too slowly to gain some macroeconomic momentum and improve the labour market situation substantially.[12] Two factors can account for this relative inertia. The first may be the lack of inter-mediation to support the realisation of the project from its start. That is the traditional French disease, recalled previously. The second factor lies more with the conception of the project itself. Freeing time makes sense if workers want more time, can use more time and know how to use it. In that respect the reorganisation of out of work time was as important as that of working time. Again it required intermediation, but although there was a national deficit on this side too, local associations have developed in the last two decades, in part to cope with the poor situation in the labour market, which could have been put directly to use as well as local authorities. The relatively high non-participation rates of the young and the elderly paradoxically could also have been turned into an advantage in such an active policy. Here the theory of the reform seems to have been incomplete, which is more the pity since these highly structural policies would have been better received if presented in their long-term perspective.

2. *The large network services issue* seems in the first place slightly more complex as it concerns services which were often publicly provisioned and in all cases highly regulated (such as transport, telecommunications, banking and distribution but also extended to health and education). Their progressive liberalisation was also high on the European agenda and a better customerisation of these services, however vague the notion, appeared as one of the widespread expectations underlying the new accord. Regarding the structural adjustment required one should distinguish between the public provision of a service and public intervention to regulate the way these intermediation services work and to monitor the way firms and households access and use them. There is obviously some room for manoeuvre in this field, to support and expand the potential of the producers as well as of the consumers (by means of regulations, subsidies, grants, training schemes or certification). The reasons why such a supportive role cannot be left to unorganised market forces are many: the need for a long-term horizon; the externalities at all levels once the effects on environment and health are taken into account, including the opportunities brought by an appropriate differentiation of services. The challenge is basically to use the qualities praised in the new accord (reactivity, innovation, rapidity, flexibility) in order to fulfil complex needs. Collective action and a framework are necessary to avoid a detrimental oversimplification of needs in such interconnected fields as large network services.

    This intuition may well have been at the core of the preoccupation by the government for the intermediation services. But so far effective policies in that direction have been limited. The issue is not directly mentioned as such in the recent law (April 2000) on 'the New Economic Regulations' which were aimed at a fair ruling of markets. The railways strike of 1995 and the debates that followed on public services did not lead to clear conclusions and showed some conflict between the redefinition of users' needs and the status of those producing these services. A revisited notion of universal services which would not only care for access but also enlarge the capacity of the basic users would have been a significant step forward. Finally this important issue which was directly connected with the monitoring of markets (and which played an important role in the electoral victory of the left) has not matured.

    Health and education are more traditional fields of reform but despite some important measures to extend access to these services, the large reforms which would take advantage of the new context of human capital and technology to improve these two sectors are not more advanced in France than elsewhere.

3.   *The third issue* is the steps that an active State could take in the huge
     subject of 'controlling' globalisation, especially of financial markets.
     Jospin (1999) considers that developments at the European level offer
     possibilities to reach a common position on regulation in key areas of
     finance, trade or information and thus press for some rules at the world
     level. Such a claim may seem utopian but its realistic part is that it may
     lead to some action on specific markets and thus progressively set up the
     legitimacy for broader actions.[13] Issues of health and safety regulations
     and of environmental stakes may motivate majorities to organise trade in
     ways which again respect the rights of consumers and producers alike.
     The need to organise the markets of cultural goods to avoid the
     disappearance of some cultural lives could also be of widespread concern.
     The international regime of property rights is clearly a big stake with
     countries being advantaged or disadvantaged by their own old specific
     practices, so that the need for fair arrangements, highly differentiated and
     changing according to the local situations may find some echoes.
         Still the big stake lies, of course, with the regulation of financial
     markets. The risks there are enormous in scale and scope. The
     liberalisation of banking and finance in France has been completed over
     the last two decades and Paris is now competing with other financial
     centres, though in a less pre-eminent position that the big international
     centres such as London or New York. Any action on this position requires
     that there is good leverage, for example to meet the need of a large
     number, or of important partner countries. The requirements to fulfil this
     condition are not that numerous. Strengthening prudential regulation is
     one, certainly to push forward (if only to fight illegal practices such as
     money laundering). More important and difficult could be the actions
     pressing for fiscal advantages or positive discrimination in favour of
     funds taking long-term and/or specific risks like ethical funds, mutual
     funds and other more or less stringently committed funds. The decisions
     regarding the creation of pension funds will be crucial in that respect. The
     support of the government for a tax on financial transactions such as the
     Tobin tax, beyond the technicalities that limits its implementation,
     contributes to legitimise international actions to control financial
     markets.
         The success of this third issue will be measured by the support it gets
     from other countries and NGOs on each topic. This support will be all the
     stronger if the various actions appear coherent and part of a renewed and
     enlarged approach of international relations.

   Overall the conditions for success of the major issues discussed requires: (a)
to work out coherent and comprehensive theories of action which will

encompass most positive externalities and synergies around the project and (b) for the project to be expressed in such terms and worked out with such collaborations that it ensures the critical mass of intermediations required for the project to gain some momentum.

So far the Third Way *à la française* may still fall short on these two necessary conditions: the formulation of comprehensive strategies enough (too much on production, not enough on demand) and the building up of the support of intermediations.

One should say in defence that these are structural policies that should be seen in a long-term perspective. In the meantime the economic recovery worldwide in the years 1999–2000 and after may facilitate their achievements.

8.6   CONCLUSIONS

The tentative conclusions that we may draw from this brief survey of the new context in which politics have to find their way and policies have to be implemented, must recall that what we called the new accord has not yet been the basis for a fully-fledged economic recovery. Structural changes and growth potentials are obvious, but overall productivity gains were until recently still at low levels. Only in the US and in a handful of small countries have we seen a significant picking up of these productivity gains in the recent past, and these successes are either due to very specific situations (like Ireland or Finland) or threatened by major imbalances (trade deficit and social division in the US). The policies required to give full momentum to the new growth regime are still being formulated. We stressed that Third Way policies could have a broader range than figured out in Blair's policies which often took a narrow puritan view of the new accord. The Jospin government showed a much broader constructivist approach (towards the Third Way) but lacked a consistent theory to support its actions, which was all the more necessary since the country structurally lacked the intermediary bodies that are needed to take full advantage of the new context.

Globally we seem to be at a turning point where what we called the new accord may fail to deliver in a sustainable way at a macro level, rather like the scientific organisation of work in the 1920s. In such a case economic growth may be highly cyclical and a creeping international crisis may last. To get out of such doldrums depends on the capacity of some countries to coordinate relevant policies. In that respect the capacities of some countries to address a fully-fledged expression of their needs, as suggested in the previous section, can really make the difference in terms of their growth path, of its quality and fairness. That is the real challenge to be faced by Third Way policies to be a successful basis for international cooperation.

NOTES

1. One can also consider that it took over three decades for the Taylorist methods of the 1920s to add a counterpart on the distribution side that would make them acceptable and efficient.
2. See Driver and Martell (2000) who stress this pragmatism, including some contradictions, in the Blair experience.
3. Disregarding direct actions on wages such as minimum wages and other means of income policies which do not seem in favour on the agendas of left-wing and right-wing governments these days.
4. It is difficult to compare the levels as the accounting practices may vary from country to country, especially regarding health expenditures.
5. A trend well publicised in the UK with the welfare to work orientation of the reforms of the Blair government.
6. Though the situation may differ with the type of households.
7. The Jospin government thus increased the share of the welfare budget publicly financed (from 25 per cent in the mid 1990s to 32 per cent in 1998).
8. On this issue of equal opportunity see Driver and Martell (2000) who stress that the dividing line between right and left depends on how undermining an inegalitarian distribution is thought to be.
9. A silent manifestation of the new accord reflecting the stand of professionals and the upper-middle-income class.
10. The title of Jospin's booklet 'Modern Socialism' is well in accordance with our view of the new accord as a new sense of modernity.
11. Jospin rightly stresses that such a structure can help parties to come back rapidly into office but it also means that they can be thrown out of office on minor issues.
12. The potential of the measure only started to appear when a general economic recovery improved the situation in the labour market.
13. Which would be an interesting way to understand Jospin's declaration: 'I want to be a builder of realistic utopia' (Jospin, 1999).

REFERENCES

Atkinson, A., Rainwater, L. and Smeeding, T. (1995), 'La distribution des revenus dans les pays de l'OCDE: documentation tirée du Luxembourg Income Study', La distribution des revenus dans les pays de l'OCDE, *Etudes de politique sociale,* 18.
Boltanski, L. and Chiapello, E. (1999), *Le Nouvel Esprit du Capitalisme,* Paris: Gallimard.
Bourdieu, P. (1998), *Contre-Feux,* Paris: Editions Raison d'Agir.
Brynjolfsson, E. and Hitt, L. (1996), 'Paradox lost? Firm-level evidence on the returns to information systems spending', *Management Science,* 42(4), 541–58.
Callinicos, A. (1999), 'Social theory put to the test of politics: Pierre Bourdieu and Anthony Giddens', *New Left Review,* 236.
Driver, S. and Martell, L. (2000), 'Left, right and the Third Way', *Policy and Politics,* 28(2), 147–61.
Ellwood, D.T. (1999), 'The Plight of the Working Poor', Children Roundtable Report, No. 2, November, Brookings Institution.
Gottschalk, P. and Smeeding, T. (1997), 'Cross national comparisons of earnings and income inequality', *Journal of Economic Literature,* 2, 633–87.
Jospin, L. (1999), *Modern Socialism,* Fabian Pamphlet 592, London: The Fabian Society.

Laïdi, Z. (1999), 'Penser le politique au-delà de l'Etat', *La Revue de la CFDT*, Numéro spécial No. 26, Nouveau capitalisme et action syndicale, décembre.

Mishel, L., Bernstein, J. and Schmitt, J. (1997), *The State of Working America 1996-1997*, Economic Policy Institute, New York: M.E. Sharpe.

Oxley, H., Burniaux, J.-M., Dang, T.-T. and d'Ercole, M.M. (1997), 'Distribution des revenus et pauvreté dans 13 pays de l'OCDE', *Revue Economique de l'OCDE*, 29.

OECD (1998), *Science, Technology and Industry Outlook*, Paris: OECD.

OECD (1999), *Employment Outlook*, June, Paris: OECD.

9. The Austrian Way: economic and social partnership

Ewald Walterskirchen

When I accepted the proposal to write a chapter on the Third Way in Austria, I could not imagine that the millennium would start for Austria with a conservative-nationalist government coalition of Schüssel and Haider and EU sanctions on Austria. These sanctions did not harm business, as may have been expected, but according to all polls they did harm the opposition parties and favour the existing government.

What remains is long-term damage to Austria's international image. In the 1970s and 1980s, Austria was a kind of model for Europe, now it is a warning. While nationalist slogans dominated the election campaign of Haider's liberal party, the written programme of the new government does not show any signs of xenophobic policies. It is rather of the Reagan–Thatcher type – a programme to hurt the clientele of the social democrats by fiscal consolidation packages and at the same time raising expenditures and cutting non-wage labour costs for the clientele of the ruling parties (entrepreneurs, farmers and families). Under these political circumstances, talking about the 'Austrian way' means talking about the past and possible scenarios for the future.

9.1   SOCIAL PARTNERSHIP

One of the characteristics of Austria's economic and social development was the high degree of consensus. Social partnership was the cornerstone of the Austrian model of consensus in the last five decades. It was invented as a reaction to Austria's Civil War in the 1930s ('never again') and as a national alliance against the occupying powers after the war. Many other European countries had some social consensus and wage restraint too, but in Austria this consensus policy was much more developed.

Social partnership is a voluntary and informal cooperation between the associations of employers and employees. The social partners in Austria have been involved in virtually every major policy decision since the 1950s, largely independent of the outcome of elections and the kind of government. Even the new coalition government does not totally exclude the social partners.

The interests of the Chambers (professional groups) are strongly represented in the consultation process of political decisions. However, the Chambers are more than simply lobby organisations, they are also fulfilling tasks in the public interest (for example consumer protection and export organisations). Social partnership does not mean denying conflicts of interest, it means balancing interests through compromises ('big bargains').

The main macroeconomic effect of social partnership has been rather moderate wage increases which kept down cost-push inflation and helped to maintain international competitiveness without devaluations. A moderate wage policy laid the foundations of hard currency policy in Austria. The incomes policy was an explicit strategy to fight inflation after the oil-price shocks, and can be seen as an alternative to restrictive monetary policy to react to the shocks. Social consensus on the distribution of income to keep down inflation may be interpreted as an important element of supply-side policy.

From the entrepreneurial point of view, the price for this rather moderate wage policy was the integration of trade unions in all decisions on economic affairs and welfare policies. Trade unions, on the other hand, were expecting lower inflation as well as higher investment and employment from money wage restraint.

Since the pressure of international competition in the EU now seems strong enough to check wages, many industrialists and entrepreneurs (the young 'falcons') have begun to doubt the usefulness of social partnership in recent years. The new political coalition between the people's party and the 'liberals' may also be seen as an outcome of these tendencies within the conservative party.

What will happen to social partnership under the new government? This is hard to say. On the one hand, the recent fiscal consolidation packages were passed on to the social partners for their comments or alternative proposals with given targets. On the other hand, the government programme is rather aggressive against the clientele of the social democrats (employees, retired persons). It is aggressive in particular against the Chamber of Labour, which is also the brains trust of the social democrats. The government intends to cut the legal contributions to the Chamber of Labour – that is her financial basis – by as much as 40 per cent. Decentralisation of wage agreements is envisaged to weaken trade unions. It is likely that trade unions will react to this policy by more aggressive wage claims and strikes than in the past. During the last decades there were hardly any strikes in Austria, with the exception of the public sector.

Economic theory is built on the economic interests of a society: neo-classical theory reflects the interests of entrepreneurs, centred on profit maximisation; Keynesian theory underlines the interests of workers, concentrating on full employment; and monetarism is built on the interests of asset holders, the 'third class', who gained much importance with the increase in wealth (Walterskirchen, 1994).

From this point of view, neo-classical synthesis – the synthesis of neo-classical theory and Keynesianism – may be seen as combining the interests of entrepreneurs and workers, leaving asset holders aside. 'New classical macroeconomics' – a synthesis of neo-classical theory and monetarism – on the other hand, may be interpreted as combining the interests of entrepreneurs and asset holders, leaving workers aside. I believe we shall only have a balanced development if the interests of the large groups in society are not denied.

9.2   BRUNO KREISKY'S POLICY IN THE 1970s AND EARLY 1980s: AUSTRO-KEYNESIANISM

If anything in economic policy deserves the name the 'Austrian Way', then it is the Kreisky era from 1970 to 1983, labelled the period of Austro-Keynesianism. The concept of economic policy in the Kreisky–Androsch era fits well in a Keynesian–Kaleckian framework. The main idea was to use macroeconomic policy in favour of full employment. However, the policies did not always follow a clear theoretical concept, sometimes they were rather experimental. The impact of Keynes and Kalecki may be traced back to Josef Steindl, Kurt Rothschild and other university teachers who influenced many economists in Austria. But they laid only the theoretical foundations; the actual policy mix of 'Austro-Keynesianism' was an achievement of the economists in the chambers and trade unions.

Kreisky was keen to hear the advice of experts (once he invited 1400 experts to a meeting). In the decades thereafter the results of opinion polls increasingly became the main orientation for politicians, and experts were used instead to confirm policies.

Why is the term Austro-Keynesianism justified? Is it just that Austrians – maybe out of a nostalgia for past glory – like the idea of having a specific role in the world? I will try to show that there are quite a few Keynesian–Kaleckian features representing the Austrian Way. Austria was a star pupil of demand-oriented policy, just as the Netherlands is nowadays a star pupil of supply-side policies.

9.2.1   Demand Management: Encouraging Investment

The main concept for the economic strategies was that there are no automatic forces driving market economies to full employment. A typical Keynesian feature is the idea that the employment situation is determined by economic growth – not by labour market flexibility – and that macroeconomic policy is needed to guarantee full employment. Encouraging investment and taking into account the interests of entrepreneurs was an important characteristic of policy in the Kreisky era. The vital role of aggregate demand in setting the level of activity was fully recognised. Business could count on an expansionary policy stance promoting investment and exports. This was part of the government's commitment to growth and full employment.

The expansionary policy stance was backed by a more liberal immigration policy than in the decades before. According to Harrod, a shortage of labour may stop a business upswing. This happened in Austria in the 1960s. In the early 1970s working permits for foreign workers helped to prolong the business upswing. Since 'the trend is just a series of cycles' (Kalecki, 1971), this policy promoted medium-term growth.

9.2.2　Anticyclical Keynesian Fiscal Policy

In the Kreisky era, fiscal policy in Austria was strictly anticyclical, that is, higher fiscal deficits were accepted in recessions through the working of automatic stabilisers plus additional investment in infrastructure. There was a definite commitment to fight against recession to prevent unemployment from the very beginning. Keynesian demand management played an important role in avoiding a major setback.

A famous, often repeated statement by Bruno Kreisky was: 'Some hundred thousands of unemployed cause me more sleepless nights than some billions of government debt.'

9.2.3　Dampening Household Saving

An interesting statement by Keynes about the stages of economic development after the war is not very well known, and was first quoted in an article by Guger and Walterskirchen (1988). In 'Long-Term Problems of Full Employment' (written in 1943, but not published before 1980), Keynes had envisaged three phases of postwar development:

1.　In the first years after the war, the inducement to invest would be higher than the desired level of savings. To prevent inflation Keynes thought of limiting investment by suitable controls and of limiting consumption by some kind of rationing.
2.　For the next 25 years Keynes expected a phase in which the 'urgent level of investment is no longer higher than the indicated level of savings' (Keynes 1971–83, p. 321). Investment and savings would be roughly

matched. The main problem in this period was to ensure a high level of employment by preventing business fluctuations and to foster growth by less urgent, but useful investment. This appears to be the situation of the 1960s and 1970s.

3. After twenty years of large-scale investment Keynes foresaw that the economy would enter into a third phase with increasing difficulties to find satisfactory outlets for new investment. The (desired) level of savings would exceed the demand for useful investment. Keynes drew the following conclusion already in 1943: we shall have to start on very important changes, aimed at the discouragement of savings and the encouragement of consumption.

It is interesting to note that Keynes considered certain historical periods with completely different problems and policy solutions, with the historical development being largely independent of the will of men.

Policies in the Kreisky–Androsch era stimulated investment by interest-rate subsidies and so on, but discouraged household saving by the introduction of taxes on interest payments and reduced savings promotion. The role of savings makes a crucial difference between Keynesian and neo-classical theory. Those who save money are 'public benefactors' (Guger, 2000) in neo-classical theory, because savings automatically mean investment and growth. In the Keynesian–Kaleckian framework, on the other hand, investment creates savings. For the Austrian economist Joseph Steindl (1979) the high savings rate was one of the problems since 1975: the economy was unable to adjust to lower growth rates because its savings propensity was geared to a high one. A reduction in the long-run growth rates (of the 1960s and 1970s) requires a lower savings propensity, otherwise the federal budget cannot be balanced.

A recent example for the validity of this theory is the experience of the United States and the Scandinavian countries in the 1990s: due to a massive reduction in the savings rate of private households, the economy flourished, and the budget deficit vanished. Relatively low interest rates contributed to the boom of share prices which were a major factor in driving the savings rate of private households down.

9.2.4 Industrial Policy

Another way to promote investment and growth was missing in Austro-Keynesianism: innovation policy. In Kalecki's theory, technical progress stimulates investment by extra profits (temporary monopoly profits) for the innovator. But industrial policy in Austria remained one-sided, with assistance for ailing industries but not for the new ones.

Technology policy was not used as an instrument to reduce Austria's notoriously high trade deficit (with Germany). A crucial idea to stimulate exports and to reduce the trade deficit was bilateral agreements. Since a major contribution to the trade deficit came from car imports, Austria announced its own car production and demanded the delivery of car parts at many state visits. Austria did not produce a single car in the end, but negotiations with governments and multinational firms had long-run consequences: today the car supplier industry is the largest industry in Austria.

Kreisky was strongly criticised for very high subsidies to the nationalised industries (particularly steel). The idea was to pay subsidies for a transition period so that they had enough time to change to new production methods and did not go bankrupt in the meantime. Today, the privatised steel industry is flourishing in Austria.

Major education reform was carried out under the social democratic government. New occupation-oriented higher schools were introduced in addition to the old higher schools (which emphasised Latin and Greek).

9.2.5 Hard Currency Policy

Another cornerstone of Austro-Keynesianism has been hard currency policy. The Austrian Schilling was pegged to the Deutschmark, which meant that Austria did not use the exchange-rate instrument for employment purposes, and that Austrian monetary policy was essentially made in Frankfurt. Therefore, the EMU did not affect Austria greatly in this respect. The hard currency policy was adopted in Austria as a tool against inflation, to keep import prices down. It was fully accepted by the trade unions, who claimed that inflation would hurt the poor in particular, because they have to spend all their income on consumer goods. The rich save more and are less hit by inflation as long as there are positive real interest rates. To sum up, policy assignment was rather unusual in Austro-Keynesianism:

-   Inflation was seen as imported and cost-determined. Therefore it was controlled by a hard currency policy which was facilitated by a moderate incomes policy.
-   International competitiveness was maintained again by a moderate incomes policy facilitated by social partnership (not by repeated devaluations).
-   The welfare state in Austria has been successful in reducing unemployment and poverty, offering a decent public infrastructure and a well-functioning health system.

146   *The economics of the Third Way*

9.3 THE SUPPLY-SIDE ECONOMIC POLICY STANCE OF THE COALITION GOVERNMENTS (1983–99)

With the exception of the years 1983–86, Austria has had a Great Coalition between the social democratic and the conservative (People's) party during the last 17 years. In this period, economic and labour market policy was predominantly supply-side oriented, according to the Zeitgeist and increasing internationalisation and globalisation. The policy stance in these years was not far removed from the Third Way as this term is normally used in the UK. However, the term 'Third Way' has never been used in Austria in the Clinton–Blair–Schröder way: as a middle-of-the-road position between 'old' social democracy and neo-liberalism. If the term Third Way is used at all in Austria, it means something rather different: either the 'social market economy' (soziale Marktwirtschaft) or the corporatist Swedish model. Social partnership was still working in Austria in the last decades, but was increasingly criticised by the media for 'impeding structural change'. In 1995, for the first time the social partners were not consulted before a fiscal consolidation package was presented to the public. The opening up of the East offered new chances for the Austrian enterprises. The effect of the fall of the Iron Curtain was clearly positive on the Austrian economy, as can be seen by the strong improvement of the trade balance *vis-à-vis* the countries of East–Middle Europe. Austria applied for EU membership and became a member of the EU in 1995. Liberalisation in many fields (particularly public services) and lower inflation rates were a major effect of EU membership. After joining the EU, the fiscal situation deteriorated because Austria became a net payer in the EU and agriculture was additionally subsidised. Also the labour market situation deteriorated temporarily: Austria's food industries and some service industries came under pressure from international competition and reduced their staff substantially.

On the whole, economic policy in the last two decades was not much different in Austria from the Third Way approach in other EU countries. Location policy ('Standortpolitik') was the key issue of economic strategies. However, social partners and trade unions had a much stronger influence than in other countries to shape these policies. The main difference was that full employment still had high priority in Austria and unemployment was fought by early retirement schemes in an excessive way. Another difference was that anticyclical fiscal policy – mainly investment in infrastructure and incentives for investment – was still regarded as an adequate instrument to fight recession and unemployment, even in 1993.

With this Third Way strategy the social democratic party lost many voters to Haider's liberal party. For these voters, anti-foreigner and anti-EU slogans seemed to be a shelter against the evils attributed to globalisation and modernisation. Chancellor Klima and his spin doctors first acclaimed the Blair–Schröder paper on the Third Way, but later, after strong opposition within the social democratic party, became more critical.

There is no need to go too much into policy details, because we can find similar supply-side strategies in all European countries.

9.3.1 Tax Policy

Economic policy was preoccupied with the improvement of Austria's competitive position in the world. Taxes for enterprises were cut substantially, the tax on property was abolished. Foundations (Stiftungen) became a decent way for the rich to avoid taxes and for Austria to attract capital. Austria now has one of the lowest effective tax rates for enterprises and property in the EU, but a high Value Added Tax (20 per cent) and very high non-wage labour costs (social security contributions). The net wage share (after taxes) declined rapidly during the last decade.

9.3.2 Liberalisation, Privatisation and Deregulation

Public services were liberalised after joining the EU. As a consequence, prices in the telecommunications and electricity sector fell substantially. Nationalised industries were privatised, but more slowly than in other European countries. Labour markets were also deregulated rather slowly (for example regarding part-time employment). But real wage flexibility and labour market flexibility (dismissals) have always been high in Austria. Technology policy is still neglected. Austria's expenditure on R&D is among the lowest in the EU, partly because there is virtually no 'big business' in Austria.

9.3.3 Moderate Wage Policy

Wage policy remained centralised (contrary to other EU countries). Wages negotiations are still carried out at the branch level (only 13 branches). There is no firm wage leadership, but the blue- and white-collar workers in the metal and engineering industry start negotiations and have great influence on the wage round. In the 1980s the main reason for moderate wage claims by trade unions was simply that the nationalised steel industry was deeply in the red, and the union of metal workers tried not to worsen the situation. The other unions are following quite closely the path of the strong union of metal-workers.

9.3.4 Fiscal consolidation

There were many fiscal consolidation packages in Austria, but curiously they were often followed after some years by additional expenditure programmes (for example for families) or tax cuts so that the fiscal situation did not really improve in the long run. Regarding pensions, Austria is not a Third Way country. Legal pension insurance is still the cornerstone of pensions, private pension plans are only just beginning.

9.3.5   Early Retirement

The main supply-side policy reaction to increasing labour market problems in the 1980s and early 1990s was to reduce labour supply by early retirement. The easing of conditions for receiving disability pensions and 'special allowances' for certain groups of older workers were the main instruments to prevent unemployment.

At present, the effective pension entry age is 57 years on average; for Vienna's civil servants it is only 52 years, for railway workers about 53 years. At the beginning these measures were concentrated on workers in the manufacturing industry threatened by unemployment, but sooner or later all manufacturing industries dismissed their workers at the age of about 55 with a golden handshake.

Although the firms and many of the older workers were happy with this solution – to make jobs free for young people – it is quite understandable that this policy was not affordable in the long run, being probably the most expensive way to fight unemployment. Evidently, it is hardly possible to finance such measures given a life expectancy of almost 80 years. Therefore, the recent budget consolidation packages restricted the eligibility for early retirement.

9.4   AUSTRIA'S ECONOMIC PERFORMANCE IN THE KREISKY–ANDROSCH ERA AND UNDER THE COALITION GOVERNMENTS – EMPIRICAL RESULTS

A simple way to evaluate the economic success or failure of economic policies in a certain period is to compare the country's macroeconomic performance with the EU average (see Figures 9.1–9.5). In the Kreisky era, Austria's economic and social policy was a model for Europe. One reason was an original policy mix, the other reason was Austria's macroeconomic performance.

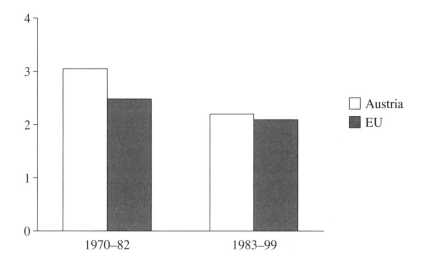

Figure 9.1   Growth of real GDP in the Kreisky era, 1970–82 and the coalition government, 1983-99 (percentage change p.a.)

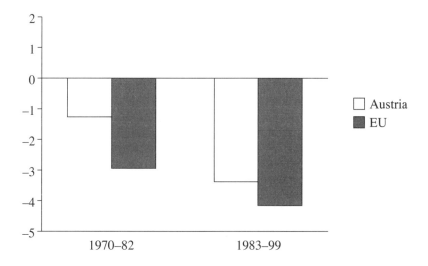

Figure 9.2   General government financial balance in the Kreisky era, 1970-82 and the coalition government, 1983-99 (per cent of GDP p.a.)

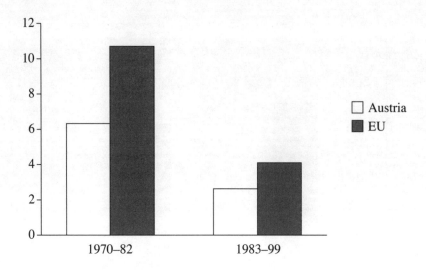

Figure 9.3   Inflation rate in the Kreisky era, 1970-82 and the coalition government, 1983-99 (per cent p.a.)

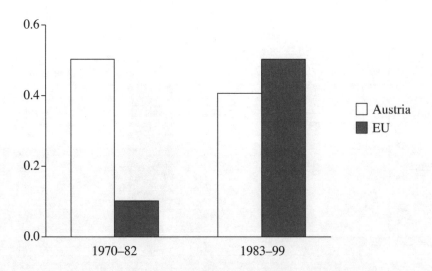

Figure 9.4   Employment in the Kreisky era, 1970-82 and the coalition government, 1983-99 (percentage change p.a.)

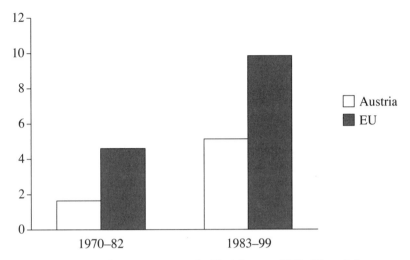

Figure 9.5   Unemployment rate in the Kreisky era, 1970-82 and the coalition government, 1983-99 (per cent of total labour force p.a.)

9.4.1   GDP Growth

Austria's growth performance in the Kreisky era (1970–82) was outstanding. GDP growth was 0.6 percentage points per year higher than in the EU. Austria was in the fast lane, although economic activities were still impeded by the Iron Curtain. In the second period (1983–99), economic growth was close to the EU average (+0.1 per cent p.a.), although favoured by the opening up of the East and presumably also by joining the EU. Particularly since 1995, economic development has not surpassed the EU although relative unit labour costs in the manufacturing industry declined by as much as 8 per cent.

Recessions in Austria have been less deep than in the EU, since demand management has been stabilising the business cycle.

9.4.2   Inflation

The price performance in both periods was superior to the EU. This is mainly due to the influence of social partnership on wage negotiations and the effects of hard currency policy - facilitated by moderate wage increases - on import costs. The inflation rate was (1970–82) 4.5 percentage points lower than in the EU, in the period 1983-99 it was 1.5 percentage points below.

In recent years trade unions have used a simple guideline for their productivity-oriented wage policy: inflation rate plus productivity growth minus one. This means that they have accepted a certain shift of income to profits.

9.4.3   Fiscal Deficits

In the Kreisky era, not only were GDP growth and labour market indicators better than in the EU, but notably also the budget deficit was much lower than in the EU. This must be stressed in particular because Austrian politicians and journalists try to make Bruno Kreisky responsible for the current large budget deficit in Austria. It is hard to understand how people are made to believe this (see Figures 9.1–9.5). The only way would be that Kreisky influenced by some kind of telepathy the unnecessary tax cuts and family packages in the year 2000.

In the Kreisky era, the fiscal deficit amounted to 1.2 per cent of GDP, it was 1.7 percentage points lower than the EU average. Also at the end of the Kreisky era the fiscal deficit was still substantially below the EU average, that is it did not increase in relation to the EU, mainly due to successful growth policies and their effect on taxes and social security contributions.

Although fiscal deficits in Austria were lower than in the EU for longer periods, in recession years and thereafter they came very close to the EU average. This confirms Keynesian countercyclical policies. In the coalition period (1983–99) the fiscal deficit went up to 3.3 per cent of GDP on average. It still remained somewhat below the EU average, but the positive difference became smaller and smaller. In 2000, after a generous tax and family support package (decided before the election!), Austria's fiscal position was at the tail end of the fiscal consolidation convoy in the EU.

9.4.4   Full Employment: the Main Target

Austria managed to keep its unemployment relatively low over the last decades. What are the main reasons for this? In the Kreisky era, higher GDP and employment growth was mainly responsible for the extremely low unemployment rates (1.5 per cent). In the coalition period, 1983–99, GDP and employment did not perform better than in the EU. The growth of employment was even somewhat smaller (–0.1 per cent p.a.) than in the EU, moreover it was concentrated on the public sector (teachers and so on). The relatively low unemployment rate in this period (about 5 per cent on average) was due to the reduction of the labour supply through early retirement, as mentioned earlier.

9.5   OUTLOOK – OPTIONS FOR THE FUTURE

What we experience in Austria now is a government willing to reform, with nationalist features.

It is too early to judge the economic policy of the new government.

Evidently, they started with a crash strategy to consolidate the budget. This fiscal consolidation package was certainly necessary after the tax cut and the family package in 2000, but it is designed mainly to hurt the social democrats.

The programme of the new coalition shows some features typical of conservative–liberal governments:

- higher expenditure on defence, farmers and families, much less on social welfare;
- liberal in economic affairs, conservative in cultural issues;
- reduction of non-wage labour costs for enterprises.

The damage of the political isolation in the EU to Austria's international standing may last longer than this government will be in office. A red-green coalition in Austria after the 2003 election appears to be feasible. The programme for a new Austrian Way might look like this:

- many elements of Austro-Keynesianism;
- revival of a new social partnership;
- focus on new technology which is driving history;
- more child-care facilities than lump-sum money for mothers staying at home;
- right of parents with small children to reduce working time;
- a halt to expenditure programmes for pressure groups; and last but not least
- a focus on environmental protection (energy taxes and so on).

The new chairman of the social democratic party in Austria, Gusenbauer, is referring to Bruno Kreisky as his political idol. Therefore, a revival of Austro-Keynesianism, with all the necessary adaptions, is not unlikely in a somewhat distant future.

BIBLIOGRAPHY

Arestis, P. and Sawyer, M. (1998), 'Keynesian economic policies for the new millennium', *Economic Journal*, January.

Butschek, F. (1985), *Die österreichische Wirtschaft im 20.Jahrhundert*, Stuttgart: Gustav Fischer.

Guger, A. (2000), 'Economic policy and social democracy: the Austrian experience', *Oxford Review of Economic Policy*, **14**(1).

Guger, A. and Walterskirchen, E. (1988), 'Fiscal and Monetary Policy in the Keynes-Kalecki Tradition', in Jan Kregel, Egon Matzner and Alessandro Roncaglia (eds), *Barriers to Full Employment*, Basingstoke: Macmillan.

Kalecki, M. (1971), *Selected Essays on the Dynamics of the Capitalist Economy*, Cambridge: Cambridge University Press.

Kausel, A. (1998), *Five Decades of Success, Austria's Economic Rise within the OECD since 1950*, Vienna: Austrian National Bank.

Keynes, J.M. (1971–83), *The Collected Writings of John Maynard Keynes*, Vols I–XXIX, Austin Robinson and Donald Moggridge (eds), Royal Economic Society.

Marterbauer, M. (1998), 'Post-Keynesian Economic Policy in Austria and in Sweden', WIFO Working Papers 107/1998.

Steindl, J. (1979), 'Stagnation theory and stagnation policy', *Cambridge Journal of Economics*, **3**(1), March.

Walterskirchen, E. (1994), '15 Jahre monetaristische Wirtschaftspolitik', in Egon Matzner and Ewald Nowotny (eds), *Was ist relevante Ökonomie? Festschrift für Kurt W. Rothschild*, Marburg: Metropolis.

Walterskirchen, E. (1991), *Unemployment and Labour Market Flexibility: Austria*, Geneva: International Labour Office.

10. The economic policy of the Spanish Socialist governments: 1982–96

Jesus Ferreiro and Felipe Serrano

10.1 INTRODUCTION

The government of the Socialist Party (Partido Socialista Obrero Español, PSOE) started in November 1982 and ended in March 1996, when the Partido Popular, a right-wing Christian Democratic party, won the elections. During these fourteen years, the economic policy of the Socialist governments focused on two objectives. From a macroeconomic point of view the entire strategy was based on the control of inflation rates. The problem of unemployment was subordinated to this main objective, a strategy that was coincident with the dominant strategies implemented in the rest of the Western economies. From a long-term perspective, the general orientation of its economic policy responded to a twofold objective. The first one was related to the idea of modernisation, that is, of social and economic adaptation to the new changes that arose as a result of the structural crisis that Western countries had been suffering since the late 1960s. The second one, deeply rooted in the classic European social democratic tradition, was the construction and consolidation of the Welfare State.

Throughout the Socialist governments, these objectives went through several phases depending on the constituency's support or rejection, the changes in the international economic situation, and the contradictions existing among such objectives. Our purpose is not to make a deep analysis of those phases or to make a personal and subjective interpretation of the general outcomes of these fourteen years of socialist administration. Instead, we will try to give elements for the debate showing the outstanding features of those years.

In order to grasp the constraints that faced the first Socialist governments we must take into account two main points. First, when the Socialist Party came to power, the political situation was at the centre of the concerns of every social, economic and political agent. The end of Franco's dictatorship in the mid-1970s opened an intense cycle of political change that only ended when Spain became an EEC member in 1986. Secondly, the heritage that the

Socialist government received from their predecessors, the centre-right wing Unión de Centro Democrático (UCD), was very complicated. Two crises converged during the process of political transition. First, the general crisis that affected all Western economies. Secondly, the crisis in the regulation model dominant during Franco's era, whose foremost characteristics were a high degree of public intervention and a strong foreign protection. The Socialist governments faced the need to manage a deep economic crisis by designing and implementing new forms of intervention, which involved a break with inertia and privileges which would not be easily accepted by the most directly affected sectors and agents.

10.2   THE GENERAL STRATEGY OF THE ECONOMIC POLICY OF THE SOCIALIST GOVERNMENTS: THE FIGHT AGAINST INFLATION

The control of inflation was the main macroeconomic objective of the Socialist governments, fundamentally during the first term.[1] As Carlos Solchaga, that period's Minister of Economy, stated, the fight against inflation

> was the previous requirement to lay the foundations to reduce unemployment in Spain. The search for short cuts was in vain. To trust in the old strategy of expansionary policies was dangerous. The point was the cost of disinflation. During the whole time I was leading the co-ordination of the economic policy of the Spanish Government, I was under the opinion that such a cost would be smaller if the halt to inflation was reached through wage moderation than if it were obtained by a restrictive monetary policy, which I had wanted to avoid at any price. (Solchaga, 1997, p. 201)

Based on this idea, the first Socialist government succeeded in keeping the consensus of the trade unions to implement an incomes policy which started in 1977 and finished in 1986. In this period the inflation rate fell from 24.5 per cent to 8.8 per cent in 1986. Since 1987, after the changes in the mechanism of the budget deficit financing and the measures adopted to liberalise the financial system and the foreign capital flows, and coinciding with a phase of strong economic growth, the monetary policy concentrated all the protagonism in the fight against inflation. Between 1987 and 1993 the average real interest rate in Spain was 9 per cent. This acceleration in interest rates led the Spanish currency to a strong appreciation, which, besides the pressure of the domestic demand, made the current account deficit reach 6.9 per cent of GDP in 1992. From 1985 until the first devaluation in 1992, the real effective rate of exchange of the Spanish peseta, in relation to the currencies of developed countries, appreciated nearly 30 per cent.[2] The change in the cycle that began in 1992, in addition to the subsequent devaluations and the wider fluctuation bands within the EMS, allowed the relaxation of the monetary policy and the subsequent fall of real interest rates. This monetary policy generated a vicious circle that seriously damaged the fight against unemployment. The rate of unemployment increased from 5.7 per cent in 1977 to 21.6 per cent in 1985, fell to 16 per cent in the late 1980s, and increased again to 24.1 per cent in 1994. However, the relation between disinflation and unemployment cannot explain alone the high rates of unemployment. Although the high interest rates and the appreciation of the Spanish peseta contributed to halting the rates of economic growth, which were very high during the second half of the 1980s, the increase in unemployment during the early 1980s was mainly explained by the severe adjustment in the productive capacities. Furthermore, the entry of a new population, mainly a female one, into the labour market during the late 1980s made a more significant fall in the unemployment rates impossible, despite the strong economic growth.

The restrictive monetary policy also had consequences on the labour market and the modernisation of the productive organisation. For the Socialist government the inflation was the outcome of excessive wage pressure. The origin of the wage push was a wage determination process which transferred the wage growth passed from the manufacturing sector, a sector open to foreign competition and, therefore, with high productivity increases, to the less productive sector (services sector). The labour market reforms enacted in 1994, which will be analysed below, can only be understood when such a view is taken into account. However, this thesis hides the actual importance of other elements that must be considered when Spanish inflation is analysed. A direct relation between wage growth and price increase involves the assumption that the profit margin is constant and, therefore, that the latter is not influenced by investment decisions, the existence of degrees of monopoly in some relevant branches of the economy or the price increase in the borrowing rate.[3] Nonetheless, those elements did have to have a strong protagonism, because when we link the sectorial price increases and the evolution of the sectorial labour costs, the unexplained component of such a link is very important, mainly in the service sector.

Figures 10.1 and 10.2 show the sectorial evolution of labour costs and prices in the service and manufacturing sectors. Data on labour costs are calculated using the real total earnings per worker. The behaviour of the service sector shows a deep gap between the evolution of prices and labour costs. Nominal unit labour costs (NULC) grew at positive rates from 1986 to 1990, but since 1990 the growth has been negative. If the thesis held by the government were right, the evolution of service prices should be in accordance with the evolution of such costs. However, during the period of tight monetary policy (1987–93), the accumulated growth of NULC was 2.58 per cent, whereas the accumulated growth of the service sector deflator was 67.2 per

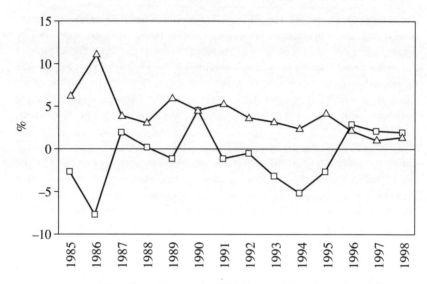

-□- Manufacturing nominal ULC   -△- Manufacturing deflator

Source: Our calculations.

Figure 10.1   Prices and costs evolution in the manufacturing sector

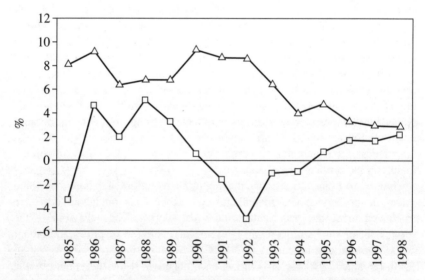

-□- Services nominal ULC   -△- Services deflator

Source: Our calculations.

Figure 10.2   Prices and costs evolution in the service sector

cent. Therefore, the wage growth would have been responsible for 3.8 per cent of the price growth in the service sector. In the manufacturing sector, such a gap is smaller. NULC shows positive growth rates in 1987, 1988 and 1990, years of strong economic growth and, therefore, strong demand for employment. From 1987 to 1993, manufacturing NULC grew in accumulated terms by 0.01 per cent, whilst the manufacturing sector deflator grew in accumulated terms by 33.84 per cent. In the manufacturing sector there was not a clear correlation between price and wage costs evolution, although the gap between such variables was smaller than in the service sector.

The divergence in sectorial prices was closely linked to the maintenance of degrees of monopoly in some branches in the service sector and to the small amount of foreign competition in the services sector. In this sense, one of the main failures of the Socialist economic policies was the non-implementation of the necessary structural reforms to increase the productivity in the Spanish economy, mainly in the service sector.

The full trust in the belief that entry into the EEC would automatically increase competence and productive effectiveness was limited only to the manufacturing sector, and it led to a high cost in terms of employment destruction.[4] The Socialist governments' refusal to implement a proactive industrial policy, besides the increase in the price of borrowing as a result of the restrictive monetary policy, hindered the necessary adaptation of the Spanish manufacturing sector to the new conditions posed by a higher competence. Actually, the only proactive policy was the policy to attract foreign direct investments, with the hope that foreign investors would supply Spanish companies with the competitive advantages needed to compete on a new stage.

The small foreign competition in the service sector, which allowed a larger market fragmentation, involved a more acute need for reforms. However, the interventions of the Socialist government in this sector were much less, leading to a slower adaptation of the sector and to the maintenance of monopoly situations that, despite the existence of ceiling prices policy in some branches, delayed the processes of innovation needed to increase the productivity of the sector. Telecommunications and transport sectors only opened to foreign competition in the 1990s. The liberalisation in the financial sector, although intense in some specific activities, kept consumers captive in some segments of business of vital importance for the public (for instance, in the mortgage market: in 1995 the legislation allowing customers to change between financial companies with low costs was modified). In the energy sector nowadays there are still administrative barriers to entry, with negative consequences for energy prices, despite the existence of a ceiling prices policy that limits the influence of the oligopoly that dominates the sector.

The combination of the price increase in borrowing, the lack of an industrial policy, the unequal evolution of sectorial prices and the price constraint imposed by foreign competition generated a permanent pressure on production costs which affected the labour market trying to find short-term solutions.

10.3   THE ROLE OF LABOUR MARKET REFORMS[5]

Although the two labour market reforms enacted by the Socialist governments in 1984 and 1994 had their own logic, based on the belief that they would help in the creation of employment, their nature, working and outcomes cannot be understood without taking into account the central strategy of economic policy described above. This link is relevant for the analysis of the evolution of temporary employment and the core elements of the 1994 reform.

The first labour market reform was approved in 1984, four years after the enactment of the 'Estatuto de los Trabajadores' (Workers Statute), the basic law in the field of labour relations. In the matter of labour contraction, the 'Estatuto' was based on the causation principle, according to which permanent labour contracts were used for permanent jobs whilst fixed-term labour contracts could only be used for temporary jobs linked to the needs of productive organisation or to temporary increases in demand. This principle was broken in the reform of 1984, which allowed the use of fixed-term employment contracts (with a legal duration limited to three years) in permanent jobs. In this sense, the reform of 1984 changed the path of entry for new workers in companies by promoting external flexibility in payrolls.

A positive consequence of this reform was the increase in the elasticity of employment demand relative to the changes in the activity. The elasticity of salaried employment relative to real GDP increased from -1.2 in 1974–84 up to 0.6 in 1985–91, due to a creation of 2 063 640 salaried jobs in the latter period (+28.2 per cent) that offset the 1 283 260 salaried jobs lost from 1976 to 1985 (-15 per cent), allowing the reduction in employment rate from 21.6 per cent in 1985 to 16.2 per cent in 1990. However, the reform involved the generalisation of temporary contracts. From 1987 to 1994, 1 239 500 temporary jobs were created in the private sector whilst 913 300 permanent ones were lost. All the new employment created was temporary employment. The result was an enormous increase in the rates of temporary employment due to the destruction of permanent employment that lasted until 1995 and to the high rates of growth of temporary workers. The rates of temporary employment in the private sector increased from 22.8 per cent in 1987 to 40.5 per cent in 1995, falling since then to 36.3 per cent in 1999.

This evolution of temporary and permanent employment was the outcome of several factors. Nonetheless, a key element in explaining the high segmentation in the Spanish labour market is the wage gap between permanent and temporary workers. Unfortunately, there is information available from official surveys on wage distribution only for the years 1988, 1992 and 1995 (Instituto Nacional de Estadística, 1992, 1995, 1997): in 1988 the total earnings (including wages agreed in collective bargaining agreements and wage drifts) of temporary workers were only 57.68 per cent of permanent ones, 59.4 per cent in 1992 and only 44.76 per cent in 1995. This earnings' gap helps us to understand how, during a strong economic expansion, permanent employment was subjected to severe cutbacks. There was a substitution of permanent workers for temporary workers, not only because of the cheaper firing costs of the latter (with the exception of one category, fixed-term contracts did not have any compensation when the contract terminated) but mainly because of the lower wages of temporary workers.

The companies used the temporary contracts to offset, first, the negative consequences generated by the restrictive monetary policy and, secondly, the transfers of resources from the manufacturing to the services sector that the sectorial price differential generated. When these conditions started to change in the mid 1990s, the trend in employment contracts changed radically: from 1995 to 1999 81.2 per cent of the new employment was permanent, allowing the fall in temporary employment rates mentioned above.

The EMS crises in 1992–93 and the subsequent devaluations of the peseta led to a more relaxed monetary policy and to a fall in the real rates of interest. The final outcome was that the government lost the possibility of using a restrictive monetary policy to reduce the rate of inflation. However, the Socialist government thought that the first labour market reform could not halt the inflation rates through the wage moderation alone, because although the reform had increased the external flexibility in the labour market the insiders' power of bargaining was kept intact. Furthermore, the high rates of temporary employment brought a negative effect on productivity and, from a macro-economic perspective, the higher elasticity of the labour demand generated a negative effect on the level of employment during the downswing in the early 1990s (in 1992–93 there was a loss of 8.6 per cent of salaried employment in the private sector).

In this context, the Socialist government believed that it was the time to promote the internal flexibility in the labour market with the objective of reducing the inflation rate in the long term. The objective of the second labour market reform approved in 1994 was to change the institutional rules of wage determination, moving to the collective bargaining of some points previously regulated by legal norms, such as the flexible use of working-time by companies, the promotion of the variable part of workers' earnings, the promotion of decentralised collective bargaining agreements, and so on. In short, the final aim was to reach a closer link between wage and productivity increases, both at individual worker and individual company levels, which would allow a break with the imitation effect which had moved the wage growth from the highest productivity sectors (manufacturing sectors) to the less productive sectors (service ones).

Nowadays, it is very difficult to state whether the 1994 reform reached its objectives or not. Since 1994 there has been a clear wage moderation: real earnings have only increased in accumulated terms by 2.6 per cent (Ferreiro and Serrano, 2001), which has partially offset the lower productivity growth due to the strong creation of employment. However, this wage moderation may be explained as an exchange for the conversion of temporary contracts into permanent ones and by the creation of permanent employment that was favoured by the 1997 reform.

Furthermore, the removal of the gap between the evolution of prices and that of unit labour costs that Figures 10.1 and 10.2 show is also related to the moderation in price increases due to the moderation in the rest of costs, such as borrowing costs (due to the more relaxed monetary policy), and profit margins (due to the implementation of liberalisation reforms in the service sector).

10.4 WELFARE STATE AND INCOME DISTRIBUTION

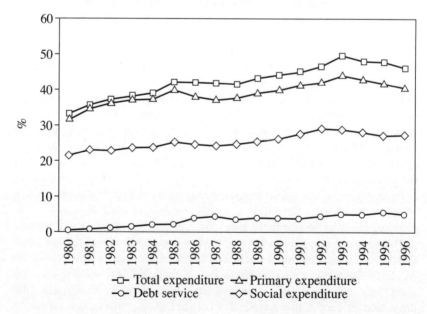

Source: Our calculations.

Figure 10.3   Evolution of the public administration expenditures (% GDP)

Figure 10.3 shows the evolution of public expenditure from 1980 until 1996: the public expenditure, without the expenditure on debt service, shows a slight upward tendency. Most of this growth is concentrated in the first half of the 1980s. From 1980 until 1985, the weight of public expenditure in relation to GDP increased by eight points.[6] During the second half of the 1980s, the tendency changed to a downward one but during the 1990s the tendency was upward again, due, among other reasons, to the crisis of the early 1990s and the unions' claims after the 1988 general strike.

Beyond considerations about the optimal size of the public sector, evolution of social expenditure was constrained by the problem, faced by all the Socialist governments, of the government budget deficit financing, which in 1982 was 5.6 per cent of GDP. The privileged finance transferred the problem of the budget deficit financing to prices. Therefore, because of the consideration of inflation as the main objective of the economic policy, the objectives of the fiscal policy of the Socialist governments were, first, the change to orthodox budget deficit financing in order to help the monetary policy to reduce inflation rates and, secondly, to reduce the deficit by the increase in the tax pressure and the halt in the increase of public expenditure.

The change from privileged to orthodox financing, in addition to the tightened monetary policy implemented, increased the debt burden. Between 1986 and 1996, the average debt service was 4.4 per cent of GDP, a similar amount to the public education expenditure and more than twice the expenditure on unemployment compensation (during a period when rates of unemployment oscillated between 16 per cent and 24 per cent). Debt service worked to slow the increase in social expenditures, a slowdown which increased, first, because of the lack of more intense measures against tax evasion and, secondly, the fiscal requirements of the Maastricht Treaty.

In 1982, fiscal pressure was 28 per cent of GDP. In 1996, the last year of the Socialist governments, this pressure was 35.8 per cent of GDP, below the 37.3 per cent of GDP reached in 1992. The increase in fiscal pressure was concentrated on direct taxes, whose share in GDP rose five points, and on indirect taxes, whose share rose three points after the implementation of VAT. The share of social security contributions in GDP only increased by one point. On the other hand, socialist fiscal policy tried to promote the progressive nature of direct taxation but the high amount of fiscal evasion weakened the progressiveness of taxation and, therefore, the desired redistributive effect.

The financial problems generated by the debt burden, in addition to the political option of not increasing fiscal pressure and a clear inability to reduce fiscal evasion (despite the increase in the number of taxpayers) reduced the capacity of the Gonzalez governments to develop the Welfare State. As Figure 10.3 shows, social expenditure has a stable trend. In 1982, the total social expenditure reached 22.8 per cent of GDP. In 1996 this share had risen to 27.5 per cent of GDP, having peaked at 29 per cent of GDP during the recession of the early 1990s. Nonetheless, this growth in social expenditure does not give sufficient information about the developments of the socialist governments in the field of social welfare.

During the Franco era, an incipient Welfare State was developed, which expanded considerably during the political transition. From 1977 until the first Socialist government in 1982, total social expenditure grew very fast, but without a defined plan about its future. The Socialist governments appear to have been more positive about development. Their commitment to the Welfare State (Recio and Roca, 1998) involved a set of reforms, some completed during their term and others during the Partido Popular government, whose objective was to lay the new structure of the Welfare State.

The public pensions scheme was always at the core of those measures. Committed to its maintenance during years of fierce conservative criticism to the pay-as-you-go (PAYG) systems, the Socialist governments tackled an initial reform in 1984 and a subsequent reform in 1996, whose objectives were to rationalise expenditure growth by tightening the links between the time and amount of contributions and the entitlement to and amount of benefits. Both reforms also tried to rationalise the claims for an intergenerational redistribution on which PAYG systems are based. On the other hand, both reforms went with active policies to increase the minimum benefits, to add pension supplements to the lowest pensions, and to maintain the purchase power of all pensions.

The evolution of expenditure on unemployment compensation was related to the evolution of unemployment. In Spain the coverage of this insurance was limited by contributions only from those entitled to unemployment compensation. The unemployment insurance has never had universal coverage: the entitlement to the benefits is limited to those salaried workers who have worked during a minimum period of time. Keeping this constraint, the Socialist governments made an effort to increase the coverage rate of unemployment benefits, even though in the last years of the Socialist term there was a change in tendency. In 1982, the share of unemployed workers that received unemployment benefits was 33.6 per cent. This rate increased to peak at 76 per cent in 1993. There were three reasons to explain this evolution: first, the maintenance and slight increase of the expenditure on this budget item, which always was above 2.5 per cent of GDP; secondly, the fall in unemployment rates during the latter part of the 1980s; and thirdly, as a consequence of the increase in fixed-term employment contracts, the increase in the number of unemployed workers entitled to unemployment benefits. However, during the last years of its term, the last Socialist government reformed unemployment benefits by making the requirements for obtaining the benefits more stringent.[7] The outcome of this reform, approved in 1992, was a fall in the coverage rate to 58 per cent in 1998.[8]

The social expenditures on health and education also increased rapidly during the thirteen years of the Socialist term: from 7.3 per cent of GDP in 1982 to 10.4 per cent of GDP in 1996. This increase was the outcome, first, of including all the population in the universal coverage of the benefits, and, secondly, of increasing the per capita expenditure. When the socialists left the government the public health system had universal coverage, real per capita expenditure on health had doubled since 1982, and the public education system had spread fully from primary to university education.

Next, we will analyse the distributive consequences of the Spanish Welfare State, focusing our analysis on the expenditures and revenues. Nonetheless, before starting the analysis of the redistributive consequences of the Welfare State, we must mention the negative consequences of the labour market reforms on the personal distribution of income. In the former section, we mentioned the earnings gap existing among permanent salaried workers, temporary salaried workers and part-timers. Unfortunately, information on the earnings gap between permanent and temporary wage-earners exists only for the years 1988, 1992 and 1995. However, we have data about the earnings gap between full-time and part-time workers, a gap which is currently increasing. If we take this data into account and the fact of the small real earnings growth registered in the late 1990s, we can pose the hypothesis of an increasing inequality in income distribution, not only between capital and labour incomes (because of the high real rates of interest and the better fiscal treatment of capital incomes), but also within the salaried population itself, where temporary and part-time workers would have been disadvantaged.

In this case, a good proxy for the analysis of income distribution in Spain is supplied by the analysis of personal income tax made by the Instituto de Estudios Fiscales.[9] In 1996, of a total of 12 068 827 salaried workers, 31.4 per cent of wage-earners had earnings below the annual minimum wage. The total earnings of this group of wage-earners only amounted to 5.6 per cent of total salary earnings.

When we analyse the redistributive effect of the Welfare State on household income (measured by the income distribution among deciles), we can state that the taxation system (the sum of direct taxes, indirect taxes and social security contributions) has a neutral redistributive effect. Direct taxation has a progressive effect on income redistribution, social security contributions have a neutral, or a slightly regressive, impact, and indirect taxes have a regressive impact. The sum of all these effects is a neutral effect of the taxation system on income redistribution. On the contrary, social expenditures do have a clear redistributive impact, although that impact is not the same for all the areas of expenditure. The cash benefits (public pensions and unemployment benefits) have a higher redistributive effect than the benefits in kind (health, education and housing), with expenditure on education and health having the smaller redistributive impact. The ultimate outcome is that the Welfare State consolidated by the Socialist Party, with regard to revenues and expenditures, does have net redistributive consequences (Calonge and Manresa, 1997).[10]

During its first term the government of the Partido Popular (1996-2000) did not adopt any measures to reduce social expenditures. However, it passed some measures in relation to taxation that may erode in the medium and the long term not only the redistributive capacity of the Welfare State but also the maintenance at current levels of the main items of social expenditure.

In aggregate terms, and focusing our analysis on central government (social security and regional governments excluded), the share of direct taxes has fallen from 46.7 per cent of total revenues (9.4 per cent GDP) in 1996 to 42.9 per cent of total revenues (8.3 per cent of GDP) forecasted for 2000. This fall is concentrated on personal income tax, which has fallen from 36.3 per cent of total revenues to 27.3 per cent (from 7.3 per cent of GDP to 5.3 per cent of GDP). The indirect taxes, mainly VAT, have worked during this period as an offsetting mechanism against the relatively smaller revenues from direct taxes. However, such an offset has been only partial, and from 1996 to 2000 the share of total revenues has fallen from 20 per cent to 19.4 per cent (Garcia and Martín, 1999).[11]

This financing of the Spanish Welfare State, based mainly on the revenues from VAT and social security contributions, faces the problem that the financial sufficiency of the Welfare State depends on the evolution of economic activity, because the sources which contribute (business tax, VAT and social security contributions) are the taxes most linked to the business cycle. Hence, the problem which is posed in the case of a change in the business cycle: if such a change takes place public revenues can fall, leading to adjustments in public expenditure and cuts in social expenditure. We cannot forget that this cut would be unavoidable because of the budget constraints that arise from the Stability and Growth Pact.

This change in the taxation system has clear redistributive effects. As we stated previously, all the redistributive effects from the taxation side were concentrated on personal income tax. Therefore, the regressive nature of indirect taxes and social security contributions, because of their higher share in total revenues during the government of the Partido Popular, may have caused the whole taxation system to become regressive rather than neutral.

Furthermore, the conservative government approved a regressive reform in personal income tax in 1999, as a result of which it is estimated that they did not collect 4.026 billion euros in 1999 and 2000. Of that amount, 20 per cent would have come from 1 per cent of taxpayers. The outcome of the reform has been a fall in the redistributive capacity of personal income tax (García & Martín, 1999). In sum, as a consequence of the above changes, since 1996, during the term of the Partido Popular, the redistributive capacity of the Spanish Welfare State has diminished.

Since the mid-1980s the Welfare State has played the role of an offsetting mechanism against the negative effects generated by labour market reforms on income distribution. Thanks to the social expenditures, low-income households have been able to balance their diminishing earnings from temporary and part-time employment contracts. If the government of the Partido Popular, during their second term, insists on the taxation reforms explained above, the only way to avoid and reduce the current inequality in income distribution is by a new labour market reform. This new labour market reform, promoting permanent employment contracts, should lead to an increase in the earnings of temporary and part-time salaried workers. If this were the case, and the new labour market brought about a less unequal distribution of earnings than the current one, the role of the Welfare State as a mechanism to redistribute the income in a more egalitarian way would be reduced. In this new situation, a small reform in taxation or in social expenditures would be less negative and, perhaps, better accepted by the constituencies and social agents.

CONCLUSIONS

The general strategy of economic policy adopted by the Socialist governments was determined by a mistaken diagnosis of the core objective of the Spanish economic policy (inflation) and by the implementation, first, of tighter monetary and rate of exchange policies, and, secondly, of a set of institutional reforms (focused on the labour market) to solve a structural problem. Actually, Spanish inflation was explained by a lack of domestic and foreign competition in some areas (mainly, within the service sector), which, in addition to a tightened monetary policy, generated high inflation rates.

The excessive flexibility generated by the two labour market reforms approved by the Socialist governments created a set of problems on the demand, supply and distribution sides, which have led to the adoption of offsetting measures. In this sense the problems generated both by wage-earners' uncertainty and consumption and the perverse competitiveness model adopted by most Spanish companies, led the Conservative government to approve the third labour market reform in 1997 with the consensus of trade unions and employers' organisations. The objectives of this reform were to generate certainty in workers (and, consequently, to increase private consumption) and to facilitate the change to a value added competitiveness model.

On the other hand, the current labour market model has involved the necessary consolidation and maintenance of the Welfare State, in line with the commitment of both the past Socialist governments and the first government of the Partido Popular to maintain and secure the current levels of social expenditure in the long term. Nonetheless, we must mention the shadows cast by the fiscal measures passed by the government of the Partido Popular. These measures could lead to a future fall in fiscal revenues, which would endanger the Welfare State model. In this case, the Spanish Welfare State would lose its role as a defence against the undesired consequences of the current labour market model.

NOTES

1. Actually, this objective came with a microeconomic objective: the industrial reconversion of those sectors more seriously affected by the crisis. From 1984 to 1986, the reconversion policy was the key element in the economic policy strategy of the Socialist government not only because of the evident economic importance of the problem but mainly because of the high employment termination that such a policy involved and its social and political consequences.
2. The Socialist government made the decision of joining the European Monetary System (EMS) with a very high exchange rate, using this appreciation as an instrument of the anti-inflationary policy.
3. During the period of strong appreciation of the peseta we can assume that the influence on the inflation process of the imports price was small.
4. The strategy held by the Socialist governments in relation to the manufacturing sector was to delegate to the private initiative the responsibility of its adaptation to the new conditions arising from the entry to the EEC. The industrial policy was identified with the maintenance of an 'institutional and macroeconomic frame competitive enough to benefit all companies' (Espina, 1995, p. 45).
5. For a more detailed analysis of the labour market reforms in Spain, see Recio and Roca (1998) and Ferreiro and Serrano (2001).
6. Among other reasons this increase in public expenditure was explained by the increase in social expenditure (which will be analysed below) and the costs of the manufacturing reconversion (around 12000 billion euros).
7. Nowadays, to be entitled to unemployment benefit, a wage-earner must have paid contributions for at least 360 days (1 year) during the last 6 years, which gives entitlement to receive benefits for four months. The maximum length of such benefits is for those wage-earners who have paid contributions for at least, 720 days (2 years), being entitled to receive unemployment benefits for 2160 days (6 years) if they have worked at least 18 years.
8. The reform in the unemployment insurance was linked to the assumption that generous unemployment benefits discourage job searching and, therefore, promote the maintenance of high rates of unemployment.
9. Information taken from their web page: www.ief.es/master/htm.
10. This analysis is made using data on 1991.
11. When social security is included, the share of direct taxes (social security contributions included) in relation to GDP falls from 9.4 per cent to 8.2 per cent, social security contributions increase from 11.7 per cent to 12 per cent, and indirect taxes increase from 7.7 per cent to 8.7 per cent. In sum, fiscal pressure falls from 33.5% in 1996 to 32.4% in 2000 (García and Martín, 1999).

REFERENCES

Calonge, S. and Manresa, A. (1997), 'Consecuencias redistributivas del Estado del Bienestar en España: un análisis empírico desagregado', *Moneda y Crédito*, 204, 13-65.

Espina, A. (1995), *Hacia una estrategia española de competitividad*, Madrid: Fundación Argentaria.

Ferreiro, J. and Serrano, F. (2001), 'The Spanish labour market: reforms and consequences', *International Review of Applied Economics*, **15**(1), January, 31-53.

García, M.A. and Martín, C. (1999), *Situación de la economía española y Presupuestos del Estado 2000*, Madrid: Confederación Sindical de CC.OO.

Instituto Nacional de Estadística (1992), *Distribución Salarial en España*, Madrid: Instituto Nacional de Estadística.

Instituto Nacional de Estadística (1995), *Encuesta Sobre la Distribución Salarial en España 1992*, Madrid: Instituto Nacional de Estadística.

Instituto Nacional de Estadística (1997), *Encuesta de estructura salarial 1995*, Madrid: Instituto Nacional de Estadística.

Recio, A. and Roca, J. (1998), 'The Spanish Socialists in power: thirteen years of economic policy', *Oxford Review of Economic Policy*, **14**(1), 139-58.

Solchaga, C. (1997), *El Final de la Edad Dorada*, Madrid: Taurus.

11. The Greek experiment with the Third Way

Thanos Skouras*

11.1 INTRODUCTION AND HISTORICAL BACKGROUND

The aim of this chapter is to provide an assessment of PASOK's (Panhellenic Socialist Movement) economic policy to date and to comment on the relationship of this policy to Keynesianism and the economics of the Third Way.

PASOK was created in 1974 and first came to power in 1981. Since then it has been in power continuously, with a break of only three years between 1989 and 1993. It has won five electoral contests in 1981, 1985, 1993, 1996 and, most recently, April 2000.

Three phases may be distinguished in PASOK's long period in office. These phases relate to PASOK's stance *vis à vis* the European Union. Though PASOK's relationship to Europe has been of importance to most of its policies, it has had a particularly strong connection with its economic policy. Thus, it may be argued that the clearest way of examining the broad contours and orientation of PASOK's economic policy is through its position with respect to Europe.

The three phases characterising PASOK's relationship with Europe may be designated as those of contrariety, rapprochement and embracement. The phase of contrariety began before PASOK's first electoral victory in 1981 and was, in fact, instrumental in its success at the polls. A brief historical detour may be in order here.

PASOK was established in 1974 after the fall of the military dictatorship (1967–74). The same year it captured 13.6 per cent of the electoral vote. This was raised to 25 per cent in 1977 and to an astounding 48 per cent in 1981. Thus, within seven years, the new socialist party created and led by Andreas Papandreou managed to win the elections gaining 57 per cent of the seats in Parliament.

1981 was a milestone year not only because it marked the coming to power of the first ever socialist government but also because it was the year of

Greece's accession to the European Economic Community as a full member. PASOK gained the elections by banking on the apprehensiveness of a large part of the Greek society regarding future economic prospects within the EEC. This fear of Europe may have been justifiable in the case of the middle and lower-middle classes, in a country which had the largest proportion of self-employed among OECD countries and an industrial structure characterised by a very large number of small, mostly family-owned, firms, but it was patently not justifiable for the farmers, who constituted about one quarter of the electorate and stood to gain from the minimum guaranteed prices of the EEC's agricultural policy. Papandreou's success was that he managed to swing in PASOK's favour a large part of the traditionally right-wing agricultural vote, by playing on the farmers' innate conservatism and fear of the unfamiliar and the unknown.

Apart from opposition to the country's membership of the EEC, the other main plank in PASOK's electoral campaign was its opposition to NATO. This satisfied not only the traditional left but successfully exploited the widespread resentment and anti-western feeling caused by NATO's lack of resistance, if not acquiescence, to the continuing Turkish occupation of the northern part of Cyprus.

PASOK thus came to power on the basis of the twin pledge to get Greece out of both Europe and NATO. Moreover, its decisive electoral victory was obtained by votes coming from very different sections of the Greek society and which, in their clear majority, had never before been cast to the left. This then was the background to the first term of PASOK's office and to the formation of its initial economic policy.

11.2   THE PHASE OF CONTRARIETY

The opposition to Europe and the West was present from the beginning of PASOK and is clearly evident in the founding manifesto of 1974. The so-called Third of September Declaration disclaims Western European social democracy and supports a third way to socialism, different from both traditional social democracy and Soviet communism. PASOK's Third Way is inspired by the neo-Marxist Dependency theories of the 1960s and uses the centre–periphery schema as the main theoretical tool in order to explain international relations, as well as the nature and historical development of Greek society.[1]

The implications of this ideological stance on the economic and foreign policies advocated by PASOK were quite marked. As regards foreign policy, the USA, NATO and neo-colonialism were the main enemies, while the EEC was seen as being fully in the service of NATO and the Americans. Liberation movements and anti-American regimes, such as Arafat's PLO and Gaddafy's Libyan regime, were by contrast friends and allies. In relation to economic policy, PASOK's preference was for socialisation of the economy, which meant not only extending the state's control and involvement in economic activity, especially in respect of the economy's 'commanding heights', but also introducing throughout the economy new forms of firm governance that would ensure social control over both the public and private sectors.

PASOK's coming to power in 1981 led to policies that were broadly in tune with these ideological positions, though it refrained from taking the most radical steps to leave NATO and the EEC. Nevertheless, the relations of Greece with both these organisations went through a period of great strain that lasted throughout PASOK's first term in office.

As regards economic policy, PASOK's options in 1981 were circumscribed by its ideology and its electoral pledges. It certainly could not rely on the private sector's support, given its hostility to capitalism and the disquiet, if not fear, that its victory caused to domestic capital. PASOK did nothing to alleviate this fear and it was, therefore, quite predictable that private investment would collapse (see Table 11.1). PASOK's economic policy was marked by a series of attempts to keep up aggregate demand and jump-start the economy. This was done by boosting private and then public consumption while effectively ignoring investment (see Table 11.2).

Thus, it may be argued that PASOK subscribed in practice to a naïve Keynesianism, which was neither admitted nor properly understood and was, of course, bound to fail. PASOK's ideology did not allow it to acknowledge and take seriously the Keynesian aspects of its policy, largely because Keynesianism was seen as an antithetical western bourgeois ideology.

Table 11.1   Private sector gross fixed capital formation (billion drachmae, 1970 prices)

1980	70.5
1981	63.6
1982	60.3
1983	56.0
1984	48.6
1985	49.7
1986	50.5
1987	52.4
1988	58.3
1989	64.0

Source: OECD (1990, Statistical Annex, Table D), (1993, Statistical Annex, Table B).

Table 11.2   Government consumption and investment (billion drachmae, 1970 prices)

Year	Government consumption	Government gross investment
1980	68.9	22.2
1981	73.6	22.3
1982	75.3	23.8
1983	77.4	27.0
1984	79.8	29.7
1985	82.3	32.7
1986	81.6	26.7
1987	82.3	20.9
1988	87.1	21.5
1989	89.5	23.8

Source: OECD (1990, Statistical Annex, Tables B and D), 1993 (Statistical Appendix, Tables A and B).

PASOK emphasised instead the institutional reforms aiming at the socialisation of the economy and treated the issue of effectively expanding aggregate demand, while retaining macroeconomic stability, as a totally unproblematic and elementary exercise requiring no intellectual effort and elaboration.

The first attempt to boost the economy also fulfilled an electoral promise and came a few months after victory at the polls. Minimum wages were increased by 40 per cent, while the average wage was allowed to rise by 26 per cent from 1981 to 1982. Consumption rose rapidly but production did not follow suit and gross domestic product remained stagnant in 1982 as in 1981. At the same time, the trade deficit doubled from 1980 and inflation persisted at over 20 per cent p.a. These developments led to a devaluation of the drachma by 10 per cent in January 1983 and a first half-hearted attempt at a stabilisation programme. The stabilisation programme was effectively abandoned before the end of the year as GDP continued to stagnate and the unemployment rate doubled from that of 1981 to 7.9 per cent of the labour force – a rate that was by far the highest of the past quarter century.

From then onwards, until the elections of 1985, expansion of public expenditure was the main way in which PASOK attempted to boost the economy. The general government deficit, which stood at a high 6.5 per cent of GDP in 1982 nearly doubled to reach 11.5 per cent in 1985.

The state of the economy following the 1985 elections was not encouraging. Public expenditure stood at 43 per cent of GDP from 31 per cent in 1980, foreign debt at 24 per cent of GDP from 7 per cent five years before, while inflation continued to be around 20 per cent and private investment bottomed out at 11 per cent, the lowest level it had ever reached in the postwar period (see Christodoulakis, 1998).

Macroeconomic mismanagement through a crude application of Keynesian tools was not, of course, the only or even the main aspect of PASOK's economic policy. The socialisation of the economy was undoubtedly the central policy objective and the methods used in order to attain this aim were the main distinctive traits that characterised PASOK's third way to socialism.

The socialisation policy was meant to apply to both the public and private sectors. As regards the nationalised industries, and especially telecommunications, electricity and transport, Representative Councils of Social Control were to be formed, consisting of 25 representatives from the state, employees, local government, consumer interests and other stakeholders (Decree 1365/83). These were responsible for planning the development of nationalised enterprises and providing greater transparency and accountability to stakeholders, thus enhancing social participation and control.

Similar bodies were to be set up in the private sector in order to act as 'decentralised organs of social control'. These supervisory councils were to be made up of representatives of management, workers, local authorities and the state. Their main function was to supervise and advise in a way that would make the national plan more effective, as well as extend social participation and control. Moreover, they were meant to provide the necessary feedback for a more rational policy of state aid and investment incentives to industry.

In addition to these major reforms, there was an industrial policy of sectoral planning and a policy for public procurements. There was also provision for planning agreements between the state and private enterprises. Last but not least, a state holding company was created to take control of and help restructure a large number of 'ailing' private firms. These were mostly bankrupt firms that their owners did not wish to operate any longer. The Organization for Enterprise Restructuring kept them afloat at a huge cost to the state budget, in order to contain the growth in unemployment.

Except for this last initiative, which was kept going for over fifteen years and was abolished only recently (May 2000), the other Third Way policies did not survive beyond the phase of contrariety and tended to fade thereafter. This was after all the reason that this phase, which largely coincided with PASOK's first term, was treated at greater length.

In concluding this discussion, it should be noted that the Third Way policies were on the whole not seriously implemented, despite their being voted on by Parliament and becoming law. In assessment, they were certainly not better than the mismanaged macroeconomic policies of that period. If there is a question-mark about their appropriateness as responses to real problems, as well as the appropriateness of their operational design, there is no doubt that the management of their implementation was dismal. The reason may be, as has been argued by Lyberaki and Tsakalotos (2000), that 'the Greek social formation was particularly infertile ground' lacking the required 'social capital to enter into the type of long-term trust relations and cooperation entailed by the new legislation'. Or, more plainly, the policies were not appropriate to the character of the Greek society, at least as it was in the early 1980s. In any case, whatever the fundamental reason for their failure, it seems unlikely that they could have been implemented successfully in an environment of increasing macroeconomic instability. Satisfactory macroeconomic management may not be a sufficient condition for the success of such policies but, it may be argued, it is most likely a necessary condition. Thus, PASOK's macroeconomic mismanagement would have doomed the Third Way policies to failure even if deeper causes did not exist and more fundamental requirements were fulfilled.

11.3   THE PHASE OF RAPPROCHEMENT

We have seen that the main macroeconomic magnitudes were in an unsatisfactory state after the 1985 elections. Management of the economy was transferred to C. Simitis, who proceeded to devalue the drachma by 15 per cent as part of a stabilisation programme. The programme relied on monetary and fiscal restraint, as well as an incomes policy, and succeeded in reducing considerably the balance of payments deficit by improving competitiveness and boosting exports (+7 per cent). The inflation rate was also significantly reduced and the basis was laid for a revival of private investment and the achievement of the highest rate of GDP growth in a whole decade (4.5 per cent in 1988).

The rapprochement with the EEC was effected during this period. The extra funds of the Integrated Mediterranean Programme, which was a form of compensation paid to Mediterranean countries for the entry of Spain and Portugal, was claimed by PASOK as a great negotiation success. Though this softened PASOK's attitude *vis à vis* the European Community, the more significant turnabout was Papandreou's decision to back Delors in the latter's fight for a larger Community budget and a substantial increase in the Structural Funds as a complement to the Single Market policy. Thus, from the middle of 1987, Greece abandoned its self-imposed isolation in Community politics and adopted a pro-Delors stance and increasingly a vision of a socialist federal Europe.

The stabilisation programme was stopped prematurely at the end of 1987, with Simitis resigning, as Papandreou traded continued economic improvement for an increase in his margin of manoeuvre regarding an early call for elections. This did not happen because Papandreou became seriously ill and the corruption scandals that erupted during his recovery prevented the call of an early election.

The next two years preceding the elections of 1989, were once more years of economic mismanagement. Monetary and especially fiscal policy were eased, with the general government deficit reaching 14.4 per cent of GDP in 1989. The international competitiveness of Greek exports declined substantially as the exchange rate policy was geared to the containment of inflation. With the government's eyes fixed on the coming elections, the worsening macroeconomic imbalances were ignored and the government budget was used as an electoral weapon for securing votes. Despite these efforts, and largely because of the corruption scandals which had enveloped the prime minister and his closest government aides, PASOK failed to win the elections of 1989.

The elections did not produce a clear winner and there was an unstable coalition government between the right-wing party and the communists, which proceeded within the year to new elections and a new stalemate. Finally, the right-wing New Democracy party won the elections of April 1990 and formed a government which lasted until September 1993, when it was toppled by a defection from its own ranks over the proposed privatisation of the state telecommunication company.

At this point in time, PASOK's experiment with the Third Way was practically finished and from then on it was no longer evident in PASOK's political speech. We have already seen that it was doomed to failure, given the poor economic management and the macroeconomic instability that ensued. It has also been argued that PASOK's ideological blinkers regarding Keynesianism in its crucial first term in office were largely responsible for the wrong strategy, if not the weak implementation, in the conduct of economic policy. An interesting question is whether the outcome might have been different if the strategy were based on a more adequate understanding of Keynesianism. This kind of counterfactual question is, of course, impossible to answer in a decisive manner but even a tentative exploration of the possibilities may be instructive.

In my view, PASOK was mistaken in ignoring investment. The idea that it could jump-start the economy by boosting private or public consumption while effectively ignoring investment constituted its biggest strategic mistake (see Skouras, 1992). Even if it were faced by an investment 'strike' from the private sector, PASOK should not have given up on investment. It should have softened its hostility in relation to the private sector and, above all, it should have embarked on a vigorous programme of public investment.[2] It is a big puzzle why public investment was neglected for so long. There seems to be a concatenation of possible causes. First, PASOK disliked big private capital, and especially contracting firms, which stood to gain most directly from public investment; second, party clientelism was best promoted by public consumption rather than investment, through the personal obligations resulting from expansion in state employment; and, third, it might be that in PASOK's naïve Keynesianism there was no significant difference between the effects of boosting investment or consumption.

In any case, the neglect of both private and public investment deprived the economy of essential infrastructures, weakened its productive potential, fuelled inflationary tendencies and worsened its performance. Had this mistake been avoided, it is not impossible that the Third Way experiment might have fared better. In the final analysis, it is nevertheless improbable that it could have counteracted and overcome the effects of the voluntarist and amateurish management that seemed to be typical of PASOK's handling of the economy. The adoption of this misguided strategy was, after all, one of the many negative effects of such management.

11.4   THE PHASE OF EMBRACEMENT

Having undergone a court trial and acquittal, not to mention a serious heart operation and his wedding to an air hostess younger than his children, Papandreou managed to win the 1993 elections and become prime minister for the third time. He was incapacitated by illness two years later and died in June 1996. Since the beginning of 1996, C. Simitis has been prime minister initially by replacing Papandreou and then by proceeding to win two elections; an early one called in September 1996 and the most recent one in April 2000.

PASOK's economic policy during this phase has been clearly orientated towards the European Union. The overarching aim has been to satisfy the Maastricht criteria and join the Economic and Monetary Union (EMU). The alignment with Europe has become stronger as Simitis' control over the party became firmer and more secure over time. But even in the first two years under Papandreou, PASOK's shift to an economic policy more in accord with Brussels' views was quite noticeable. This was evident in the close collaboration between Greece and the European Commission, in relation to the drafting of the two most important economic policy documents: the Convergence Programme and the Community Support Framework (1994–99).

The Convergence Programme sets out and signposts the trajectory that the Greek economy needs to follow, in order to qualify for participation in EMU. This plan, with its large number of intermediate targets in terms of macroeconomic magnitudes, in effect determines fully the macroeconomic policy to be followed for a number of years ahead. Similarly, the Community Support Framework, which contains the plan for the utilisation of the substantial contribution by the Structural Funds, presents the developmental choices and the investment programme for six years, from 1994 until the end of 1999.

The two programmes contain the main decisions regarding macroeconomic stability and economic development and between them set the essential features and determine the character of economic policy. Thus, they have completely replaced the national development plan, which was supposed to be the cornerstone of PASOK's economic policy in the 1980s. But what is of even greater significance is that both these new plans were designed in close collaboration and agreed with the European Commission. The Community Support Framework, in particular, went through a long period of negotiation starting effectively in October 1993 before it was agreed and signed by both sides in June 1994. It is clear that this is an immense distance from the ideologically-inspired economic policy of PASOK's early years.

Given its pro-European direction and convergence targets, how successful was the conduct of economic policy in this phase? Despite some initial delay in getting its act together, PASOK significantly improved its performance in managing the economy during this phase. This is particularly the case in the second half of the period, under Simitis' premiership. Let us briefly look at some figures.

The budget deficit was reduced from 13.6 per cent of GDP in 1993 to 1.8 per cent in 1999 while government debt was reduced from 110.1 per cent of GDP in 1993 to 104.6 per cent in 1999 (see Table 11.3). During the same

Table 11.3   Various macroeconomic indicators

Year	GDP growth rate	Consumer price index	General Government Deficit (% GDP)	General Government Debt (% GDP)	Unemployment rate
1990	0.0	20.4	−15.9	—	6.0
1991	3.1	19.4	−11.3	—	6.7
1992	0.7	15.9	−12.6	87.8	7.8
1993	−1.6	14.4	−13.6	110.1	8.8
1994	2.0	10.9	−9.9	107.9	8.7
1995	2.1	8.9	−10.6	108.7	9.1
1996	2.4	8.2	−7.4	111.3	9.8
1997	3.5	5.5	−4.0	108.5	9.7
1998	3.1	4.8	−2.5	105.5	11.2
1999	3.4	2.6	−1.8	104.6	12.0

Source: Directorate of Macroeconomic Analysis, General Directorate of Economic Policy, Ministry of National Economy: Basic Macroeconomic Aggregates and Indices.

period the inflation rate fell by about 12 percentage points from 14.4 per cent in 1993 to 2.6 per cent in 1999. Interest rates also fell considerably and the yield on 10-year government bonds was just 111 basis points higher than that of the comparable German bonds at the end of January 2000. As a result of this performance in achieving macroeconomic stability and convergence towards the Maastricht targets, it is widely expected that Greece's formal application to join the EMU will be approved by the Lisbon Summit in June 2000, with effect from 1 January, 2001.

Macroeconomic stability was not achieved at the cost of a stagnant economy. On the contrary, GDP growth rates during this period were, for the first time since 1980, above the European average being close to 3 per cent on average for the six years between 1994 and 1999 while rising clearly over 3 per cent since 1997. As a result, nominal convergence was accompanied by real convergence and Greek GDP per head began to move nearer to the European average, reversing the trend of the 1980s and early 1990s.

Other developments include a steady increase in profitability, mainly as a result of the fall in interest rates but also of restructuring, and a significant revival of private investment. On the other hand, the budget deficit reduction and the attendant restrictive monetary policy have contributed to an increase in unemployment which, for the first time, exceeded the 10 per cent mark reaching 11.2 per cent in 1998 and 12 per cent in 1999 (see Table 11.3).

Also, in the last two years, the pace of privatisation has picked up. The privatisation process has been centralised with a transfer of the administrative responsibility to the Ministry of the National Economy, which has drawn up a schedule of rapid privatisation of several state-controlled banks and public corporations. In all, 27 public entities have already been or are due to be privatised in the period from April 1998 to February 2001 (see Stournaras, 1999).

Finally, again during the last two years, steps were taken to effect some structural reforms relating to the flexibility of the labour market. This was only a start and it is clear that the new PASOK government, which emerged in the recent elections, has every intention to pursue further the deregulation of the labour market. This area, together with that of the social insurance system which is in urgent need of reform, seem to present the greatest difficulty and danger for the government at present. PASOK has refrained from tackling the reform of the social insurance system so far but it is now beyond question that such a reform cannot be delayed any longer. This and the deregulation of the labour market are certain to bring PASOK into a serious confrontation with the trade unions, as well as with a large part of its traditional supporters.

11.5   THE RECENT ELECTIONS AND THE RETURN OF THE THIRD WAY

The election results in April 2000 indicate that the Greek voters appreciated PASOK's performance in economic management. PASOK fought the elections on the strength of its success on the economic front stressing its managerial abilities and experience. To the New Democracy's charges that it had paid no attention to the citizens' everyday life, disregarding their demands and needs and neglecting social services, PASOK's response was that the economy needed to be put on the right footing first and that it was, as a result of a stronger economy, in a better position to face effectively problems on the social front, as it in fact intended to do in the coming term. Thus, PASOK promised to give priority to the health and education sectors, reform the pensions system, protect the old-age pensioners and the small farmers and fight unemployment. With respect to the latter, apart from special care for the weak and disadvantaged, there was a concrete promise to create 300 000 new jobs in the coming years, amounting to about 7 per cent of the existing labour force. There is also to be a reform of the civil service and an elimination of bureaucracy and corruption.

Needless to say, PASOK also promised to continue the good management and further strengthening of the economy within the EMU. It also emphasised the fact that it had established trust and close working relations with the relevant European officials and was, therefore, best placed to negotiate and resolve outstanding issues relating to EMU membership. Finally, PASOK's experience and good management and planning credentials were a guarantee for the adequate preparation and proper organisation of the Olympic Games, to be held in Athens in 2004.

In sum, PASOK fought and won the recent election not so much on the ideological plane, where New Democracy sounded at times definitely more populist if not further to the left, but more on the grounds of managerial reliability and effectiveness. There was little public debate of grand models and no reference to PASOK's old Third Way.

A rare reference to the Third Way was made in the press, in connection with Papantoniou's meeting with Gordon Brown in London, on the 21 February 2000. Papantoniou, the main economics minister, agreed with Brown's deregulation programme and accepted the need for greater flexibility in the labour market but balked at adopting the American development model for Greek use. 'Greece must combine deregulation policies with policies of redistribution', he is reported to have stated (see Karakousis, 2000a). National differences need to be taken into account in deregulating markets and the social cohesion policies of the European model should be combined with the positive components of the American one in a new synthesis. This position was dubbed 'Papantoniou's third way' by a financial journalist who tried to stir up, without success, public discussion of the economic model to be adopted for the next 10 to 20 years (see Karakousis, 2000b). No party took up this challenge and in particular the two large parties showed little ideological differentiation, both of them addressing the crucial, and quite sizeable until the end, group of 'undecided' voters in the centre of the political spectrum.

Nevertheless, it is true that not only PASOK's present policy but even the whole phase of embracement have more in common with what is generally understood as the Third Way than PASOK's first phase of contrariety, during which the term Third Way was coined and gained currency in Greece.[3] The Third Way, as commonly understood outside Greece, is related to the response of western social democracy to the challenges of the globalisation era after the demise of the Soviet empire.

The economic policies that have been espoused by centre/centre-left governments in the western world during the 1990s, underscore the importance of privatisation and the reduction of the public sector in the economy and lay stress on the deregulation of markets and, particularly, the removal of labour market rigidities. These are the general economic policies associated with the Third Way and these are exactly the policies followed by PASOK recently and are intended to be pursued more vigorously in its present term of office. Consequently, it may be argued that PASOK's experiment with the Third Way (or, at least, with the general economic policy stance that is related to the Third Way) is taking place currently. It is only the anachronism of the term, given its past usage in Greek politics, that probably prevents immediate recognition of this fact.

Is this new western Third Way more likely to be successful than the old PASOK Third Way? It is still too early to tell. It has already been noted that a critical test is bound to come with the attempt at deregulation of the labour market and the reform of the pensions system. No doubt there will be other policy measures and even chance events that will lead to crises. Whether the government will persist in this direction, risk alienating its traditional supporters and survive the inevitable crises is, of course, an open question. But there do not seem to be other viable options on the horizon; the government has to tread the path of the western Third Way as regards the general economic policy stance. It can only attempt to vary the particular policy priorities, taking into account the given political conjuncture, and strive to apply the policies effectively by possibly adapting them to local conditions. This is no easy task and demands not only a concerted effort but also, and more importantly, it requires that PASOK reinvents itself and becomes fully transformed into a European-style social democratic party.

In conclusion, it would seem that the Greek experiment with the Third Way is hardly over, even though the original PASOK version of the beast is certainly dead and buried. Greek politics has taken a clear turn to the middle ground and the emphasis has shifted from a confrontation of political ideologies to a contest of reliability and effectiveness in the provision of public services. This, of course, does not mean that ideology and models, even of the grand type, have no more a future in Greek politics. But it is very unlikely any more that such debates will be carried out separately from the rest of Europe. If a Third Way to socialism successfully emerges in the future, it will be a European one rather than a local variety. Like the Greek economy, Greek socialism also seems destined to become fully betrothed to Europe.

NOTES

*   I would like to thank P. Arestis and M. Rustin for useful comments. Special thanks are due to Daphne Nikolitsa for her help in providing me with the most recent, revised statistics from the Ministry of National Economy.
1.   See Tsakalotos (1998), also Spourdalakis (1988). The Tsakalotos paper covers well PASOK's economic policy until 1996 and is particularly instructive on the phase of contrariety.
2.   For a proposal of such an investment programme, see Skouras (1983).
3.   This point, with which I fully agree, was made by Mike Rustin at the conference and I thank him for it.

REFERENCES

Christodoulakis, Nicos (1998), *The New Landscape of Development* (in Greek), Athens: Kastaniotis Publishing.
Karakousis, Antonis (2000a), 'Papantoniou's 3rd Way', *Kathimerini - International Herald Tribune*, February 22.
Karakousis, Antonis (2000b), 'What Economic Model?', *Kathimerini - International Herald Tribune*, February 26–27.
Lyberaki, Antigone and Tsakalotos, Euclid (2000), 'Reforming the Economy without Society: Social and Institutional Constraints to Economic Reform in post-1974 Greece', unpublished paper.
Ministry of National Economy (2000), *Basic Macroeconomic Aggregates and Indices* (in Greek), Athens: Ypetho.
OECD (1990), *Economic Surveys - Greece 1989-90*, Paris: OECD.
OECD (1993), *Economic Surveys - Greece 1993*, Paris: OECD.
Skouras, Thanos (1983), 'Recovery and restructuring: an investment policy proposal' (in Greek), *Bulletin of the Commercial Bank of Greece*, December.
Skouras, Thanos (1992), 'Introduction', in T. Skouras (ed.), *The Greek Economy: Economic Policies for the 1990s*, London: Macmillan.
Spourdalakis, Michael (1988), *The Rise of the Greek Socialist Party*, London: Routledge.
Stournaras, Yannis (1999), 'The Converging Greek Economy: Developments, Policies and Prospects', Ministry of National Economy, www.ypetho.gr.
Tsakalotos, Euclid (1998), 'The political economy of social democratic economic policies: the PASOK experiment in Greece', *Oxford Review of Economic Policy*, **14**(1).

12. South Africa: a Third Way in the Third World?

Jonathan Michie and Vishnu Padayachee

12.1 INTRODUCTION

The late 1990s appeared to mark a shift in global politics and economic policy 'away from the free-market frenzy that ruled the world roost for some two decades after the mid 1970s' (Westergaard, 1999, p. 429). Left-of-centre and social democratic governments are in office in many parts of the world, including virtually the whole of Western Europe. In Britain, the 'New' Labour Government claim to be adopting a new economic approach, one distinctively different to the orthodox, neo-liberalism of the 1970s and 1980s, but also one that does not carry the socialist or corporatist burdens of 'old labour'. That view is echoed in other parts of Western Europe, albeit with modifications and variants in the detail. 'On the threshold of the third millennium, we are told, the future lies with a new Third Way' (Westergaard, 1999, p. 429).

To what extent are these approaches new? Are they similar enough in content to characterise as a single new approach or are the differences among them too great? And how relevant are these ideas and frameworks for developing and transitional economies, such as South Africa, faced as many are by the challenges of addressing significant levels of poverty and inequality, re-integrating into the global economy, and creating and consolidating sometimes fragile democracies?

Since 1955 when the Freedom Charter became the touchstone of its ideology, combining a 'wide-angled allure of the French Revolution's Declaration of the Rights of Man with radical affirmations' (Marais, 1999, p. 66), the main anti-apartheid movement, the African National Congress (ANC), together with its alliance partners the South African Communist Party (SACP), the South African Congress of Trade Unions (SACTU), and later the Congress of South African Trade Unions (COSATU), occupied a broad political space on the left and centre-left of South African politics, encompassing black nationalist ideals as well as orthodox Marxist perspectives. Nationalisation of the mineral wealth and banks, among other institutions, stood at the very core of its economic policy for over three decades. So too did a variety of other broadly defined redistributive and poverty alleviation strategies.

For a number of reasons the ANC, since it assumed a dominant role in the first democratic government elected in 1994, has, in contrast to its earlier economic views, traversed a fairly orthodox, neo-liberal, macroeconomic policy path, closely approximating the old Washington Consensus. The reasons for this include the ANC's own previous inattention to economic policy issues, its particular understanding of the balance of global and local power in the political and economic arenas, and the nature of the political settlement reached in the run-up to the first democratic election (see Michie and Padayachee, 1997, 1998; Habib and Padayachee, 2000).

Following Tony Blair's official visit to South Africa in 1999, and especially around the time of the March 2000 budget, there have been attempts, from both within and outside government, to cast the ANC's economic strategy as a Third Way model. This chapter examines the central features of the South African government's economic policy stance since 1994, and then considers it in relation to this European debate on the Third Way.

12.2   THE APARTHEID LEGACY

The problems confronting the heavily mineral-based South African economy on the eve of democratic elections in April 1994 were undoubtedly immense. Economic growth had slowed markedly since the early 1970s. Both gross domestic investment and savings declined sharply throughout the 1980s. Labour absorption into the formal economy had plummeted from over 60 per cent in the mid-1970s to under 40 per cent in 1994 (Michie and Padayachee, 1997, pp. 12–17). South Africa has been described by the World Bank as among the world's most unequal economies, with a Gini coefficient measuring 0.58. Estimates based on South African census data, which Marais quotes, puts the Gini coefficient as high as 0.68, worse than that of the Bahamas, Brazil or Jamaica and 33 other developing countries (Marais, 1998, p. 106). However, some potentially positive features upon which to rebuild were evident, with relatively low levels of domestic and foreign debt, and an inflation rate at just 8 per cent at the time of the 1994 election (see Michie and Padayachee, 1997, for further detail and discussion). In addition, the country was unique among most developing economies in that it had a sophisticated and well-developed financial and banking sector (MERG, 1993, p. 244). However, the financial system had become increasingly tied to the major conglomerates in mining and industry and had not historically been geared to serve the needs of the disadvantaged consumer or business communities, a situation that has continued in the post-apartheid era.

12.3 THE ECONOMIC POLICY DEBATE IN SOUTH AFRICA

The economic thinking of the apartheid government shifted since the late 1970s, from an inward-looking and interventionist strategy to one which became increasingly free market-oriented in character. The de Kock Commission on monetary policy (1978), the Kleu Commission on Industrial Strategy (1983), and the Reynders Commission on Export Trade (1972)[1] all raised doubts about an inward-looking strategy of development and espoused the virtues of a 'system in which freedom of enterprise, consumer freedom of choice and private ownership play a fundamental part' (Morris and Padayachee, 1988, pp. 5–6). The 1993 Normative Economic Model (NEM) of the Nationalist government represented the most advanced form of this strategy (CEAS, 1993).

ANC economic thinking also changed following the unbanning of the organisation in February 1990. The draft economic policy circulated for debate after the Harare conference in April 1990 made it clear that nationalisation remained an important plank of ANC policy. The role of the state in economic reconstruction was boldly asserted; the document had a decidedly inward-looking orientation based primarily on the needs and capacities of the domestic economy, with little reference to the dramatic economic developments which were unfolding globally at the time.

By the time the ANC's *Ready to Govern* policy document was released in 1992 some aspects of ANC economic policy had changed, with a relatively more market-oriented approach being espoused. Nevertheless that document did represent a genuine attempt to formulate a strategy that balanced growth, redistribution and basic needs, with a growing imperative to become market-friendly and globally competitive.

Two important inputs into the ANC's Reconstruction and Development Programme (RDP) (its 1994 election manifesto) were the research findings of the Macroeconomic Research Group (MERG) and the Industrial Strategy Project (ISP). Both were linked, albeit in different ways, to the ANC and COSATU. Both the MERG document and the ISP proposals represented attempts, albeit with significant differences, to chart frameworks that lay between old style ANC economic thinking and the dominant neo-liberal ideas of the Washington Consensus. In this loose sense they may be regarded as Third Way models, although MERG placed its emphasis mainly on the demand-side, rather than the kind of supply-side measures the ISP favoured, more frequently associated with a Third Way approach.

MERG took what might be characterised as a Post-Keynesian approach where effective demand failures and the possibility of under-full employment equilibrium are recognised as key problems. MERG envisioned a two-phase, 'crowding-in' approach to South Africa's development, a state-led social and physical infrastructural investment programme as the growth driver in the first phase, followed by a sustainable growth phase which would see private sector investment kick in as growth picked up (MERG, 1993; Padayachee, 1998). The MERG report emphasised the meeting of basic needs and the development of social and economic infrastructure designed to secure 'a rapid improvement in the quality of life of the poorest, most oppressed and disadvantaged people of South Africa' (1993, p. 2).

The ISP work was located within a framework identifiable with the literature on global competitiveness and restructuring, most closely associated with the IDS at Sussex University. The ISP concentrated on the need to revive productivity growth in the context of the likely opening-up of the South African economy and changing patterns of comparative advantage in global industry (Joffe et al. 1995, pp. 22–3). They argued that these goals are best achieved by gearing production towards higher value activities (into the downstream processing of South Africa's natural resources, and into niches of high value within certain sectors).

The ANC's *Reconstruction and Development Programme* (RDP) was published in March 1994. At one level it could be argued that the RDP broke with the view that growth and development are processes that contradict one another. Its powerful statement of principles sets out a development strategy which:

> integrates growth, development, reconstruction and redistribution into a unified programme. The key to this link is an infrastructural programme that will provide access to modern and effective services ... This programme will both meet basic needs and open up previously suppressed economic and human potential in urban and rural areas. In turn this will lead to an increased output in all sectors of the economy, and by modernising our infrastructure and human resource development we will also enhance export capacity. (1994, p. 6)

But in the detail it proposed sometimes contradictory ideas. For what it did was attempt to marry the ANC's old social democratic and socialist values (redistribution, basic needs) with new neo-liberal ones (trade and financial liberalisation, the independence of the central bank), ostensibly held together through (centrist) institutions and accords at which all the 'social partners' would be represented. As Bond and others have noted, it was, in the course of its formulation, impacted upon by 'status quo' forces, both South African and international, who had made great efforts since 1990 at influencing the political leadership of the ANC. In the end the RDP reflected an uneasy compromise between 'the feasibility of combining a social welfare state in the developmental sphere with neo-liberalism in the economic sphere' (Bond, 2000, p. 54).

In power, the ANC rapidly brought the dissident constituencies of COSATU, the SACP, and left ANC factions into line and consolidated its economic ideas around an essentially neo-liberal programme. This was first evident in the November RDP White Paper, which Adelzadeh and Padayachee (1994) described at the time as representing 'a very significant compromise to the neo-liberal, "trickle-down" economic policy preferences of the old regime', despite assurances from ANC Ministers that only the language of the old RDP had been changed to suit the new demands of governance (1994, p. 2).

Orthodox economic ideas were given full, unqualified reign, in the Growth, Employment and Redistribution Strategy (GEAR) published in the wake of a currency crisis in June 1996, and following major policy statements from both the labour movement and organised (white) business in late 1995 and early 1996.[2] Central to GEAR, as even senior state bureaucrats now admit, was an orthodox macroeconomic policy. Thus, for example, the DTI's Alan Hirsch, a key figure in the making of economic policy since the late 1980s, has argued that faced with new global realities, the ANC took the view that it had to 'play the globalisation game, but try to play it our way ... So we adopted a fairly orthodox set of policies', especially in respect of monetary, fiscal and trade policy (Hirsch, nd, pp. 1–2). A key feature of 'our way' (according to Hirsch) were a 'slew of supply-side measures' (nd, pp. 1–2), in respect of trade, industrial policy and support for new investment, innovation, small business, and black economic empowerment.

The underlying premise of GEAR, which aimed to attain a growth rate of 6 per cent per annum and job creation of 400 000 by the year 2000, is that growth would best be promoted by freeing the private sector from the fetters of the distorted racist logic and constraints of the apartheid era. The essential need to remove all vestiges of a state-imposed, racially-based economic order has been extended to argue for a much more sweeping 'rolling back of the state'. These include the abandonment of arguably important policies such as a discrete and effective public investment programme, tariff protection for vulnerable industries, essential reform of the heavily conglomerate-controlled domestic financial system, and the tightening of controls to prevent capital flight, amongst others (Michie and Padayachee, 1998, p. 627).

Six years into the new democracy and four years after GEAR, it is patently clear that, apart from complying rather well with Washington Consensus-type targets for macroeconomic stability, the real economy is performing nowhere near the levels that are needed to address the problems that South Africa inherited from apartheid.

Table 12.1 shows the record on growth, unemployment and inflation from 1994 to 1999. With the exception of 1996, growth rates have been low.

Table 12.1   Growth, unemployment and inflation, 1994–99

	1994	1995	1996	1997	1998	1999
Growth rate*	3.2	3.1	4.2	2.5	0.6	1.0
Unemployment**	−0.4	−1.1	−0.7	−1.7	−3.7	−3.0
Inflation rate#	8.9	7.9	7.2	8.8	7.5	7.9

Notes:
*   Percentage change in GDP.
**   Percentage change in formal employment in the non-agricultural sector.
\#   Core inflation, that is percentage change in CPI excluding the prices of certain basic foodstuffs and the interest rate on mortgage bonds, overdrafts and loans, as well as property and value-added taxes.

Source: SARB (*Quarterly Bulletin*, December, 1999, S-138, S-146, S-150; *Quarterly Bulletin*, March 2000, S-146, S-150).

Growth rose marginally in 1999, but nowhere near the 7–8 per cent per annum that would be required to absorb new entrants into the labour market and make inroads into the growing pool of unemployed people (Michie and Padayachee, 1997, p. 17). Unemployment has grown, with net job losses recorded each year. 'The available data indicate that the number of people employed in the non-agricultural sectors of the economy declined by around 80 000 in the first nine months of 1999' (SARB/QB, 2000, pp. 2–3). Decreases were recorded in both the private and public sector, and in all major industries including mining, manufacturing and construction. Over the period 1996–99, Statistics SA revealed that there was a net job loss of 365 000 non-farm jobs (NBI, *Quarterly Bulletin*, April 2000). At the same time, a strict monetary policy regime has kept inflation in single figures.

A declining exchange rate has underpinned an improvement in exports, including in manufactured exports. The currency has been badly buffeted by the Asian contagion and more recently by a rampant US dollar, and perceptions of political instability in the region, following the Zimbabwean land invasions. South Africa has not been the preferred destination of direct foreign investment despite its commitment to austere macroeconomic policies, and the granting of an investment grade credit rating first by Moody's, and then in early 2000 by Standard and Poor's. The 1998 World Investment Report showed that South Africa had attracted a mere $380 million in direct foreign investment compared to Brazil's $29 billion and Australia's $6 billion (*Sowetan*, 22 May 2000).

The following two sections examine developments in fiscal and monetary policy since 1994.

12.4 FISCAL POLICY AND THE 2000/01 NATIONAL BUDGET[3]

In terms of fiscal policy, a central concern of GEAR was to reduce the overall budget deficit and the level of government dis-saving in order to encourage domestic savings and create a more attractive economic environment for international investors. Table 12.2 shows that the budget deficit was reduced from 5.1 per cent of GDP in 1994-95 to 2.4 per cent in 1999-2000. The deficit for the 2000-01 budget is expected to rise slightly to 2.6 per cent of GDP, and then fall to 2.5 per cent in 2001-02 and 2.2 per cent in 2002-03 (Department of Finance, 2000).

Table 12.2 Budgetary aggregates, millions of rands

	1994-95	1999-2000	2000-01	2001-02
Total revenue	112 358.8	196 302.0	210 400.0	227 400.0
Total expenditure	137 490.8	216 040.0	233 452.2	251 478.0
Budget deficit	25 132.0	19 738.0	23 052.2	24 078.0
Deficit % of GDP	5.1	2.4	2.6	2.5

Source: Department of Finance (2000).

The 2000-01 budget saw the culmination of a process of tax reform started by the ANC government in 1994. In his budget speech, the Minister of Finance, Trevor Manuel, described the budget's tax proposals as constituting 'the most extensive set of tax reforms ever undertaken' in South Africa.[4] Some key features of the tax reform announced in the 2000-01 Budget were the reduction in the rate of personal income tax, especially benefiting low income earners; the introduction of capital gains taxes from 1 April 2001; a change in the form of taxation from a source-based to a residence-based system; and a graduated rate of taxation for small and medium enterprises to promote their growth.

The tax relief granted to individual taxpayers is a continuation, albeit in an accelerated form, of a process of reforming personal taxes that began in 1995. The government has over this period also removed the discrimination against women, reduced the number of income tax brackets and provided significant tax relief for individuals, particularly for low-income groups. Since 1995 it also reduced the corporate tax rate from 45 per cent to 30 per cent. This, the Ministry of Finance has argued, is mainly to attract local and foreign investment, a key determinant of growth in the GEAR model.

Since 1998, state expenditure at both the national and provincial levels in South Africa has been guided by the Medium Term Expenditure Framework (MTEF). This provides for three-year rolling budgets, with spending plans being updated annually in the form of a Medium Term Budget Policy Statement. This process was intended to ensure that state spending was brought in line with the objectives of the government's GEAR strategy and to reprioritise departmental spending policies to meet the country's development challenges.

Personnel expenditure is the largest item in the budget. Between 1995-96 and 1998-99 personnel expenditure grew from 46.6 per cent of total non-interest spending to 50.1 per cent. The government has attempted to slow down this growth through limiting public service employment and keeping salary increases in line with inflation. The target set in the 2000-01 budget is to have spending on personnel reduced to 48.4 per cent of total non-interest expenditure by 2002-03 (Department of Finance, 2000). The success of the policy is likely to depend on whether or not the government is able to deal with trade union opposition to public sector reform.

The Department of Trade and Industry budget fell by 10 per cent between 1996-97 and 1999-2000.[5] One area of spending which has increased significantly is defence. The 2000-01 budget sees the start of a R30 billion investment in modernising South Africa's defence equipment. Spending on defence rises by over 28 per cent in the 2000-01 budget, and by an average of 15.5 per cent over the three-year period beginning 2000-01 (Department of Finance, 2000). The large amount allocated to defence for the equipment procurement programme has been highly controversial, and appears to have been supported at the highest levels of the state in the context of potential threats caused by regional instability, as well as a possible leading role for the national defence force in peace-keeping efforts in Africa.

In the context of sluggish growth, net job losses and large-scale poverty and inequality, state expenditure programmes are failing to provide an adequate social security net for South Africa's poorest and most vulnerable groups, especially the unemployed, women, children and the elderly. Of particular concern from a poverty perspective are the cuts in social security grants, such as Old Age Pensions and Disability Pensions.[6] Economist Julian May (2000) has studied the state's expenditure in respect of targeted programmes for the poor (old age pensions, the land reform programme and the housing fund) and estimated from MTEF data that over the period 1995-2000, these three line items accounted for only 5 per cent of the total budget.[7]

12.5 MONETARY POLICY AND THE INTRODUCTION OF INFLATION TARGETING[8]

Before President de Klerk's accession to power in 1989 the South African Reserve Bank (SARB) had little real autonomy from government. However, in line with the market-liberalisation recommendations of the de Kock Commission of Enquiry (1985) and coinciding with the political reform process, the Bank came to assume increasing control over the making and implementation of monetary policy, although it remained legally subordinate to the Finance Ministry and government. One of the key outcomes of the political negotiations for an end to apartheid was to confer on the SARB full constitutional independence. Although some dispute surrounded the issue at the time (and to some extent still does) this was understood to mean *both* goal and operational or instrumental independence.

Since 1994 'interest rates have been targeted at inflation almost to the complete exclusion of other factors, based on the assumption that inflation results from excess demand, rather than structural problems related to supply' (Roberts, 1997, p. 74). Success in keeping inflation at relatively low levels has come at the expense of other economic goals, especially employment creation (Roberts, 1997, p. 54; see also Michie and Padayachee, 1997). The trade union federation, COSATU (and even to some degree the Finance Ministry) has been critical of the Reserve Bank's policy of maintaining high interest rates, in pursuit of low inflation, and the effect this has had on depressing overall economic activity in the country (and especially stifling small, black business development) (see COSATU, 1996).

Even IMF emerging country research has shown that while there are growth benefits from reducing inflation from hyperinflation levels to around 8 per cent, 'trying to crush [inflation] down below 8 per cent yielded very little reward in relation to the pain such an exercise could involve' (see Barnardt, 2000). Developments with regard to the central bank since mid-1999 – especially the appointment of Tito Mboweni as the first black, ANC-government appointed Governor – offer new possibilities, though no guarantees, that the Reserve Bank could well play a more constructive role in the country's economic development.

12.6 OTHER KEY POLICY DEVELOPMENTS

In this section we briefly review some of the other key economic and developmental policy positions (and shifts) of the ANC government.

12.6.1   Trade, Industrial, Small Business and Competition Policy

One clutch of policies falls under the Ministry of Trade and Industry and include trade, industrial, competition and small business development policy. There has been a significant reform of the trade policy regime. The tariff structure has been simplified; quantitative restrictions virtually abolished and tariff levels have been reduced 'generally at a faster pace than that required by the WTO' (Barnes and Kaplinsky, 2000, p. 211), with significant costs to jobs and production in vulnerable industries such as clothing and textiles. If industrial policy is understood to aim at particular (selected) industries (see Chang, 1996, p. 60), then post-apartheid South Africa can hardly be said to have had one. A variety of supply-side programmes covering the brief of the DTI have been put in place in recent years. Fiscal constraints, bureaucratic inertia and other factors have resulted in the budgetary and human resource allocations to such measures being rather limited. Furthermore, bureaucratic difficulties and related factors have meant that not all budgetary allocations for supply-side measures have been spent. Neither has the private sector always responded concretely to government initiatives, as the private sector 'outrage' against the Department of Labour's 1997 proposal to impose a levy on business to support worker training programmes, illustrates.

Progress in respect of competition policy has been slow, but a new Competition Act was implemented from October 1999. The Act, designed in part to check centralisation of power in an already heavily conglomerated economy has important features, including greater power to intervene prior to mergers and acquisitions taking place, with a larger, better resourced and more skilled human resource base to support its work. The new Act also involves a wider array of constituencies, including the unions, in its formal structures, in order that effective representations can be made at an early stage, to deal with questions of potential job losses.[9]

12.6.2   Labour, Land and Housing Policy

Despite the absence historically of clear policy positions, given decades of confrontation, exploitation, oppression and dispossession, the ANC's most vocal, emotive policy stances have been over issues linked to labour, land and housing.

The government's policies in respect of labour have included measures to improve labour standards, and secure more coherent bargaining and conflict resolution processes. A consultative body, Nedlac, was established to develop a national social accord involving labour, business, the state and community organisations. Legislation including the National Qualifications Framework, the Labour Relations Act, the Basic Conditions of Employment Act, and the

Employment Equity Bill are consistent with the recommendations and approaches of MERG and the RDP. However, in face of pressure to 'increase labour market flexibility', the government has begun a pull back on some of its earlier positions. The review of some aspects of labour legislation was first proposed by the President at the 1998 Jobs Summit. Thus, for example, companies employing fewer than 10 workers would be granted some flexibility from the Basic Conditions of Employment Act. This would affect some 200 000 companies, employing about 500 000 workers. Some simplification of the regulations governing the dismissal of workers was also made (NBI, *Quarterly Bulletin,* April 2000).

The RDP's aim of 'over 300 000 houses per annum' was a non-starter from the moment that stringent budget cuts became a key feature of the new government's macroeconomic policy. In the first year of the new government, Minister Slovo projected just 90 000 low-cost houses. Slovo adopted an 'incremental' housing policy, based on individually owned sites, as the only tenure form. The Ministerial Task Team, which following amendments, adopted the Housing White Paper as policy in October 1996, confirmed that the state's 'gradual withdrawal' from housing provision was a fundamental principle (ANC, 1994; Bond, 2000). The effect of the Housing White Paper, described by housing academic Patrick Bond, as 'neoliberal' was 'to transfer state resources that should have gone into public or social housing into the private sector with little to show for it in return' (2000, p. 145). Financial incentives were given to private banks, but developers 'did not succeed in fostering low-income housing delivery' (Bond, 2000, p. 145). The present housing backlog is estimated at between 2.5 and 3 million. Just to clear this would require some 350 000 houses to be built per annum for the next 15–20 years (NBI, *Quarterly Bulletin,* April 2000).

South African land reform policy has three main objectives: restitution (aimed at redressing the legacy of post-1913 forced removals); redistribution (being the main vehicle for state-subsidised land transfers to landless people); and land tenure reform (aimed at strengthening the land rights of farm workers, labour tenants and residents on tribal communal lands in state hands). According to land rights co-ordinator at the National Land Committee, Andile Mngxitama, the restitution programme has been slow. Only 4925 of the 63 455 claims lodged since 1994 have been settled, mostly via cash compensation rather than land restoration. By March 1999 only 301 projects had been finalised under the redistribution programme. This programme was suspended in July 1999, and when it was lifted in February 2000 it was announced that it would henceforth 'be targeted at the creation of a black commercial farming class, while the poor rural majority would now have to make do with an ill-defined food safety net plan' (*Sunday Independent,* 3 April 2000). In the area of tenure reform, early progress was made on clarifying and strengthening legal procedures for dealing with farm evictions. All in all, however, it has taken over 5 years to transfer less than 2 per cent of South Africa's farmland.

12.6.3 Privatisation and Black Economic Empowerment

The ANC had been a steadfast opponent of privatisation throughout its modern (post-1955) history. However, largely under the guise of using the proceeds from the sale of state assets to fund RDP investments, the ANC-led government was able, despite union resistance, to push through a commitment to privatisation at its 1995 conference. The apartheid regime and homeland governments owned a variety of ventures from airway companies to leisure resorts which most agreed could be sold off, but controversy continues to surround the sale of more strategic assets such as the electricity provider, EsKom. The partial sale of the telephone utility, Telkom, to Malaysia Telecom and SBC (IJS) has been the most significant move to date on this front.

One of the stated objectives of privatisation is black economic empower-ment (BEE). In areas like the privatisation of state transport services, COSATU-linked trade union investment companies – led by former high profile unionist and ANC parliamentarians – have been particularly active, although they too have been attacked by COSATU President Willie Madisha, as vehicles for the enrichment of a few. The proposed preferential state procurement policy – in line with the Malaysian model much admired by the President – would also fast-track black economic empowerment. If passed, one element of this new policy would allow 'previously disadvantaged' people to win state contracts (worth R74 billion in 1999) even if their price is up to 11 per cent higher than the cheapest tender (*Financial Mail*, 28 January 2000).

But the main vehicle for BEE since 1994 has been the sale – via highly-leveraged pyramid arrangements organised by white merchant banks – of segments of some of the giant, white-owned conglomerates, to consortia of black businessmen (and a few businesswomen). For a while developments of this kind were highly thought of, but the bubble burst when Johannesburg Consolidated Investments, bought on credit by a black consortium led by former Robben Islander and ANC member, Mzi Khumalo, collapsed due to rising interest rates, a falling gold price, and what Bond describes as a 'shareholders' revolt against Khumalo's nakedly self-interested investment of hundreds of millions of rands in a family-controlled firm unrelated to the JCI's business' (Bond, 2000, p. 43). More scandals and controversies of this kind followed throughout 1999, and criticisms continue to be directed at the 'new black elite' (estimated to number a few hundred) who dominate the new corporate boards.

At the other end of the spectrum of 'new black business', black street traders and informal economy workers – who in sharp contrast to the apartheid era have become a distinguishing feature of South Africa's cities in the 1990s – face attempts, especially in Johannesburg, to confine them to facilities off the main thoroughfares, with the aim of attracting back the large rate-paying corporates that have fled the inner city.

12.7 FROM GEAR TO THIRD WAY?

Economic performance since 1994 has been poor. A mix of inappropriate policy choices and problems with implementation (bureaucratic inertia, critical capacity shortages in the state machinery, corruption and inefficiency) have accounted for this (Michie and Padayachee, 1998). Weeks (1999) has discounted external shocks (often raised in official circles as being primarily responsible for poor economic performance) as a significant contributory explanation. Government and big business frequently blame 'labour market inflexibility' as a key explanation of the country's economic ills, even though the respected ILO report argues that the South African labour market is more flexible than many claim (Standing et al., 1996).[10] The growth driver of accelerated private foreign and local capital investment has not materialised to the levels GEAR projected. GEAR has failed palpably in meeting its own targets, especially in respect of growth, redistribution and employment.

Yet there is little discussion in South Africa about the wisdom of having pursued GEAR-type policies. Many of GEAR's principal authors in the Finance Department, including one who was seconded from the World Bank, have recently left – most for senior positions in the private banking and finance sector (a key beneficiary of GEAR policies).[11] The neo-liberalism of GEAR has become entrenched in government thinking and policy. Yet it has become a neo-liberal policy that increasingly dare not speak its name. A policy in search of a rationale or, failing that, some customer-friendly packaging.

President Mbeki has committed the government he has led since 1999 to accelerated delivery in respect of jobs, housing, land reform and the like. Reference to GEAR's failures in these areas have become a national embarrassment. In addition, Mbeki has spearheaded an African Renaissance project – a sweeping yet largely undefined programme to regenerate African economic recovery, promote its cultural heritage and support moves towards liberal democracy and good governance. Mbeki's African project needed a label not directly associated with those emanating from the Washington institutions, whose Structural Adjustment Programmes had wreaked havoc in many parts of the continent since the 1980s.

Enter Mr Blair, a few months before South Africa's second democratic elections. The very notion of a 'Third Way' was largely unknown in South Africa up to that point, outside of a few in academia. Since then, it has cropped up in many government and party pronouncements as well as in the media. The spark for this was Blair's speech at the Old Assembly Dining Hall in Cape Town's Parliamentary complex on 8 January 1999. Blair explicitly described the GEAR strategy as representing 'the Third Way, South Africa style'. The difference between Britain and South Africa, he argued, was a matter of 'scale'.

The justification for Third Way policies in Britain is often depicted in terms of winning over 'middle England'. It might therefore appear an odd concept to sell to South Africa, even if it were translated to winning over 'middle South Africa', or its equivalent. Why would the ANC, with massive electoral victories in 1994 and 1999 underpinned by the votes of organised labour and a still dominant African poor – urban and rural – need to shift its policy to the centre to seek any accommodations? Something along these lines was certainly relevant during the negotiations for ending apartheid and holding democratic elections. These concerns were met explicitly through the so-called 'sunset clauses' of that political settlement, and in the commitment to establishing a Government of National Unity. More broadly, the RDP – and the MERG proposals – could be depicted as representing a Third Way between the ANC's previous commitment to large-scale nationalisation on the one hand, and permitting continued gross inequalities on the other. Thus, a 'people-driven RDP' strategy might be thought of as a Third Way accommodation with what could be realistically achieved given global and domestic constraints.

Why was the commitment to a 'left', people-driven RDP abandoned? The reasons are broadly the same as generally cause governments to abandon progressive goals, namely pressure domestically and internationally from those who prefer the status quo. In the case of South Africa, there were no electoral reasons not to have pushed ahead with a more interventionist and redistributive agenda. There are of course powerful domestic forces, in the shape of those (large conglomerates and others) who still hold economic power – largely unchanged from under the apartheid regime. But any danger that they could destabilise a radical government has diminished since 1994, not increased. The obvious answer is the gains that are thought to flow from playing by the global rules of the game. And those rules are set by the Washington institutions.

In Tony Blair's endorsement of GEAR as representing the South African Third Way, he depicted this as setting a course 'to tackle the needs of the disadvantaged, while retaining the confidence of the markets'. The 'markets' are presumably the global financial ones.

There are two sets of questions here. First, is GEAR an appropriate strategy for the South African government to pursue? Does it 'tackle the needs of the disadvantaged, while retaining the confidence of the markets'? The second set of questions, which the book for which this chapter was written discusses, is whether it makes any sense to characterise current economic strategy as a Third Way?

Perry Anderson (2000) has argued that the neo-liberal consensus has found a new point of stabilisation in Third Way regimes. The hard core of policy remains the pursuit of the Reagan–Thatcher legacy, on occasion with measures their predecessors did not dare exact. In his view, the Third Way is simply the best ideological shell of neo-liberalism today. This is an interesting observation in the post-apartheid South African context. The ANC government has embraced neo-liberalism. However, it could not be presented as such. At first it was presented as being compatible with the RDP, despite the fact that the MERG proposals were clearly more compatible with an RDP approach.

The publication of the GEAR strategy then marked an admission – albeit not admitted – that macroeconomic policy was not to be constrained by an RDP approach. Its failure to deliver on targets in its own terms, especially on job creation, has left it largely discredited within South Africa. GEAR is rarely mentioned by name in post-1999 official statements. However this is not to suggest that its ideas have been abandoned. Its core principles have been thoroughly infused into government thinking at all levels. As the Mbeki government pursues its African Renaissance agenda, it finds that it cannot easily sell neo-liberal ideas, *à la* Washington Consensus, in many parts of Africa, due to the experience of Structural Adjustment Programmes. In both cases – within South Africa with GEAR being the neo-liberal strategy that dare not speak its name, and in Africa with the Renaissance agenda being a strategy in search of a mission – the 'Third Way' becomes a useful slogan. Neo-liberal policies become the Third Way's strategy for retaining the confidence of the markets, alongside a few policies, increasingly crowded out by tightening fiscal constraints, to tackle the needs of the disadvantaged.

12.8   CONCLUSION

As argued in detail elsewhere by us and by others,[12] even within the existing domestic and global constraints, far more could be done by the South African government to tackle the needs of the disadvantaged and to create the conditions for sustainable economic growth than is currently being done. It had been widely believed pre-1994 that a more active strategy would indeed be pursued by an ANC government to overcome the economic and social legacies of apartheid. This was generally believed and accepted, including by the apartheid regime itself that negotiated the handover, and by the markets.

It may be that the term 'Third Way' can have some analytical purchase, depicting the scope and nature of progressive economic policy within the current globalised economy (and in the cases of some countries at least, in face of changing class composition, alignments and identification). If so, then the sort of people-driven RDP that might have redistributed wealth and power in post-apartheid South Africa could have been an appropriate candidate for the label. Instead, the Third Way so understood has been largely abandoned in favour of simply making what progress is possible across the range of policy areas within the narrowing confines of an orthodox economic policy agenda.

NOTES

1. For more discussions and references on these commissions see, Morris and Padayachee (1988).
2. For a discussion of GEAR in the context of the alternative policy proposals being put forward at the time, by business and labour, see Michie and Padayachee (1998, pp. 626–9). For an analysis of the effects of having pursued the GEAR strategy, see Weeks (1999).
3. This section draws upon Padayachee et al. (2000).
4. Perhaps the most notable achievement has been the reform of the revenue collection service, South African Revenue Services (SARS), from a moribund institution in 1994 to one that has significantly improved the collection of revenues.
5. The 2000–01 budget sees a nominal increase of 23 per cent, but this is earmarked for a major recapitalisation programme for the minibus taxi industry, not for any industrial or investment policy measures (Department of Finance, 2000).
6. The revised Child Support Grant, from which approximately 217000 of the country's poorest children currently benefit, has not been increased since its introduction in 1998, thus decreasing in real value in both 1999 and 2000.
7. Personal communication. These calculations are complicated because of the difficulties in obtaining accurate data on spending allocations by provincial and local level governments.
8. This section draws upon Padayachee and Smith (2000).
9. On this see Jooste and others in the *South African Labour Bulletin*, **23**(3), 1999.
10. For a critique of both the theory and practice of labour market flexibility, see Michie and Sheehan (1999a, 1999b).
11. See Greta Steyn, *Business Day*, 3 April 2000.
12. MERG (1993), Michie and Padayachee (1997, 1998), Harris and Michie (1999), Fine and Padayachee (2000).

REFERENCES

Adelzadeh, A. and Padayachee, V. (1994), 'The RDP White Paper: reconstruction of a development vision', *Transformation*, **25**.
African National Congress (1992), *Ready to Govern*, Johannesburg: ANC Publication.
African National Congress (1994), *Reconstruction and Development Programme*, Johannesburg: Umanyano Publications.
Anderson, P. (2000), 'Renewals', *New Left Review*, **1**, Second Series, January/February.
Barnardt, N. (2000), 'Think again on inflation targeting', *Business Day,* 22 February.
Barnes, J. and Kaplinsky, R. (2000), 'Globalisation and trade policy reform: whither the automobile components sector in South Africa', *Competition and Change*, **4**.

Blair, T. (1999), Speech by the British Prime Minister to the South African Parliament, Cape Town.

Bond, P. (2000), *Elite Transition*, Pietermaritzburg: University of Natal Press.

Central Economic Advisory Services (1993), *Key Issues in the Normative Economic Model*, Pretoria: Government Printer.

Chang, H.-J. (1996), *The Political Economy of Industrial Policy*. Basingstoke: Macmillan Press.

COSATU, FEDSAL, NACTU (1996), *Social Equity and Job Creation: The Key to a Stable Future*, Labour document, Johannesburg.

Department of Finance (2000), *Budget Review 2000*, Pretoria: Government Printer.

Fine, B. and Padayachee, V. (2000), 'A Sustainable Growth Path', *South African Review*, **8**, HSRC Publications, Pretoria (forthcoming).

Habib, A. and Padayachee, V. (2000), 'Economic policy and power relations in South Africa's transition to democracy', *World Development*, **28**(2).

Harris, L. and Michie, J. (1999), 'The Effects of Globalization on Policy Formation in South Africa', in D. Baker, G. Epstein and B. Pollin (eds), *Globalisation and Progressive Economic Policies*, Cambridge: Cambridge University Press.

Hirsch, A. (nd), 'Globalisation and policy formation: reflections on the South African experience', Unpublished mimeo, Pretoria.

IDASA (Institute for Democracy in South Africa) (2000), 'Submission to the Portfolio Committee on Finance on the 2000/01 Budget', Budget Information Service, http://www.idasa.org.za.

Joffe, A., Kaplan, D., Kaplinsky, R. and Lewis, D. (1995), *Improving Manufacturing Performance in South Africa*, Cape Town: UCT Press.

Jooste, T. (1999), 'The new Competition Act', *South African Labour Bulletin*, **23**(3), June.

Macroeconomic Research Group (MERG) (1993), *Making Democracy Work: A Framework for Macroeconomic Policy in South Africa*, Bellville: Centre for Development Studies.

Marais, H. (1998), *South Africa: Limits to Change*, Cape Town: University of Cape Town Press.

Marais, H. (1999), 'His masterful voice', *Leadership Magazine*, October/November, Cape Town.

May, J. (ed.) (2000), *Poverty and Inequality in South Africa: Meeting the Challenge*, Cape Town: David Philip.

Michie, J. and Padayachee, V. (eds.) (1997), *The Political Economy of South Africa's Transition: Policy Perspectives in the late 1990s*, London: Dryden Press.

Michie, J. and Padayachee, V. (1998), 'Three years after apartheid: growth, employment and redistribution', *Cambridge Journal of Economics*, **22**(5).

Michie, J. and Sheehan, M. (1999a), 'HRM practices, R&D expenditure and innovative investment: evidence from the UK's 1990 Workplace Industrial Relations Survey (WIRS)', *Industrial and Corporate Change*, **8**(2), 211–34.

Michie, J. and Sheehan, M. (1999b), 'No innovation without representation? An analysis of participation, representation, R&D and innovation', *Economic Analysis*, **2**(2), 85–97.

Morris, M. and Padayachee, V. (1988), 'State reform policy in South Africa', *Transformation*, **7**.

National Business Initiative (NBI) (2000), *Quarterly Trends*, April, Johannesburg.

Padayachee, V. (1998), 'Progressive academic economists and the challenge of development in South Africa's decade of liberation', *Review of African Political Economy*, **25**(77).

Padayachee, V. and Smith, T. (2000), 'Beyond inflation targeting: central banking, macroeconomic policy and democracy in post-apartheid South Africa', Unpublished paper, University of Natal.

Padayachee, V., Smith, T. and Valodia, I. (2000), 'The 2000/01 South African budget: new directions in economic policy?', *Economic and Political Weekly,* April.

Roberts, S. (1997), 'Monetary policy within macroeconomic policy: an appraisal in the context of reconstruction and development', *Transformation*, **32**.

South African Reserve Bank (SARB) (2000), Statement of the Monetary Policy Committee, 13 January, Pretoria.

South African Reserve Bank, *Quarterly Bulletins*, various, Pretoria.

Standing, G., Sender, J. and Weeks, J. (1996), 'The South African challenge: restructuring the labour market', ILO country review, Geneva.

Weeks, J. (1999), 'Stuck in low GEAR? Macroeconomic policy in South Africa, 1996–98', *Cambridge Journal of Economics*, **23**(6), 795–811

Westergaard, J. (1999), 'Where does the Third Way Lead?', *New Political Economy*, **4**(3).

13. Coping with globalisation: Australian economic policy and the Third Way

Tim Harcourt*

INTRODUCTION

The 'Third Way' debate is gathering momentum in Australia for many different reasons than it is in other countries. Why is this so? Well, it comes down to our history as a colony of Britain and the experiences of our respective labour movements. The Third Way is controversial because some in the Australian Labor Party (ALP) argue, with some justification, that the ALP invented it.

The ALP leadership, past and present, has argued that the policies of the Hawke-Keating Labor Government of 1983-96 provided the basis of Tony Blair's New Labour platform in the UK in 1997. As Paul Keating recently recalled saying to Tony Blair 'Our way was not the third way, but the *only* way' (see Keating, 1999). In some ways selling The Third Way in Australia has been like trying to sell *The Joy of Sex*. To quote Paul Keating: 'We were more interested in doing it than finding a label for it' (see Keating, 1999). Keating and others in Australian Labor circles argue that Australia provided Blair with the Third Way or variants of it, not the other way around. After all, Blair was a regular visitor to Australia, has strong personal relationships with Kim Beazley, Geoff Gallop and other Australian political figures, and strong religious and philosophical links with Peter Thomson, an Australian theologian. Blair's programme for modernisation, it is said, was provided with a successful model in the Hawke-Keating government - one of the few successful social democratic governments that survived a political era dominated by the right. During the time that Bob Hawke was Prime Minister in Australia, Mrs Thatcher dominated the British political landscape, the Reagan-Bush administrations were in power in Washington and Helmet Kohl dominated politics in what was then West Germany. In addition, free market

*Fellow, Australian APEC Study Centre, Melbourne, Australia. Thanks to Dennis Glover, Andrew Leigh, Mark Latham, Geoff Harcourt, Tom Forrest, Tim Battin, Malcolm Sawyer and Philip Arestis for their suggestions and assistance with this chapter. The views contained within are those of the author alone and should not be attributed to any organisation to which he is affiliated.

economics had become influential again in universities, think tanks and amongst government officials. This was the political and philosophical environment that faced the ALP in the 1980s and early 1990s. Despite these global trends, Hawke won four elections in 1983, 1984, 1987 and 1990 with Paul Keating winning one more 'against the odds' election victory in 1993.

However, it is not all one-way traffic. Some younger politicians believe that the ALP should adopt Blair's political philosophy and shape it according to their own political agenda. The most well known advocate of the Third Way in Australia is NSW MP Mark Latham who writes in a regular column for the *Australian Financial Review* (the Australian equivalent of the *Financial Times*) under the banner 'The Third Way'. However, Latham himself has shown that some Third Way type policies have their origins in the Hawke–Keating Government.

This chapter is divided into three sections. Section 13.1 explains the origins of the Third Way debate in Australia, which has been alluded to above. It traces some instances of policy interaction between the Australian and British Labour parties including Tony Blair's close links to Australia and his observations of the Hawke–Keating Labor Government. It also highlights the Australian 'Third Way' or Old/New Labor Politics and the debate that is affecting the ALP now in opposition (although it is in government in several Australian States).

It also looks at how the politics of the Third Way has affected the other side of politics of Australia. All sides of politics notice successful politicians like Tony Blair and Bill Clinton and their formulas are usually adopted if they are proven vote winners. The government of the Liberal National coalition headed by John Howard has not been shy about highlighting some of the successes of Blair and the parallels with Australia's own reforms particularly in the area of social welfare.

Section 13.2 looks at some of the specific Third Way economic policy issues. It is not possible to look at all of the issues on the agenda but just some of the more prominent issues that have been discussed in Australia. The policy issues selected for this chapter include:

- Macroeconomic policy (including prices and incomes policy)
- Globalisation and trade policy
- Labour market reform
- Social welfare and the social wage
- Education and the information age
- Microeconomic reform

Section 13.3 of the chapter looks briefly at some of the future scenarios for the Third Way and Australia. The section is divided into a number of themes that could be important in how the Third Way fares in Australia in this new millennium.

13.1   ORIGINS OF THE THIRD WAY IN AUSTRALIA

This section looks briefly at the origins of the Third Way in Australia. First, it examines the influence of Australia in Tony Blair's political development. Second, it examines the influence of Blair's success to date on the Australian Labor Party. Finally it looks at the Third Way on the Australian political scene as a whole.

Prime Minister Blair has close links to Australia. This has been highlighted by his biographer John Rentoul and by Australian academic Andrew Scott in his comparison of the modernisation process in British and Australian Labour parties (see Rentoul, 1995 and Scott, 2000).

Blair spent some of his childhood in Adelaide, South Australia from 1955 to 1958. South Australia, unlike the other former Australian colonies, was not founded as a penal settlement, but was formed by non-conformist free settlers. South Australia gained a reputation for radical dissent and has quite a different history from the rest of the Australian colonies. The dissenter non-conformist tradition related to incidents of religious persecution but also to social movements such as the British chartists. As a result, while still a colony, South Australia was one of the first places in the world that gave women the vote and introduced progressive legislation in parliament in areas such as industrial conciliation and arbitration. Led by a socially innovative premier Charles Cameron Kingston, South Australia also passed some of the first worker protection legislation and social welfare reforms before it joined Australia at Federation in 1901. In the 1970s, led by the dynamic, charismatic premier, the late Don Dunstan, South Australia introduced social reform that was later adopted in other parts of Australia. From Charles Cameron Kingston, in the nineteenth century to Don Dunstan in the twentieth, South Australia has had its fair share of reformers and modernisers. However, it would be unrealistic to draw too much from this South Australian experience for Tony Blair. After all he was aged just 2-5 when he lived in Adelaide!

Australia again entered Blair's life as a university undergraduate at Oxford in the 1970s where three Australians befriended him, namely Kim Beazley, now Federal Labor leader, Western Australian Labor Leader, Geoff Gallop and Peter Thomson, a mature student of theology. Whilst the two Western Australians have remained close to Blair, given their common vocation as professional politicians, it is claimed that Thomson has had a greater influence on Blair's political and religious philosophy (Rentoul, 1995, pp. 41-8). Rentoul describes the importance of Thomson in influencing Blair's views on the concept of community, which was derived from the Scottish philosopher John Macmurray. Blair's political philosophy including his ideas of community and social cohesion is an important part of the Third Way. According to Rentoul and Scott, these developments came in part from his friendships with the three Australians in his undergraduate days at Oxford.

Later, as a politician in the early 1980s, Blair continued to be influenced by his Australian connections. He visited Perth, Western Australia in 1982 just before being elected to parliament in 1983 in British Labour's second crushing defeat by Margaret Thatcher. He gave a lecture to Gallop's political science class at Murdoch University, which Rentoul says was an early sign of his interest in modernising the British Labour Party. Blair's lecture, which was later published, noted the Labour Party's angst between traditional policies and the need for an acceptance for a mixed economy: 'The Labour Party sits uneasily, squashed between the traditional Clause IV part socialism and the acceptance of a mixed economy' (Rentoul, 1995, pp. 88–89).

Rentoul suggests that Blair's later campaign to remove Clause IV in order to modernise the Labour Party can be traced to his lecture in Western Australia in 1982. Blair's reference to the mixed economy is important given that the Australian Labor Party went through similar arguments over its preferred stance on the mixed economy in the early 1980s as well. The 1980 'Labor essays' series, in fact, included a paper on the mixed economy by two economists who were active in the ALP (see Harcourt and Kerr, 1980). This was in part a process where Australian Labor revised its policies and performance in the late 1970s which enabled it to govern at a federal (and state) level for most of the 1980s.

After Blair's 1982 Australian visit, Australian Labor was elected under Bob Hawke and successfully won re-election in 1984, 1987 and 1990. In the meantime Blair was elected to the House of Commons and had to witness the electoral calamities of British Labour in 1983 and 1987 after the SDP split. The success of the Australian Labor Party in government was constantly compared to the British Labour Party after the latter's electoral support had collapsed in the 1980s (Scott, 2000, p. 3).

As a result of the different experiences of the British and Australian labour parties in the 1980s, Tony Blair and Gordon Brown visited Australia in 1990 to meet Prime Minister Hawke and Treasurer Keating. This was at the peak of the Hawke–Keating partnership before the recession and eventual leadership split took its toll on the government in the early 1990s. Both Tony Blair and Gordon Brown were regarded as the future generation of British Labour and were thought by the then Labour leader Neil Kinnock as the most likely to benefit from a visit to Australia (Scott, 2000, p. 4). At that time, Australia was competing for attention with Sweden and later the USA as possible 'models' for UK Labour. It should also be remembered that the Australian union movement itself had also looked at Sweden and other Scandinavian and Western European countries in its own overseas visit in 1987 which produced the landmark document *Australia Reconstructed* (see ACTU/TDC, 1987).

The unexpected success of Prime Minister Paul Keating in retaining office in 1993, despite a recession and a ten-year-old government, prompted the British Labour Party again to look at Australia. Blair visited again in 1995 and John Prescott visited Australia for the first time whilst the ALP was still in government.

Whilst Blair has clearly been an admirer of the Hawke–Keating governments and has personal links to Australia, to what extent can Australia claim to be the originator of the Third Way? In terms of Third Way philosophy, Australia would find it hard to make an explicit claim. For instance, Anthony Giddens, Blair's intellectual guru, makes no mention of Australia in his book *The Third Way*. The book's preface says 'The idea of forming a Third Way in politics has been widely discussed over recent months – not only in the UK but also in the US, Continental Europe and Latin America' (Giddens, 1998). His sequel *The Third Way and its Critics* only mentions Australia in reference to international comparisons of tax and poverty rates (Giddens, 2000, pp. 90–100). Most of the international links in the Third Way are across the Atlantic or to Western Europe. It may be that Australia had implicitly implemented Third Way policies in government under Hawke and Keating but they were not labelled as such. While Blair continually learnt from the success of the Hawke–Keating Government in Australia, defeat came to the ALP in March 1996. This brought new circumstances. Whilst Blair's New Labour were preparing for government, the ALP were picking up the pieces of defeat after 13 years (as the longest serving federal Labor government in Australia's history). Like the UK Tories, Australian Labor had a large 'it's time for a change' factor going against it in the 1996 election. Australian Labor lost government with a large swing against it. Paul Keating resigned from parliament leaving Kim Beazley to lead the ALP in opposition. Unlike the experience of British Labour in 1979–83, Australian Labor did not split asunder after its 1996 defeat. Kim Beazley performed credibly in opposition and the ALP regained many seats in the 1998 election and came within a whisker of returning to office. In fact the ALP won the two-party preferred vote but lost the election (which is based on Australia's unique system of preferences). Australian Labor also performed well at State level, winning government in Queensland, Tasmania and Victoria and being re-elected in NSW in March 1999.

However, there has been some philosophical tension in the ALP since 1996, which has surfaced since the 1998 election. Some activists on the left of the party claimed that Labor was too right wing whilst in government. Of course, similar charges were made in Britain against the Wilson–Callaghan Labour

Government after it lost office. Andrew Scott himself is a proponent of this view. This also occurred in the New Zealand Labour Party, which went further to the right than its Australian counterpart in implementing free market policies in New Zealand from 1984 to 1990.

In 1996–98, Beazley made noises that Labour would revisit some of the policies of the Hawke–Keating Government and would now be more interventionist in economic policy particularly in trade policy. But since the 1998 election, Labor has said little about the Hawke–Keating legacy and for the most part has been concerned with opposing the government's reform package (includes a 10 per cent VAT-type GST). The left of the political spectrum (including within the ALP) has argued that Beazley should distance himself from Hawke and Keating and return to more 'traditional' policies. The right of the political spectrum has been critical of Beazley for standing for nothing or at worst running a cheap populist agenda. Apart from criticism from the left and right, there is also the Third Way and its advocacy by Mark Latham MP. Latham is an unusual figure in the Australian political process. He is a policy intellectual who has actually written a book *Civilizing Global Capital* (see Latham, 1998a). This may be considered standard in Britain (as most MPs seem to have written newspaper articles and books themselves). But this is quite unusual in Australia. It is particularly unusual for someone to write a book on policy in particular. Most publications by Australian MPs are written as 'kiss and tell' memoirs after they have left office. Latham has also published a number of articles in academic journals, and writes a regular column in newspapers. Another Labor MP, Lindsay Tanner, has also attempted to steer the party in new policy debates. Tanner, as a left winger and Latham, a right winger, neither of whom held office in the Hawke–Keating Government, have been considered to be part of the new Labor's new generation. Tanner, like Latham, is a published author. His book *Open Australia* (Tanner, 1999) takes on a number of policy sacred cows particularly with reference to trade and industry policy. Whilst Tanner is less associated with the Third Way than Latham, his views, particularly on trade policy, have put him at odds with some 'traditional' left-wing Labor views.

Of course, in discussing the Third Way in Australia it is important not just to look at one side of the political ledger. The Third Way and Tony Blair's success is affecting conservative policies in Australia as well. Scott in fact draws some of the parallels between John Howard and Tony Blair in their own electoral role strategies (Scott, 2000, p. 121). Scott notes that some political observers thought that Howard's cautious electoral strategies in 1996 (presenting as small a policy target as possible) were influential for Blair's successful strategy in 1997. Both these strategies were in contrast to their own parties' unsuccessful campaigns in the previous elections. For instance, in 1993, the conservative coalition in Australia provided a detailed list of their policies in their manifesto entitled *Fightback!* making themselves vulnerable to government and media attack. Similarly, in the UK, the then shadow Chancellor of the Exchequer, the late John Smith, announced tax measures in the 1992 election campaign that did not help Neil Kinnock's chances of making it to Number 10. Both parties learnt their lesson to win at their next opportunity.

But this is mainly about political tactics. What about actual policy? Prime Minister John Howard's changes to welfare such as 'work for the dole' have been claimed to be similar to the mutual obligation concepts of the Third Way. In its second term, the Howard Government has introduced some family systems measures and the Prime Minister has argued that government should be as concerned with social policy as with economic policy. Howard continues to draw some parallels with the reforms to social welfare that Blair is bringing in. However it is not clear that it is Tony Blair who is influencing John Howard. It might be that George W. Bush's 'compassion conservatism' is a closer parallel to the approach of the Australian conservatives.

In summary, the Third Way is affecting Australian politicians particularly on the centre left. Some in the ALP argue that Tony Blair is just doing to Labor what the Hawke-Keating government already did in government as part of the modernising process. Furthermore, they argue that all political parties need to go through a modernising and repackaging process if they are going to grow and develop.

In fact, it could be easily argued that there is a continuous modernising policy 'boomerang' between the Australian and British labour parties. As Scott has argued, the Blair process is similar to that which occurred to British Labour under Gaitskell and Wilson in the late 1950s and early 1960s. In turn, Australian Labor went through its own modernising under Whitlam in the late 1960s, drawing on parallels of Wilson and Gaitskell. Some in Australia go further and say that the Australian influence is an important part of Blair's own programme. It is clear that Tony Blair has important ties to Australia. However, the Third Way literature does not have much to say about Australia, so Australia may have influenced Blair implicitly and only in terms of policy mechanics.

But Blair has had an impact in Australia on both sides of politics. Successful politicians always get noticed particularly when success occurs in Britain and the US. Australia is a small country with close ties to both Britain and the US so success will always gain some political currency in the domestic political system. Blair has influenced Australian Labour just as Thatcher has influenced Australian Conservatives and in doing so has affected the political position of all political parties. However, Australia has only taken notice because of Blair's political success. There has not yet been a serious discussion of the Third Way as a social movement or political philosophy. Only Mark Latham

208 *The economics of the Third Way*

has provided a detailed policy application of the Third Way with some contributions by Tanner. Even Scott in his own detailed analysis of the historical links between the Labour parties in Australia and the UK gives short thrift to the Third Way. He writes:

> Beazley has rightly rejected as facile the calls by some to emulate Tony Blair's version of the 'Third Way' – most vocally made by maverick MP Mark Latham, for whom the term 'Third Way' has become a mantra which apparently can mean whatever he says it means, but which is particularly about dismantling the continued provision of welfare support on the basis of need. (Scott, 2000, p. 256)

Similarly, in the Labor Essays series for 1999–2000, not much was said about the Third Way except for a chapter on trade unions that discussed generational renewal (see Glover and Patmore, 1999). For the most part it has not been analysed in detail and in some quarters, it has been largely dismissed as a new philosophy or social movement. This is for a number of reasons. One is the reluctance of Australia, in these republican times, to look particularly to the UK for ideas or leadership. Another is the challenge that the Third Way presents to the orthodoxies of left and right in Australian public policy. Yet another is the reluctance of Australians to embrace wide-ranging philosophies as such instead of judging practical policies on their merits. Australian political parties are not so concerned with Tony Blair's philosophy as with the electoral success of his policies. This will determine whether Kim Beazley or John Howard adopts some elements of the Third Way in their policy platform for the next Australian post-Olympics election that is due in 2001. The specific economic policy issues that are important to the Third Way debate in Australia are considered in Section 13.2 to which we now turn.

13.2   SELECTED 'THIRD WAY' POLICY ISSUES

13.2.1   Macroeconomic Policy (including Prices and Incomes Policy)

The centrepiece of macroeconomic policy under the Hawke–Keating Government was the Prices and Incomes Accord with the Australian Council of Trade unions (ACTU). The ACTU and the ALP signed the original Accord in 1983 when Labor was still in opposition. It was forged as an alternative economic strategy to the conservative policies of the day. However, the Accord also had its origins in the failure of the Whitlam Labor government to survive beyond three years (1972–75). During the term of the Whitlam government there was a noticeable lack of coordination between the ACTU and the Labor government and the key players vowed that this would not recur when Labor returned to the Treasury benches in 1983.

The formation of the original Accord was greeted with suspicion from all quarters. This was partly because of the Whitlam government experience but also because of the difficulties faced by Wilson and Callaghan in the UK in the 1960s and 1970s. The latter events affected Tony Blair and New Labour's attitudes to the British unions. However, the Accord proved to be remarkably durable and lasted the entire 13 years of the Hawke–Keating Government. The stages of the Accord are shown in Table 13.1. Whilst space does not permit a

Table 13.1   The stages of the Prices and Incomes Accord

Accord Mark 1	Election of Labor Government sees implementation of the Prices and Incomes Accord
Accord Mark 2	From mid-1985 it is clear that a severe terms of trade decline has drastically reduced Australia's national income. The Accord is renegotiated to discount wage increases for the price impact of the currency depreciation, compensated by income tax cuts
Accord Mark 3	June 1986 – wage adjustment is discounted as agreed and superannuation of up to 3 per cent of wages is introduced
Accord Mark 4	March 1987 – continuing national economic difficulties required complete revision of the Accord with respect to the wages system. Two-tier wages system introduced: first tier to protect weaker groups against continuing inflation, second tier to promote productivity and efficiency. Union movement explicitly embraces cause of national wealth creation, in addition to traditional concern regarding equitable distribution
Accord Mark 5	February–May 1989 – Award restructuring introduced as thorough overhaul of Australian system of industrial awards. Restructuring of the regulatory infrastructure. Career paths, training equity and efficiency are key goals
Accord Mark 6	March 1990–April 1991 – Enterprise bargaining agreed –logical next step in award restructuring, to implement facilitative (enabling) provisions of restructured awards at workplace level
Accord Mark 7	February–March 1993 – 'Putting Jobs First' commitment to continue enterprise bargaining plus 'safety-net' wage adjustments for the weaker and lower paid. Commitment to low inflation and continuing workplace reform. Commitment to discuss maternity payments
Accord Mark 8	June 1995–March 1999* 'Sustaining Growth, Low Inflation and Fairness' – setting new targets for employment growth, underlying inflation rates and including three additional 'safety net' wage adjustments

Source: ICFTU-APRO (1997, p. 3).

Note   *expired in March 1996 with the change in government.

full explanation of all developments of the Accord agreements, a common
theme is how the Accord partners adjusted the arrangements according to the
economic policy imperatives of the day. For instance, the terms of trade
collapse in 1985 caused the renegotiation of the Accord to discount wage
increases for the price impact of the currency depreciation. Similarly, Accords
4 and 5 were a response to the need for skill development and productivity
improvement to assist Australia's international competitiveness. Accord Mark
8 set explicit targets for job creation and committed the unions to a low
inflation environment. All these agreements combined economic policy
objectives with social policy needs.

In essence, the Australian labour movement went through its own
'modernisation' process in terms of economic policy when Labor was in
government. The ACTU executive and leadership proved its capacity to
understand the government's economic objectives. The economic literacy
of Australia's trade union officials greatly assisted the Hawke–Keating
Government.

However, the Accord should not be regarded as being about economic
policy alone. It was directed at industrial and social objectives as well.
Nor should it be seen as a capitulation to 'neo-liberal' economic policies
or a 'selling out' of the trade union constituency. The Accord provided
a clear alternative to the predominant Reagan–Thatcher policies of
that era. It was also an alternative to centrally planned strategies that
were causing the collapse of Eastern Europe. The Accord focused
on a number of economic objectives including the reduction of
unemployment, wages and prices stability and improved productivity and
international competitiveness. It was not the 'fight inflation first' policy
nor was it similar to the policies imposed by the IMF on the Callaghan
government in Britain in the late 1970s. Did British Labour learn
from the Accord? Certainly, many British Labour and TUC leaders and
researchers visited Australia to study the Accord (Scott, 2000, p. 239). New
Labour campaign director Peter Mandelson admired the 'close but
nonetheless disciplined and carefully presented relationship with the trade
unions' (Scott, 2000, p. 4). But is the Accord a forerunner to the Third
Way? It certainly was not explicitly so. Tony Blair is not working with John
Monks like Bob Hawke and Paul Keating worked with Bill Kelty. The
relationships are different and the circumstances are different. Of course, the
ALP did not have a 'winter of discontent' to live down. However, the Accord
did provide a model of how to manage a prices and incomes policy in an open
economy. It also provided an explicit understanding of market competition
and optimal forms of government intervention at the macroeconomic level,
which is important for all social democratic parties to understand in
government.

13.2.2 Globalisation and Trade Policy

According to Anthony Giddens, in his treatise on the Third Way, 'Globalisation' is one of the five dilemmas facing social democrats (see Giddens, 1998, pp. 28–33). Globalisation has also preoccupied Australian public policymakers in the latter half of the 1990s. Much of the discussion on globalisation in Australia has focused on trade liberalisation. The Hawke–Keating governments concentrated largely on multilateral trade negotiations through leadership of the 'Cairns Group' of agricultural trading nations. This continued under the Howard Government, particularly when former Deputy Prime Minister and National Party leader, Tim Fischer, was Minister for Trade. However, globalisation also includes other dimensions such as the liberalisation of investment, organisational change in 'global' corporate structures, and the emergence of the information age. The Hawke–Keating Government not only participated strongly in the multilateral trade round under GATT and its successor the WTO, but it also implemented a voluntary reduction of trade barriers. Tariffs on imports were reduced and various subsidies and quotas phased out. Similarly, investment was liberalised as one of the first acts of Paul Keating as Treasurer was to allow the entry of foreign banks into the Australian financial system.

The Hawke–Keating Government also championed regional economic ties through the formation of the Asia Pacific Economic Co-operation (APEC) (see Hawke in Harcourt, 1999). The Howard government has largely retained the preference for an open economy with a minimum of protection (although there were signs that the government and the opposition had second thoughts about the continuation of tariff reductions (see Latham, 1998b, p. 385).

The globalisation debate has attracted political controversy in Australia. It has been a rallying point for the far right. As the USA has Pat Buchanan, and France has Jean Marie Le Pen, Australia has our very own Pauline Hanson, leader of the One Nation party. Hanson and her party have opposed free trade, immigration and any form of internationalist policies. However, the far left have also been suspicious of globalisation. Witness the demonstrations in Seattle last year. Latham has written that globalisation has provided 'an alibi' for the left to return to policies aimed at replacing or modifying capitalism (Latham, 1998b, p. 389).

The neo-liberal right has unashamedly supported globalisation and sees it as consistent with deregulation at home. The issue of globalisation and labour standards is a case in point. The left has typically opposed free trade and deregulation of the labour market. The right has argued for both trade liberalisation and labour market deregulation. However, as shown in Gahan and Harcourt (1999), labour market deregulation does not necessarily 'fit' with trade liberalisation. You can have a variety of forms of labour market institutions no matter what trade regime you may have in place. Mark Latham agrees. He has argued that:

> The old Left, while embracing decent labour, consumer and environmental standards, has always been sceptical about the benefits of trade liberalisation. The new Right, whilst embracing a free trade agenda, has had little concern for social standards.
> The Third Way takes the best of the two positions – free trade with social standards. This is the best way to handle the economic and social policy challenges of globalisation. (Latham, 1999, p. 6)

The Hawke–Keating Government opposed the incorporation of social standards in trade policy. The Howard Government also thinks that trade and labour issues do not mix. For the most part, the Third Way approach to trade and labour standards has not been adopted by either of the major political parties in Australia.

13.2.3   Labour Market Reform

Labour market policy was an important part of the Accord (as discussed in 13.2.1). The industrial and political wings of the labour movement agreed on macroeconomic policy objectives in order to make social gains for working Australians and their families. But part of the 'pact' was industrial peace. The ACTU and its affiliated unions eschewed the strike weapon and practised wage restraint in the stronger sectors in order to receive social wage gains directly from government. This did occur. Industrial disputes fell to record low levels in contrast to the experience of the Wilson–Callaghan Governments in the UK (see ICFTU-APRO, 1997, p. 8). Of course, relationships were important. Prime Minister Bob Hawke was a former ACTU President and Minister for Industrial Relations. Ralph Willis was a former ACTU economist. ACTU Secretary Bill Kelty forged a close relationship with Paul Keating. These relationships helped the management of the Accord process.

The Australian labour market underwent a number of changes over the Accord period (see Table 13.1). The wage system was at first centralised, with full indexation of wages for price adjustments. It underwent a number of transformations and eventually consisted of decentralised bargaining under-pinned by an award safety net. Most of the change was managed in order to promote economic efficiency and the protection of the most vulnerable groups in the labour market. The Australian experience was different from that of Britain and New Zealand who undertook radical deregulation of the labour market. This occurred without producing outcomes in economic performance that were superior to Australia's (see Gregory, 1999).

The Howard Government has chosen to favour more individualist employment arrangements since it came to office in 1996. Some echoes of past industrial conflict have returned in the form of a major dispute on the Australian waterfront but for the most part industrial disputation levels have not returned to the levels of the 1960s and 1970s.

For the most part, Australian Labor's experience with the labour market has been different from British Labour. Blair has restored the national minimum wage and signed the social charter but has not worked as closely with the unions as Australian Labor did. In opposition the ALP has continued to have a relationship with the trade unions but there has been some disagreement over the use of individual contracts.

However, the Third Way approach to the labour market in Australia has mainly concentrated on education and training rather than on industrial relations reform (Latham, 1998b, p. 391). The award-restructuring phase of the Accord developed career paths and skills for low-paid workers in the award system. This policy development is perhaps a forerunner of the Third Way emphasis on education, training and the development of knowledge capital in the labour market.

Labour market policies have taken place in the industrial context of Australia's unique system of awards and industrial tribunals. As noted by Isaac (1993), labour market reform has taken place in Australia for over a century of wage fixing. The institutional framework of Australian industrial relations enables constant change and reform. Hence there is no 'regulation' or 'deregulation' choice as is sometimes (superficially) put by neo-liberal economists who naively believe that the labour market functions like any other market. There is no need for social democrats to embrace the neo-liberal view of the labour market and accordingly, Australian Labor has not done so. The Third Way enables governments to continue innovation in labour market policy as was done by the Hawke–Keating Government and the ACTU within the framework of the Prices and Incomes Accord.

13.2.4   Social Welfare and the Social Wage

The 'social wage' was one of the cornerstones of the Accord. In return for money-wage restraint to meet its macroeconomic objectives the government gave several commitments to the ACTU in the form of tax cuts. Direct (PAYE) income taxes were reduced and several taxes introduced on fringe benefits and capital gains. Whilst these taxes were brought in to target higher income earners and reduce the rate of tax avoidance the latter group also benefited from a reduction in the top marginal rate of income tax. Apart from tax cuts, the Accord also introduced universal health coverage (Medicare), superannuation, childcare, family payments and labour market programmes (such as Termination Change and Redundancy provisions). The social wage gave gains to workers through the provision of public goods rather than directly via the pay packet (see Gaynor and Harcourt, 1991).

A key element of the social wage was to target social welfare more efficiently and equitably. This was done particularly by one of the left's senior minsters Brian Howe (who later became Deputy Prime Minister). The use of labour market programmes was a response to the 1991–92 recession, which was part of the Working Nation measures. The traineeships which were, in effect, government subsidies to employers to take on unemployed workers, were a highlight of the working nation programmes since they addressed long-term unemployment in particular. The Howard government further targeted social welfare and tightened labour market programmes. A key reform of the Howard government has been 'work for the dole'. Howard often refers to the concept of 'mutual obligation' as justification for the work for the dole scheme. The Howard government has also privatised government employment agencies.

How do these measures of both governments relate to the Third Way on social welfare? The targeting of social welfare was necessary from an egalitarian point of view but still retained a strong role for government. The work for the dole scheme was not a Third Way concept but Howard may have invoked Blair to make it more saleable to the electorate.

Mark Latham has vigorously tackled the traditional views of both right and left on social welfare. He has warned against the increased welfare dependency ratio in Australia and the adverse effect of the welfare system on incentives to work and invest in human capital (see Latham, 1998b, p. 393). However he has also linked Third Way concepts of rights, responsibilities and risk-sharing to the superannuation reforms of the Hawke–Keating Government. He notes:

> The Third Way sees advantages in revitalising the universality of welfare, not as a way of lifting government outlays, but to restore the link between contributions and benefits ... This is why a renewed commitment to universality needs to be based on a system of mixed provision – social insurance funded from private contributions; combined with a publicly funded safety net of minimum benefits. These are the principles the Keating government used to devise a universal superannuation scheme. They now need to be expanded to the pre-retirement years. (Latham, 1998b, pp. 393–4)

Latham argues that this enables government to help people make risk assessments and understand their rights and responsibilities rather than just receiving entitlements on an open ended basis.

Latham has also argued for a Kaldorian progressive expenditure tax (PET). This is in contrast to the Howard's Government's VAT-style GST and the Labor opposition who oppose the GST in its current form.

Both the Labor and Coalition Governments have made changes to the welfare system. However neither has adopted the Third Way approach to welfare and taxes as advocated by Latham. However, as Latham has shown, there are links between his Third Way proposals for welfare and education reform aimed at rewarding effort and encouraging saving and investment to the approach of the Keating Government in its superannuation scheme.

13.2.5 Education and the Information Age

Education is one area where Mark Latham's Third Way ideas have been having a major impact on the Labor opposition and perhaps even the Coalition Government. Latham has placed major importance on the need for investment in human capital for reasons of both economic efficiency and the need to reduce social inequality. Latham has argued that education is important to Australia in the information age. Whilst in the past, Australia has relied on mining and agriculture, its future depends on knowledge-based industries.
Latham has written:

> A small nation like ours can only succeed in the global chase for investment and economic advantage through the development of a well-educated population and workforce. Indeed, Australia's national sovereignty is now best expressed through the skills and insights of our people. (1998b, p. 392)

Latham also sees the investment in human capital as a means of reducing inequality in Australia particularly in regional centres and the impoverished outer suburbs of the capital cities (which encompasses Latham's electorate). To some extent the education focus of the Beazley opposition is a result of Latham's policy work when he was shadow minister for education from 1996 to 1998. A major theme of Beazley's electoral platform has been the 'Knowledge Nation'. The Howard Government too has concentrated on the importance of the information age or the 'new economy' to Australia's economic future.
Policies on education are part of the Third Way agenda. All political parties will adopt many of these policies given that human capital is regarded as the major driver of economic growth in the information age. The endogenous growth theories of the 1980s and 1990s are now beginning to influence the political agenda (see Dowrick, 1994). However, there are differences in how the education system should deliver these contributions to economic growth. The ALP has called for higher rates of investment in public education whilst the coalition has argued for more private sector involvement in the expansion of education. The Third Way is likely to have more influence as Australia develops more knowledge-based industries in the information age.

13.2.6   Microeconomic Reform

Whilst most of the 1980s reforms of the Hawke–Keating Government were macroeconomic in nature (the floating of the exchange rate, introduction of the Accord, financial reform and so on) microeconomic reform was also important especially after the terms of trade shock of 1985–86. The microeconomic reform agenda involved privatisation, deregulation and the introduction of competition policy into all sectors of the Australian economy. It was combined with the reduction of tariffs and the opening up of the Australian economy. On microeconomic policy the Labor Government acknowledged the importance of market forces even if macroeconomic policy, industrial relations and social policy objectives were delivered through the Accord framework. As Paul Keating has explained:

> Now we brought a new word into the Labor lexicon – competition. Competition is our word, not their word. We set up the Competition Commission because we were tired of paying twice as much as we should be paying for cars, for telephones, for clothing, for electricity. In all these things, by cutting tariffs and by lifting domestic competition, we created a lower price structure and therefore, people's wages went further. (Keating, 1999, p. 3)

The Coalition in opposition and later in government had a policy of taking privatisation further, selling part of the telecommunications utility, Telstra, and applying market-based solutions to government employment agencies. It is claimed that privatisation has caused a backlash amongst both Labor and Conservative voters. For instance the Coalition's rural constituencies have expressed disquiet about the effect of privatisation on rural services in telecommunications, transport and financial services.

In opposition the ALP has opposed the further sell-off of Telstra and distanced itself from some of the policies associated with the Hawke–Keating microeconomic reform agenda. Latham, however, has argued that market forces are important but they must be married to strong social policies to assist social cohesion and civil society. He supports the microeconomic reforms of the Hawke–Keating Governments when he writes:

> This is why the reform direction of the Hawke and Keating government was so significant. It kept the pressure on the private sector to meet the challenges of market competition by continually upgrading its products, services and management skills. It kept them honest by making them less dependent on government protection. (Latham, 1998b, p. 389)

Latham has been critical of what he calls industry welfare and believes the state should not support 'producer interests' but instead directly assist citizens to gain skills to cope with the consequences of market forces. His approach is based clearly on the importance of public investment in human capital and the development of knowledge-based industries.

Left-wing critics like Scott argue that microeconomic reform alienated the ALP's traditional voters and call for more government intervention in industry. Others, such as Michael Thompson (1999), argue that working class voters supported microeconomic reform because of the benefits they received in lower prices and improved economic welfare. Neither has produced much evidence to support these contrary views.

The Howard Government has continued support for microeconomic reform but has attempted to counterbalance this with infrastructure and other government programmes aimed at rural and regional Australia. Its counterparts at the state level have also privatised public utilities. But the coalition's main energies in microeconomic reform have been in tax and the labour market where there is clear disagreement between the major parties.

Belief by social democrats in the benefits of markets for allocative efficiency is part of the Third Way. It was supported by the Hawke–Keating Government and extended by the Howard Government. It also receives the support of Mark Latham, as there is a clear connection between the Third Way agenda and the policies of the Hawke–Keating Government on microeconomic reform.

13.3   THE FUTURE OF THE THIRD WAY IN AUSTRALIA

The future of the Third Way depends on a number of themes.

The first theme is the information age or the new economy, which is affecting economic policy throughout the world. Will the new economy put Australia (along with the US, Europe, and other advanced industrialised countries in Asia) on a high growth track, which would change the parameters of economic policy? This may shift the political divide between social democrats and neo-liberals on economic policy to social policy where the ideological divisions are less clear-cut (see Giddens, 1998). Alternatively the information age may not bring the predicted high growth prosperity for all but will actually provide a new series of inequalities (see US Department of Commerce, 1998).

The second theme is generational. To what extent will the Third Way be conducive to generational change in Australia? This refers to the new attitudes of generation X (and generations Y and Z) in Australia and generational change in the political parties themselves. Will the Third Way be the rallying point for generational change in the Labor Party or the Coalition or will the information age change the political process altogether? Will the ALP have its debate about its philosophy and platform in a similar fashion to Blair's clause

IV debate in Britain or did in fact Hawke and Keating do their modernising in government whilst the British Labour Party was in opposition? Some of these issues on generational change are taken up in the new volume of Labor Essays published by the Australian Fabian Society and Pluto Press (see Glover and Patmore, 1999).

The third theme of the future is electoral failure. Will Blair and Brown eventually face an electoral backlash like Keating did in 1996? There were some signs of disquiet on the left about the future electoral appeal of the Third Way. But it may be too early to draw much inference from these results. This is the challenge for British Labour and will affect the ALP's response too. Australian Labor will have to determine whether it wishes to combine its own traditions with some of the more successful aspects of the Blair and Clinton programmes. This will also have a political impact on the Australian conservatives. Will John Howard successfully adopt the best parts of the centre left agenda from Blair and Clinton and move his government to the centre away from economic issues and onto social issues?

Lastly the final theme goes to Australia's relationship to the rest of the world. Most of this chapter talks of the relationship between the UK and Australian Labor and to a lesser extent the USA. An important question is whether Australia will in future become closer to Asia in terms of its own defence and political ties. It is also apparent that in the Third Way debate there is much to be learnt from non-UK/Europe as foreign influences on Australian economics and politics need not be solely Anglo-American.

CONCLUSION

In conclusion, the Third Way debate is relevant to Australia because of the close links between the political traditions of two countries particularly on the social democratic side of politics. This chapter has explored these links with regard to key economic policy issues. It highlights certain Australian characteristics of the Third Way debate, which include:

- the important personal and philosophical influences of Australia on Tony Blair;
- the influence of the Hawke–Keating Labor Government on British Labour;
- the modernising policy 'boomerang' between the British and Australian labour parties;
- the influence of Third Way politics on all political parties in Australia;

- the adoption of the Third Way as a political platform by Labor MP Mark Latham and its links to some of the economic policies of the Hawke-Keating Labor Government.

The future of the Third Way in Australia will depend on how the information age transforms our economy and how effectively the political parties respond to the demographic and international developments that will affect Australia. All Australian political parties will be watching how effectively Tony Blair's New Labour fares in its attempt at re-election under the Third Way banner. But the Third Way's shelf life ultimately depends on the capacity of Australia's own home-grown politicians, whether it be John Howard, Kim Beazley or Mark Latham (or someone else perhaps even from another party), to turn the Third Way into policies that win elections.

REFERENCES

ACTU/TDC (1987) *Australia Reconstructed: ACTU/TDC Mission to Western Europe - A Report by the Mission Representatives to the ACTU and TDC*, AGPS, Canberra.

Dowrick, S. (1994), 'Openness and Growth', in P. Lowe and J. Dwyer (eds), *International Integration of the Australian Economy*, Sydney: Reserve Bank of Australia.

Gahan, P. and Harcourt, T. (1999), 'Australian labour market institutions, "deregulation" and the open economy', *Economic and Labour Relations Review*, **10**(2), December, 296-318.

Gaynor, M. and Harcourt, T. (1991), 'Advances of the Accord', *Workplace*, Spring, 10-12.

Giddens, A. (1998), *The Third Way*, Cambridge, UK: Polity Press.

Giddens, A. (2000), *The Third Way and its Critics*, Cambridge, UK: Polity Press.

Glover, D. and Patmore, G. (1999), *New Voices for Social Democracy: Labor Essays 1999-2000*, Sydney: Pluto Press.

Gregory, R.G. (1999), 'Labour Market Outcomes in the UK, New Zealand, Australia and the US: Observations on the Impact of Labour Market and Economic Reforms', in S. Bell (ed.), *The Unemployment Crisis: Which Way Out?*, Cambridge: Cambridge University Press.

Harcourt, G.C. and Kerr, P. (1980), 'The Mixed Economy', in North and Weller (eds), *Labor - Directions for the 1980s*, Sydney: Ian Novak Publishing.

Harcourt, T. (1999), *APEC's Labour Agenda*, Geneva: International Labour Organisation.

ICFTU-APRO (1997), *International Trade, Investment and Competitiveness: Trade Union Strategies in a Globalising Economy,* Singapore: ICFTU-APRO.

Isaac, J.E. (1993), 'How Important is Industrial Relations Reform to Economic Performance', in M. Bryce (ed.), *Industrial Relations Policy under the Microscope*, ACIRRT Working Paper No. 40, April.

Keating, P.J. (1999), 'Life Membership Acceptance Speech to the ALP New South Wales Annual Conference', Australian Labor Party (New South Wales Branch), October, Sydney.

Latham, M. (1998a), *Civilising Global Capital*, Sydney: Allen and Unwin.
Latham, M. (1998b) 'Economic Policy and the Third Way', *Australian Economic Review*, **31**(4), 384–98
Latham, M. (1999), 'Economic Governance and the Third Way', Speech to CEDA, 14 April 1999, Sydney.
Rentoul, J. (1995), *Tony Blair*, London: Little Brown and Company.
Scott, A. (2000), *Running on Empty - 'Modernising' the British and Australian Labour Parties*, Sydney: Pluto Press.
Thompson, M. (1999), *Labour Without Class*, Sydney: Pluto Press.
Tanner, L. (1999), *Open Australia*, Sydney: Pluto Press.
US Department of Commerce (1998), *The Emerging Digital Economy - Part II*, Washington, DC: US Department of Commerce.

Index